Issue 20

Regimes of Emotion

EDITORIAL OFFICE
Lawrence & Wishart
99a Wallis Road
London E9 5LN

SUBSCRIPTIONS
2002 subscription rates are (for three issues):
UK: Institutions £70, Individuals £35
Rest of the world: Institutions £80, Individuals £45

ISSN 1362 6620
ISBN 0 85315 954 8

Cover pic: Del Loewenthal.
We gratefully acknowledge the help of John Bryantwood of the University of Surrey for help in organising all the pictures for this issue.

Text setting Art Services, Norwich

Printed in Great Britain by
Cambridge University Press, Cambridge

Soundings is published three times a year, in autumn, spring and summer by:
Soundings Ltd c/o Lawrence & Wishart,
99a Wallis Road, London E9 5LN.
Email: soundings@l-w-bks.demon.co.uk

Website: www.l-w-bks.co.uk/sounding.html

CONTENTS

Continued on next page

Continued from previous page

NOTES ON CONTRIBUTORS

Anita Biressi is Senior Lecturer at the Department of Arts and Media, Buckinghamshire Chilterns University College. She is the author of *Crime, Fear and the Law in True Crime Stories* (Palgrave 2001).

Haim Bresheeth is an Israeli academic and peace activist living and working in London. He is co-editor (with Nira Yuval-Davis) of *The Gulf War and the New World Order*, published by Zed Books, and co-author (with Stuart Hood) of *Introduction to the Holocaust*, published by Icon Books.

John Bryant is lecturer in informatics at the European Institute, University of Surrey.

Dympna Casey is a lecturer in the Centre for Nursing, National University for Ireland.

Nelarine Cornelius is a Senior Lecturer in the School of Business and Management at Brunel University. She is editor of the book *Building workplace equality: ethics, diversity and inclusion* (Thomson 2002).

Andy Cumbers is a lecturer in geography at the University of Glasgow.

Fiona Douglas lectures in Human Resource Management at the University of Greenwich Business School.

Susan Ehrhardt is a doctor who works for Oxfam, currently based in Calcutta. A selection of her poems was published in *New Chatto Poets II*.

Judy Gahagan has published poetry, prose and translations. Her second volume of poetry, *Night Calling*, will be published by Enitharmon in 2003.

John Grieve Smith is a Fellow of Robinson College, Cambridge and has had wide experience in Whitehall and industry. He is the author of *Full Employment: A Pledge Betrayed* (Macmillan 1997); and *There Is A Better Way: A New Economic Agenda* (Anthem Press 2001).

G. C. Harcourt is Emeritus Reader in the History of Economic Theory, University of Cambridge, Emeritus Fellow, Jesus College, Cambridge and Professor Emeritus, University of Adelaide. For many years he was an advisor to the Australian Labor Party. In 2001 Palgrave published volumes 6 and 7 of his selected essays, *50 Years a Keynesian and Other Essays* and *Selected Essays on Economic Policy*.

Arlie Russell Hochschild is Professor of Sociology at the University of California at Berkeley, and author of many books including *The Managed Heart: the commercialisation of human feeling*, University of California Press, Berkeley 1983.

Peter Howells is Professor of Economics at the University of East London and editor of the Royal Economic Society's *Newsletter*. He has written or contributed to more than twenty books in the area of monetary and financial economics (many of them with Keith Bain) and a large number of papers published in the professional journals. His current research examines the influence of central banks over market interest rates.

Trudi James is a Sure Start Health Visitor in Haringey, London.

Lena Jayyusi is a Palestinian writer living in Ramallah.

Gay Lee is a palliative care nurse.

Del Loewenthal is Reader at the Centre for Therapeutic Education at the University of Surrey.

Maria Lorentzon is Senior Visiting Fellow, European Institute of Health and Medical Sciences, University of Surrey.

Fraser MacDonald is a cultural geographer and Research Fellow at the University of Aberdeen. With Andy Cumbers he organised a conference to mark the 25th anniversary of *The Red Paper on Scotland*

Gregor McLennan is Professor of Sociology at the University of Bristol. He has written extensively on Marxism, pluralism, sociology and cultural studies.

Hisham Matar is a Libyan writer, now living in exile in Britain.

Marjorie Mayo is Professor of Community Development, Community and Youth Work, Goldsmiths College, University of London.

Sasha Miller is a freelance journalist.

Stuart Nairn teaches at the Department of Adult Nursing, University of Nottingham.

David Newbold is Senior Lecturer in the Faculty of Health, South Bank University.

Heather Nunn is Senior Lecturer in Journalism and Communications at the Department of Media, Communication and Cultural Studies, Middlesex University. She is the author of *Politics and Fantasy: Gender, Political Culture and Thatcher* (Lawrence and Wishart forthcoming).

Rick Rattue is a student of Management Studies in the School of Business and Management at Brunel University.

Ian Robbins is Professor of Mental Health Practice and Consultant Clinical Psychologist, NHS Traumatic Stress Service, European Institute of Health and Medical Sciences, University of Surrey.

Pam Smith is Professor of Clinical Practice, European Institute of Health and Medical Sciences, University of Surrey

Stephen Lloyd Smith is Lecturer in Management Studies at Brunel University.

Andrew Stevens is a writer and journalist. He lives in London.

Steven Taylor's poems have been widely published in magazines. He is currently putting together his first poetry collection.

Bridget Towers is Principal Lecturer in Sociology at the University of Kingston.

Nira Yuval-Davis is Professor of Gender and Ethnic Studies, Department of Sociology, University of Greenwich.

EDITORIAL

The dynamics of class and the radical right

Many plausible explanations are currently offered for the rise of the far right in modern Europe, and indeed for the broader shift to the moderate right in most European countries today.[1] Fear of crime and insecurity, and hostility to immigrants, refugees and ethnic minority communities, are most often cited as the anxieties which underlie this rightward current. The complacency of the political establishments in most European countries, and their privileged detachment from everyday experiences and struggles, are also offered as explanations for the rise of parties that claim in these conditions to be speaking up for 'ordinary citizens' against self-serving or corrupt governing classes. The collapse of Communism, and the destruction, confusion and weakness of the former parties of the left, is another factor contributing, as no one quite anticipated it would, to the emerging ascendancy of the right. Since there is no longer any robust voice speaking for the disadvantaged from the left, space has been opened up for protests to be made on their behalf by movements who claim to speak and fight for them against a different enemy. Instead of the rich and powerful, ethnic competitors for territory, jobs, and social benefits are characterised with dire effect as the most tangible and remediable cause of the problems of the poor.These explanations have some purchase on the present situation, and must be considered in the attempts to devise responses to it. But it is necessary at the same time to look for deeper social changes which are contributing to this disturbing shift in the political climate. This article will suggest what these changes are, and the large problems that these signify for progressive politics.

---

1. Recent election successes for the far right include an 18% vote for Le Pen in the second round of the French presidential election in 2002; Pim Fortuyn's List's second place in the Netherlands in 2002; 9% for the Popular Party in Portugal in 2002; 12% for the Danish People's Party in 2001; 27% for the Austrian Freedom Party in 1999; 9.9% for the Flemish Block in Belgium in 1999, with 20 out of 50 seats won in Antwerp; 14.7% for the Norway Progress Party in 1999; 22.5% for the Swiss People's Party in 1999; the British National Front's three council seats in Burnley in the UK local elections this year; the right-wing coalition of Berlusconi's Forza Italia, the Allianza Nazionale (a post-Fascist party from the south, led by Fini) and Bossi's Lega Nord, which has governed Italy for over a year.

Relations between social class and politics have for shorthand purposes often been constructed as a set of correlations between political affiliations and positions of relative advantage or disadvantage in labour and property markets, established at various snapshots in time. 'Rational choice' models of political preference suggest that equilibriums are formed when those social fractions representing the relatively privileged, and those representing the relatively disadvantaged, make up equal sized blocks. It is this 'equilibrium assumption' which explains why so much political attention is usually focused on the 'middle ground', on attracting the votes of those balancing fractions whose fluctuations of allegiance make the difference between the success or failure of centre-left or centre-right coalitions. In reality, as everyone knows, political allegiance by no means correlates closely with relative wealth or poverty, there being many other variables of collective organisation, gender, and political or religious tradition, which have always complicated models of the relations between class and politics. But if such models are of little use in their simplistic forms, they have long explained a great deal about the material correlates of political allegiance. 'The economy, stupid', was a famous recent expression of this insight.

Indeed, even on the left, the size and composition of these fractions of the advantaged and the disadvantaged, or to put it another way, the size and composition of different social classes, has long been a central dimension of political analysis and strategy. Eric Hobsbawm's *The Forward March of Labour Halted*, which in 1978 drew attention to the ongoing demographic decline of the industrial working class, and its implications for progressive politics, sounded an alarm bell whose significance was accepted both by the revisionists of New Labour, and by those of the New Left.[2] Each of these tendencies correctly drew the conclusion from this emerging social demography that the left could no longer count on its latent 'class majority', since the core working class on which its base was built was now in decline. New social constituencies would have to be found to sustain the parties of the left, if they were to remain contenders for power and hegemony. It is the failure to construct such a new hegemony, in a way which does not exclude and marginalise working-class constituencies, which

2. Eric Hobsbawm's article was first published in *Marxism Today* September 1978. See also, for a more upbeat post-industrial interpretation of the same period, Andrew Gorz, *Farewell to the Working Class*, 1980 (English edition Pluto Press 1982).

has created the opportunities for movements and parties of the radical right.

But while arguments of this kind have their validity, they are still inadequate to map what may now be happening to the political landscape of advanced European societies. The critical issue is not the relative numerical size of different classes or class fractions, and their relative weight in a democratic system which articulates these through the competition of the electoral system. Although one can model the relative success and failure of the left through such snapshots of 'demographic power', plotted over time, longer-term changes require a more dynamic analysis. Such an analysis needs to make explicit some hitherto taken-for-granted assumptions of socialist politics which may now, with potentially grave consequences, be losing their validity.

Suppose one thinks of class systems not as distributions of wealth, power, and life-chances, at different moments of time, but instead as patterns of collective mobility, upwards or downwards. That is to say, suppose one imagines social classes not as *structures*, nor even as *antagonisms*, but instead as upward or downward *flows* of groups held together by some kinds of collective identification and solidarity.[3] Suppose that the predominant orientation of a social class has always depended not so much on its relative position in a structure at a given moment of time, and its sense of relative deprivation or advantage within this, but instead on its longer-term direction of advantage or disadvantage, its *collective social trajectory*. It is not that questions of relative deprivation or advantage do not matter - plainly they do. These variables account for many local fluctuations in political support, election by election, and for many decisions taken by politicians as they try to win such support, for example by conferring material benefits on different fractions of the electorate. But while these distributional variances account for many political choices within short-term frameworks, the long-term - the *longue durée* of class politics - may have a different dynamic.

The left has been able to take for granted for nearly two centuries that the working class, as it has constituted itself, is a broadly progressive social force. 'Progressive' - especially by contrast with the current ascendancy of xenophobic and exclusionary social attitudes - has always meant universalistic, inclusive,

3. This argument about the centrality of flows has been influenced by Manuel Castells' *The Rise of the Network Society*, Vols 1-3, Blackwell (1996), John Urry's *Sociology Beyond Societies*, Routledge (2000), and Zygmunt Bauman's *Liquid Modernity*, Polity (2000).

and optimistic. Marx, and the broader socialist tradition, held that it was reasonable to identify the interests of the working class with the interests of humankind at large, and to represent this class as the bearer of a universal human interest, as they held the bourgeoisie to have been before it.[4] This assumption that the emancipatory demands of the working class were broadly linked to universal human aspirations for democracy and freedom has not recently been much in anyone's mind, as the political role and voice of the working class has diminished. Knocked about by demographic decline, by criticism of its own particularisms and moral limitations (for example in the domain of gender and race), and by the failures and inhumanities of communist regimes which had claimed to equate working-class with universal human interests, this paradigm of progress has for the time being at least faded from its earlier prominence.[5]

The possibility now needs to be considered that the working class can no longer be unproblematically identified with a broadly universal and progressive interest, painful and disturbing as this may be. It is the analysis of classes in the dynamic terms of collective mobility that gives rise to this possibility.

During the nineteenth and twentieth centuries the industrial working class embodied, on balance and in general terms, a general and universal interest. Its two great achievements were political democracy, which could never have been achieved without the action and advocacy of working-class movements, and a large measure of social and economic democracy, through the winning of universal entitlements to some measure of provision of health care, education, and economic security. Because of these political achievements, and also because of the key role of the industrial working class in a growing economy and thus in the achievement of higher (though unequal) standards of economic well-being

4. Marx and Engels' *Communist Manifesto* (1848) forcefully explained the bourgeoisie's claims to speak for a universal human interest as an outcome of its growing ascendancy.
5. Marxists once saw themselves as the legitimate intellectual inheritors of the political economy of the Enlightenment, mapping the stage of development that followed the theory of nascent capitalism developed by Adam Smith, David Ricardo, Thomas Malthus, Jeremy Bentham et al. Now it seems that the descendants of political economy in its original form have triumphed. We have a historicism without the proletariat, a class-based theory of progress in which the bourgeoisie retains its historic role for all time.

for all, the industrial working class experienced over most of two centuries a large measure of collective upward mobility.[6] There were of course massive setbacks to this long-term rise, of which Fascism and Nazism were the most important, and widespread suffering along the way, especially in the earlier phases of each nation's industrial revolution. Much everyday political conflict has been about these temporary setbacks and how to overcome them. But the continued assumption that this rise was the normal long-run historical condition has provided the underpinning framework for socialist political thought, in both its revolutionary communist and its evolutionary social democratic variants.[7]

Throughout most of these two centuries, the industrial working class of Europe was in a process of emergent ascendancy relative to the agrarian populations of feudal and post-feudal landowner-dominant Europe. Thus the cities were generally progressive in politics and culture, the countryside generally conservative, reflecting their predominant class compositions.[8] Of course the rising urban bourgeois classes were also a key element in this progressive evolution, their alliances with the industrial working class in the achievement of civil rights, political democracy and social democracy being intermittent features of this process of social advance. (The post-war boom, under the 'regime of accumulation' of Fordism, was a recent phase of this ambivalent class alliance.)

But over the last decade or two, it has become plain that the industrial working class is no longer a rising social class in Europe but is in a state of relative decline and marginalisation. Its absolute and relative numbers are falling in the population, as those of agrarian workers and peasants did before it. This decline has different and interlinked causes. These include the displacement of

---

6. Some class fractions - 'the labour aristocracy' as it has been called - were of course more upwardly mobile than others, and this was a long-standing source of political division within the working class. These divisions did not however preclude the long-term rise of the working class as a whole.
7. The idea that conservative ideology was a product of declining social classes, and universalistic, progressive ideologies the creation of ascendant social classes, is a major theme of Karl Mannheim's *Ideology and Utopia* (1936). Differences in the cultural formations of rising and declining social classes, or 'dominant, emergent and residual' culture as he termed them, were explored by Raymond Williams, for example in *Marxism and Literature* Oxford University Press (1977).
8. W. Barrington Moore's *The Social Origins of Dictatorship and Democracy* (Penguin 1967) explains these alternate patterns of national development largely by reference to the respective roles of the peasantry and the urban working class in them.

industrial work by labour-efficient technologies; 'globalising' shifts of industrial production into parts of the world where labour protection, collective organisation and labour costs are low; and the deliberate disorganisation and weakening of the working class by alliances between conservative governments and corporate interests.[9]

The electoral consequences of this decline have long been recognised by most parties of the left and centre: the quest for more middle-class, 'post-industrial' sources of support is the *leitmotif* of the Third Way and 'New Labour', and of kindred political formations in Europe and indeed in the United States and elsewhere. But what has been less recognised are the implications of this seismic shift for the entire 'imaginary' and vision of progressive politics. It may be that the experience of the long-term and apparently inexorable decline of the industrial working class is undermining its identification with an inclusive, universal future, its confidence that its own demands ultimately stand for the demand for a better and fairer society for all human beings. And it may be that this attrition of universalistic expectations and aspirations could be the most critical and damaging feature of our post-industrial times.[10]

Let us consider the possibility that the broader dynamic which shapes political imaginaries is the alternation between those social formations which are universalistic and inclusive because their experience is of collective ascendancy, and those which are particularist and exclusionary because their experience is of collective long-term decline. Our argument is that it is the rise and fall of classes, not their relative power at any one moment, which explains whether they are, in general, embodiments of a broader human interest, or representatives of merely sectional privileges. Can we not explain the rise of the xenophobic and exclusionary right across Europe (and the pre-emptive adaptation to its demands by 'respectable' parties) principally by reference to these collective trajectories, what one might call the *dynamic* dimension of class

9. One could say that the 'decline of the working class' signals a political and cultural defeat, more than a demographic fact, since although the 'industrial working class' has undoubtedly declined, the number of those who live by wage labour has grown as women have entered the workforce in large numbers.

10. A recent example of the importance of such inclusive perspectives was seen when the African National Congress came to power in South Africa a decade ago. The partially communist formation of the ANC was an important factor in its framing of its strategy in universalistic rather than particularistic terms.

structures? It is, after all, the most salient and important fact about the rise of contemporary right-wing movements that their principal constituencies are not the petit bourgeoisie of earlier Poujadist movements, but the distressed populations of working-class industrial cities, whether in Rotterdam, Lancashire, or former East Germany. These populations are turning on their ethnic minority neighbours, or on phantom immigrant influxes and 'swampings', since they now see themselves not as members of a larger collective embarked on a journey of social improvement, but as a threatened and impoverished population. They see themselves as engaged in a desperate life-and-death struggle for declining shares of goods and services of all kinds. Their perceived rivals in this struggle are both the privileged and condescending middle classes, and ethnic newcomers.

In an article in an earlier issue of *Soundings*, the New Labour project was characterised as one which aimed above all to create a hegemony of the upwardly mobile.[11] It is this project of upward mobility which explained New Labour's commitment to the inclusion of corporate business within its 'big tent', its earlier emphasis on 'education, education, education' as its principal vehicle of individual and collective social mobility, and its insistence that entry into the labour market, or training for this, must be the *quid pro quo* for entitlements to social benefit. Whilst wanting to demonstrate continuing concern for the victims of modernisation, New Labour has been in no doubt that its principal appeal needs to be to those who can contribute to and share in modernisation's benefits. Tony Blair's personal image - his energy, youthfulness, informality, and relentlessly upbeat style - is of course perfectly tailored to correspond to these aspirations for improvement. It seems hollow only when his own aura of personal success and privilege, and the similar aura of those who surround him, jars with the circumstances of the many of those who are asked to believe in him.[12]

---

11. Michael Rustin, 'The New Labour Ethic and the Spirit of Capitalism', *Soundings* 14.
12. The problem with this would-be coalition of the upwardly mobile was that it was conceived as an assemblage of individuals, not as a collectivity of any kind. New Labour has tended to be embarrassed whenever it has tried to give its project an imaginative coherence, the Dome being an early example of this difficulty. Crucial conflicts of interest between labour (which needed to be reinvented in post-industrial terms) and capital were obfuscated by the formulations of the Third Way. Chantal Mouffe 'A Radical Centre: A Politics without Adversary', *Soundings* 9 described this as a 'politics without antagonisms', but in fact the not-so-hidden antagonists were those who still insisted on the realities of class.

It is now becoming clear, however, that the success of a strategy of this kind - of seeking an identification founded on a shared experience and expectation of upward mobility - is partly dependent on the response of those social fractions who feel themselves to be left out of this upward trajectory. Those who feel left behind are liable to behave politically as downwardly mobile and threatened groups in society usually do, that is to say in angry and exclusionary ways. Socialists are used to assigning such conservative and defensive mentalities to relatively 'backward' and traditional classes, in the countryside, or among the higher social classes who are necessarily threatened by moves towards greater equality. Their problem now is that it is the heartlands of the industrial working class in many European nations who are most exposed to these downward pressures, and who are giving force to new social movements of the right. (It must be said that the New Labour government has been doing somewhat better than its continental and United States allies in looking after its core constituencies. It also seems that in its recent policy changes - notably towards giving more support for tax-based public services, notably the NHS - it has at last recognised the dangers that threaten.)

There have of course previously been occurrences of relative immiseration, and their common political consequences are well known. Fascism in the 1930s was the product of a catastrophic loss of security in large groups of the population. Outbreaks of xenophobia in recent years in the Balkans, in Russia, and in the former East Germany, as state-socialist economies which had produced a modest measure of material prosperity collapsed, provide more recent instances of these effects. It seems highly unlikely, however, that economic insecurity and anxiety will take such dramatic or life-threatening forms in contemporary western Europe, and for these reasons movements of the far right are likely to prove more containable here than in some of those other catastrophic situations.

But the problem is that we may be seeing not merely local or cyclical instances of relative immiseration, but a larger trend associated with economic globalisation itself. The decline of the working class in Europe is inscribed in deep social and economic pressures, notably towards de-industrialisation, and is not merely the outcome of political timidity, compromise or misjudgement by left-of-centre parties, facts of life as these may be. What is more, this broader global crisis is actually being perceived and articulated by these new right-wing parties and movements, in their own crude way.

Thus, hostility towards immigrants and their descendants, and 'asylum-seekers', should be seen not merely as an irrational displacement of anxiety and hostility on to conveniently visible scapegoats, but as a defensive and retaliatory response to globalisation itself. Anti-globalisation movements can, in other words, have right-wing instead of left-wing agendas. This is made clear by the salience of 'asylum-seekers' and 'new' immigrants in the agitations of the far right. 'Asylum-seekers', who are perceived as would-be 'economic migrants' seeking better lives for themselves and their families, and not only as victims of war or political terror, are seen as representatives of the myriad invisible competitors of European workers. The fear is that 'more would come if they could'. Hence the current political appeal of the idea of 'Fortress Europe'.

Paradoxically, the earlier achievement of working-class movements in creating social protection through welfare systems now contributes to this anxiety, as these social benefits seem to be threatened by market reforms and growing inequality on the one hand, and by increased competition from newcomers on the other. It seems that the more marginal the populations of industrial working-class areas feel, the less they are inclined to share their remaining systems of social support with perceived outsiders. It is these attitudes which connect hostility to immigration on the part of right-wing parties with nationalistic attitudes towards Europe and other supranational bodies which appear to limit the willingness or capacity of national governments to look after their own.[13]

The more tolerant attitudes of 'liberals' in the governing classes of Western European nations are attributed by right-wing movements, and not without some real basis, to the fact that the social strata to which they belong are not in any way threatened - as are the poor - by territorial or economic competition from immigrants. In many respects these strata may see immigration as offering tangible benefits to themselves, for example in providing employees vitally

13. Although these right-wing parties seek support from the streets by articulating hostility to immigrants, outsiders, and foreigners, they can also present themselves as thoroughly 'modern' populists in sharp suits, as is the case with Berlusconi and Fini in Italy, Haider in Austria, and was the case also with Fortuyn in Holland. They find support among emerging strata who feel excluded by corporatist establishments, as well as among those who have simply been left behind by change. This combination, and their alignment with their national cultures, is what makes them a serious threat to the mainstream parties.

necessary to keep the institutions they control functioning. (The health and social care system in many English cities is, for example, entirely dependent for its continued functioning not only on ethnic minority employees, but on continuing inward flows of these.) These are real conflicts of perspective and interest between the constituent elements of centre-left and even centre-right coalitions.

In these circumstances, the reversal of these alarming tendencies towards xenophobia and racism in European politics is going to be a very difficult task, and is one which requires the most searching analysis.

Economic and social programmes which can offer economic inclusion and benefit to *all* citizens are the fundamental requirement of a politics capable of holding at bay the new authoritarianism and xenophobia. If the movements which are being mobilised by the radical right (which are responses to globalisation whether this is made explicit or not) are to be effectively countered, left-of-centre parties need to develop coherent and effective responses of their own to the dangers to citizens which market-led globalisation brings. Particularly damaging and threatening in this respect are high levels of unemployment in Europe - it is quite clear that the trade-off attempted by many European governments, of relatively high levels of benefit for those displaced from the work-force in return for the toleration of high levels of unemployment, has not been successful and is leading to serious social disintegration. Higher levels of growth, and a continuing commitment to relative equality - a viable 'European model' such as Will Hutton advocates in his new book - are the precondition for reversing the growing right-wing tide.[14] The *extent* of inequality is relevant, in that the more unequal society is, the greater is the fear of downward mobility, and the hostility towards perceived competitors that this brings about. In more equal societies, on the other hand, which have a greater investment in common standards and well-being, there is less anxiety about relative position, and thus less fear.[15] Yet inequality, anxiety and fear are now on the rise.

The prospects for economic growth and political harmony in Europe thus

---

14. Will Hutton, *The World We Are In*, Little Brown (2002).
15. The negative consequences for health and well-being of relative inequality are powerfully demonstrated by Richard Wilkinson in his *Unhealthy Societies*, Routledge (1996) and in 'What health tells us about society', *Soundings Special: The Next Ten Years* (1997).

depend on the renewal of more inclusive and egalitarian social policies. Electoral coalitions which have focused on too narrow and too privileged a social base are driving large numbers of working people into the arms of right-wing movements. Even the more enlightened fractions of capital may now, faced with the threat of the radical right, rediscover social inclusion to be in their better interests. For example, higher levels of immigration are now needed by business to expand a labour force being diminished by declining birth rates and an ageing population; and greater economic and political integration across Europe is also called for, if the Eurozone is to remain competitive. A resurgent right will tolerate neither of these developments.

In order to see off the threat of neo-fascism, and resume the development of its own project, the left needs to think again about its premature abandonment of the working class. It needs to recognise that although workers in manufacturing industry may no longer be in the majority, those who depend for their well-being on the fruits of their labour remain as numerous and preponderant as they ever were. If left-of-centre parties cannot again learn to speak for these populations, we can now see who will do so in their place.

MR

The ghetto is calling

Haim Bresheeth

When will we start taking seriously the desperate plight of the Palestinians?

They keep coming, streaming in through the invisible system of cables, lines and aerials, which are so far away from their lit screen in a room shaken by the repeated shelling, bombardments, shooting and bestial brutality of the occupation forces. Men and women whom I know and love are sending their pleas from Palestine on the net - a far cry from the isolation of Warsaw ghetto, where some of my family perished. And yet, their story is so disturbingly reminiscent of the ghetto, fighting to the bitter end, attacked by the grandsons of those who died in that other struggle.

From Ramallah, Gaza, Hebron, Bethlehem - from all over Palestine, people are writing and asking for help. They are all amazed, and so am I, at the measured calm with which the world accepts their demise and growing catastrophe, their second Nakba. What will it take for a change to occur? The news-readers have lost all interest in what is now called 'the cycle of violence' - as if there is a symmetry between the occupier and occupied - as if the violence of a mighty army destroying all before it is equal to the despair, hopelessness and anger forcing people to kill others by committing suicide. Those who criticise the Palestinians for suicide attacks will do well to dwell on what it takes for a person to commit suicide in this way. Israel has persuaded the Palestinians, quite efficiently, that there is no hope for them to live normally in the Middle East. They seem to have heeded this cruel and inhuman message, and some of them, seemingly many - and numbers are growing by the day as Israeli atrocities mount - are prepared to give their life in order to hurt the occupiers of their country.

But then, this was always true. Nations around the globe have shown that self-sacrifice is an integral part of an independence struggle. What is more surprising, more enraging, is the mental and moral degradation of Israeli Jews at this time. The peace movement of old is gone; gone are the voices of reason, of total opposition to the continued brutality of occupation, to the lawlessness that this occupation has created, and to its dehumanising effects, not just on Palestinian society, but first and foremost, on the Israeli polis itself. In league with Sharon sit the Labour Party, with Peres as their historical leader: they take equal and full part in the atrocities, in the blind stupidity of bloodshed, of trying to bludgeon a whole people into submission. Every child which sees his father killed, mutilated or humiliated, every woman who is not allowed into hospital to give birth, every family who are gradually starved into submission - they will remember, they will tell the tale, they will hate their oppressors with new vigour - and so will the rest of us. For this blindness, the 'left' in Israel will pay for a long time to come, as will the whole region.

Do Israelis not realise that in good time their leaders may come to face the International Tribunal for War Crimes? What has happened in the occupied territories since 1967, not to mention what is now taking place, are war crimes of every single sort imaginable. And all this, to what effect? Have the Palestinians given up their claim for sovereignty and independence under the inhuman pressure of continued attacks? Have they accepted that Israel has a right to do what it likes anywhere in the Middle East, or are they ever likely to accept that? They were ready to settle for 22 per cent of their country, realising that this was all that might be on offer, only to find that there was not a single Israeli leader prepared to vacate the occupied territories and ALL the illegal and damaging settlements. The Israeli public, now terrified of leaving their homes, should really spend some time thinking about what they have made of Palestinian life, of the hell that has been meted out since 1948, and especially since 1967. Justice, peace, security, are all indivisible. There will no Israeli security without security for Palestine - this at least should be clear to all and sundry, but it obviously is not. Israelis can no longer be trusted to identify their own good and proper interests, not to mention those of the Palestinians. The rest of the world needs to step in, and quickly.

So the time has come to say clearly that those who may yet stop this messy situation from deteriorating into further bloodshed, ethnic cleansing, population transfer and genocide - namely the western powers - will also suffer the results of a merry-go-round of blood and irrationality. The anger now collecting in the Arab world, in Islamic countries, in the Third World, the South - that anger may well be released at a time and place that cannot be foreseen, like the attack on 11 September. It is a time for all rational leaders to regroup and quickly force Israeli withdrawal and the immediate setting up of a viable Palestinian state, affording its citizens peace, security and prosperity.

At this time Jews who remember the Holocaust should stand up and be counted - they should clearly say that they are totally against Israeli occupation, and for liberation of the Palestinians from the Israeli yoke. If the future life of people in the region is dear to them, they should help Israel to free itself from the diseased and debilitating cycle of brutality that they have plunged themselves and the Palestinians into; they should clarify that Israel has not got them on its side, and is not acting in their name. It is not the Palestinians who need to be under pressure, after all these years of atrocities, but the short-sighted Israeli public, with its refusal to face reality. What must come now are sanctions of every kind, and withdrawal of help and co-operation from Israeli organisations, up to the point of sending an international force into the region to enforce the evacuation of the territories. The time has come to take a stand.

If, despite the pressing need to force an end to the violence by ending the occupation, nothing is done - well, we know well enough what will follow. We have seen it time and again on our screens, in former Yugoslavia. Do we want to wait until all is lost? Our Palestinian friends are calling out to us. Please, let us not abandon them, as the European society of the 1940s abandoned my own family to their fate.

Visit to 'North Tel-Aviv' Israel, January 2002

Nira Yuval Davis

Nira Yuval-Davis *reflects on her visit to Israel earlier this year, before the recent Israeli invasions.*

I went to Israel just after Christmas, to teach a mini-course in Tel-Aviv University. Since the deaths of my parents and aunt I've been left without a 'home' in the 'homeland', and such engagements give me an opportunity to stay in Israel for a while. I can 'immerse' myself in the local scene (and in its smells and tastes - the strong evocation of sensual belonging), keep in touch with friends and family, and meet and support my Israeli and Palestinian friends who are struggling against the Israeli occupation. This need that I have to keep on going there - is it the yearning of the diasporic for the homeland? Or is it the yearning of the exile? And this need that I have to keep on getting away from there - is it claustrophobia? Cowardice? A symptom of my hybridity and/or multi-layered citizenship and belonging? I'll ponder all this another time. Now I want to share what I found in this three-week visit.

Unlike friends from Women In Black who had flown over as part of an international support group, I did not stay in the West Bank and Gaza strip. I met these friends only on the first day of my visit, in a large anti-occupation demonstration in Jerusalem, organised by the women's coalition for just peace. This was one of only two visits to Jerusalem during my stay, the other being for a talk on transversal politics in Bat-Shalom, the Women's Centre. The Israel I was staying in, and want mainly to talk about, was the 'Northern' Tel-Aviv experience, where I was surrounded by the more affluent, educated, largely Ashkenazi and mostly secular Israeli Jews - those about whom my friend Barukh Kimmerling has just written a book, in which he describes the ending of their rule of Israeli society (though this view is by no means uncontested, especially by Mizrakhi colleagues).

I also have doubts about the end of Ashkenazi domination, given their (still?) very high levels of representation in Israeli political, military and economic elites. But there is no doubt that their hegemony is now heavily contested, especially culturally. It was not incidental that, when I went to see the Israeli version of the play *One Flew Over the Cuckoo's Nest*, the machoism of the hero had been reconstructed as that of a Mizrakhi man. Although almost every healthy and self-respecting Ashkenazi youngster of the mainstream would volunteer for combat units during their national military service, they are not the real 'men' in Israeli society anymore. And the Mizrakhi effect is even more influential in Israeli music, whether pop or jazz.

As an interesting aside - the market for the kind of Israeli craftsmanship that used to rely heavily on Middle Eastern themes in jewellery, embroidery, weaving and glass has radically diminished. In part, this is the result of the global capitalist market, and its homogenising effects. In part, however, this field has been [re?]claimed by the Palestinians. Even the beautiful woven table mats and bags sold at the airport souvenir shop were no longer described as 'authentic' Israeli craft, as in the days of 'Maskit', but as the 'special artistic contribution' of the Druze (a Palestinian minority living in Israel).

In the North Tel-Aviv Israel where I was staying, the Mizrakhi Jews were mostly assimilated middle class; and Palestinian workers, even citizens of Israel (except for a couple of cleaning women in the university) were largely absent - although Israeli Palestinians were very much present as students, especially in the Mikhlalot, the Israeli equivalent of polytechnics. Here, some of the lecturers told me, their numbers sometimes approach 50 per cent. The porters, the women at the tills in the supermarket, etc, all spoke Russian.

The Northern Tel-Aviv experience was weird in its defensive 'normality'. On the surface, life continued as usual. The radio channel 3 constantly played old and new Hebrew songs (although the words of some of the new ones were very melancholic and lost), and the shopping mall in Ramat-Aviv was full of shoppers and people attending various leisure activities. (Although I was told that the overall attendance in restaurants and cafes in Tel-Aviv had sharply declined, not just because of the radical crisis in the tourist industry but also as a result of the general economic recession, in which about 10 per cent of Israeli citizens are now unemployed - and also because of a fear, at that time largely repressed, of terrorist attacks.)

The spatial dimension of this 'normality' was shrinking, however. The Occupied Territories, which had brought to post 1967 war Israel an illusion of openness and grandeur, had been closed to Israelis for some time - except as military occupiers (more on this later) or (very rarely) as participants in left political demonstrations of solidarity and support for the Palestinians. There was a chasm between the North Tel-Aviv Israel reality and that of the Jewish Settlers in the territories (though this can sometimes be more illusory than real, as the story of 'Amanat Kineret', which I talk about later, demonstrates). There was also a chasm between 'North Israelis' and the religious neighbourhoods, which are continuously spreading and 'conquering' new territories (due to their higher demographic rate of reproduction); and there was a further chasm between these areas and the places where Palestinian citizens of Israel live. When I went to one of these villages, to visit an old friend, and to interview teenagers in the local high school about their politics of belonging, the taxi driver refused to take me there; the taxi company would have been prepared to find a sufficiently brave driver only for a very special fee! Eventually a taxi driver from the village came to pick me up (actually by now it's an unplanned town).

The most frightening aspect of this 'normality' was what people had got used to accepting, in terms of Israeli policy in the Occupied Territories. The facts were mostly known, and had been exposed by the international press. What can be difficult to understand unless one has been there is how preoccupied people can still be with their own troubles and fears, so that things that would have seemed unbelievable or outrageous some years ago had now become part of 'normal' life: like the Israeli policy of assassinating Palestinian political leaders (and this in a state that prided itself for not having the death sentence); like the mass destruction of houses in Rafah in the Gaza strip (which was analysed on radio and TV as a 'propaganda failure' of Israel ...); and like the more general pressures of acute harassment, deprivation and fear for people in the Occupied Territories. A friend who visited Ramalla while I was in Israel, as part of a delegation of Israeli women peace activists who met with a similar Palestinian group, described to me the incredible physical landscape she saw (and this was *before* the later mass invasion): it was a landscape of destroyed houses, with the narrow road through the middle guarded by the Israeli tanks and road blocks which control entry to the city; similar, somewhat smaller blocks were set up between the different city neighbourhoods, so that any routine movement of people for any purpose took hours, and was controlled by the whims of those who controlled the blocks. My Palestinian friend from Ramalla, however, shared with me the astounding fact - a reminder of the incredible facility of the human spirit to adjust to almost any situation - that even in Ramalla, in the midst of all this, (at least at that time) people had developed strategies for living 'normal' lives.

Returning to my main focus, the 'Northern' Tel-Aviv of January 2002 - there was a terrible pessimism and confusion there about what to do and what the future held. The Northern Tel-Avivis were bitterly disappointed and disillusioned with the failure of the Oslo process. They had been given to understand that a solution to the conflict with the Palestinians, and with the Arab world as a whole, could come about without their having to pay any excessive price, or making any real change in their way of life. On the contrary, the Oslo agreement was seen as a means by which their economic, if not political, dominance in the 'new' Middle Eastern market would crystallise, so that they would be able to withdraw from national service, into the individualistic life styles of western global capitalism.

However, this was always extremely unlikely. The original Madrid, and then Washington discussions between Israeli and Palestinian delegations had been an historical opportunity to confront and transform the conflict which started with the settler colonial project of Zionism. But the subsequent transition of the negotiations to Oslo, in back rooms and with secret manipulative steps, was the result of an attempt by Israel to guarantee its superiority and control of the future Palestinian 'state'. Thus it ended with a break-up, and the dissolution of any emerging trust between the sides. Since then, there has been little cause for hope. And at the time of my visit it was already clear that the situation was worsening rapidly.

The break down of the peace process has had the effect of reinforcing ethnic and religious fundamentalism on both sides as the only way forward. Increasing fundamentalism amongst religious Jews was just as worrying for the Zionist liberal 'left' as was the Palestinian Intifadah. Everybody was talking about the 'chasm' in 'the people'. In an attempt to overcome this, a group of liberal Zionists, headed by Yuli Tamir, an ex-minister in the Peres government and a well-known political scientist, in co-operation with a group of right-wing and religious activists (as well as some senior figures from the Israeli military), composed what came to be known as 'the Kineret treaty', which I mentioned earlier. This 'treaty' attempted to imitate the style of the Israeli Declaration of Independence, whose liberal principles it was supposed to update and reinforce, at the same time finding common ground between the Israeli Jewish right and left. But, as its bitter critics pointed out, the Kineret treaty was not liberal, because it focused on the Jewish character of the Israeli state and society, in spite of the fact that 20 per cent of Israeli citizens are not Jewish; furthermore, no Palestinian citizen of Israel was among those involved in the process of drawing it up. And it was not democratic, because those who signed the 'treaty' were not elected by anyone and yet presumed to speak 'in the name of the people'. Solutions which seek only to bridge gaps within the Jewish population, and remain committed to a Zionist state without confronting some of the basic issues involved in the Israeli-Palestinian conflict, are unlikely to provide the basis for any long term solution.

'the Oslo agreement was an attempt by Israel to guarantee its superiority and control of the future Palestine "state"'

Pessimism was also very deep among the much smaller non-Zionist Left, although they continued tirelessly, and with incredible courage, to speak out, demonstrate, campaign and confront the Israeli occupation. Their strength and persistence filled me with awe and admiration, and I am proud that some of them consider me their friend. Partly overlapping with this group of activists there was also a group of intellectuals and academics whose analysis helped to demystify what was happening. I was astounded and gratified by the openness of the post-graduate students who attended my course on the politics of belonging in Tel-Aviv University. If I compare this situation to 1980, when I went back to Israel after finishing my PhD to decide whether or not I wanted to return to live there, the difference is more than remarkable. Then I could find hardly anyone with whom I could share a discourse. In my presentation at the Israeli Sociological Association conference that year I had to spend 15 out of the 20 minutes allocated for my paper in explaining the assumptions on which I had written it. A period of about fifteen years then followed, during which something like a mutual boycott existed between Israeli academia and me. Now, though many of the things I was talking about were still new to the students, the overall deconstructive paradigm was familiar and acceptable.

The pessimism of the non-Zionist Left, however, does not stem solely from the chasm (let's use this currently much loved Israeli expression) between analysis and practice, between their freedom of speech and the atrocities of the state's policies (freedom of speech for Jews, that is - Azmi Bishara, the intellectual and political leader of Palestinian citizens of Israel, has been threatened with court, and his immunity as an MP withdrawn; and even for progressive Israeli Jews there have recently been some repressive measures in the universities). Their pessimism also stems from a recognition - as a friend who is a lawyer, who has been doing wonderful things in the defence of Palestinians since 1967, told me - that the eventual resolution of the conflict might well be one in which there will not be a place for Israeli Jews to live in the Middle East. In other words, she was sharing my opinion, that, after the break-up of the second Intifadah, and the end of any legitimacy or trust in Israel, the fate of Israeli settler society might resemble that of Algeria more than South Africa.

An important part of this pessimism is due to the Islamization of Palestinian national discourse (also partly caused by the collapse of the peace process, and originally supported by the Israeli secret service as a counter measure to the influence of the mainstream PLO); this excludes not only Jews, but also Christian Palestinians, and would at most tolerate Jewish existence in the Middle East as only a religious community rather than a national one - as was the situation under the Ottoman millet system. And a worrying part of this Islamist discourse is its racialized anti-Jewish element.

I attended the UN world conference against racism in Durban last summer, and was exposed to the antisemitic element of some Muslim discourse there (although the Palestinian delegation itself was very careful to reject any such discourse). It is also true that the Zionist and Israeli lobby at that conference did not help the matter in their presentation of any criticism of Israeli policies - let alone of Zionism - as antisemitism. Israel has recently been using the antisemitism card very heavily, as a way of deflecting criticism of its present policies, and this needs to be exposed and rejected. Nevertheless I, along with some of my anti-zionist Israeli Jewish activist friends, am also worried about the antisemitic overtones of some currents within Islam.

To end these at times disjointed observations, I want to tell about two pairs of siblings I met in Israel, one Jewish and one Palestinian. In each case the brother was older, around 20-21 years of age, and the sister younger, 18-19.

The Jewish siblings, children of a family relative, were both in the military. The boy was a couple of months before the end of his service, spending his time in his unit headquarters, after spending most of his time in a combat unit, and manning the road blocks in the West Bank. The girl was in her first few months in the army, training to be a guide, and a trainer for male soldiers in their basic training. The Palestinians, children of an old friend who has been an activist sine the 1960s, were both in higher education. The boy was studying electrical engineering and the girl law.

In each case the brothers were scathing about their sisters - for the choices they had made, and, even more so, for the enthusiasm with which they were pursuing these choices.

The Jewish boy was deeply traumatised by his military service. He was full of bitterness and impotent frustration. He couldn't wait to finish, to escape from it all in a trip to India or the Amazon, as so many of his peer group friends have done; after his return, he would study some high-tech skill in the university, and make as much money and little politics as possible. He felt that he and his friends were impotent puppets in a game they could not win, stuck between two impossible enemies. As far as the Palestinians were concerned, he felt the war was hopeless, because 'how can you win against the hatred of 14 year-olds? ... This is not a military enemy you can fight against'. He felt that he spent all his time in trying to remain passive in the face of impossible provocation. (At least he didn't tell his parents or me the other bits if they happened.) But it was even worse on the other side - the Settlers. Each time they passed the road block they would curse and spit at him and his fellow soldiers. This was because the army would not allow the Settler militia - at least most of the time - to pursue and kill the Palestinians who attacked them. He told me that if it was dependent on him and his friends, they would have immediately withdrawn from the Occupied Territories to the Green Line (Israel's 1948 borders), and there stood and defended the country till their last drop of blood. But why should they find themselves in this impossible situation for the sake of the Settlers? When I asked him whether he believed that the settlements would eventually be evacuated, he answered negatively. There were too many of them, they were too powerful.

He was disdainful towards his sister on two grounds. Firstly, for the enthusiasm she was showing towards the army and what she was doing - 'believing in all this shit they are feeding you'. The second ground was gendered - how could you hope as a woman to become a trainer of male soldiers, especially as you would be dealing only with problem cases, those who were too cowardly to volunteer to become combat soldiers. (The course his sister is so enthusiastically taking part in is relatively new - a result of the Israeli military's abolition last year of its special Women's Corps, and its adoption of a model close to that of the American military.)

The disdain of the Palestinian boy for the enthusiasm of his sister was not explicitly gendered, although the difference between them may have been. He was disdainful that she chose to study law: as if any legal struggle (and, by implication, any citizenship-based political struggle - something in which his father had all his life been engaged) could accomplish anything effective to change the position of the Palestinian citizens of Israel. He was studying electrical engineering, hoping to find some well-paid job (although - and this is pure speculation on my part, he didn't want to talk too much to me - such a knowledge can be useful for other purposes as well).

The girl was full of enthusiasm. She shared a flat with four other girls from her high school, all of them studying law in a Mikhlala. She explained to me apologetically that her brother couldn't see how the study of law could become a basis for other activities, presumably political. What she was most enthusiastic about was the activities of the Muslim society in their Mikhlala. How wonderful and eye-opening they were, and how radical. She explained to me that while religion used to be dominated by tradition, in the last few years, and with the work of the new Islamic religious teachers' seminaries that have been opened in a couple of places in Israel, religion managed to get away from tradition and become a tool for social and political change. She confided that she still does not have the courage to cover her hair in public, because of the implications for the public treatment of her as a result, but that she wished she did have.

I am told that the position on religion that this girl described to me is close to that of the followers of Jihad (to differentiate themselves from the much more traditional attitudes of Hamas), and that this is the direction towards which many young intellectual Palestinians - who in my youth would have turned to socialism - are turning.

This was scary. It reminded me of some of my Iranian friends in London a short time before the Khomeini revolution there. On the other hand it is also understandable. As this Palestinian girl and her mother explained to me (not in this terminology), until 1967 the Palestinian citizens of Israel were completely invisible in Arab and Palestinian national discourse. Even in the Oslo process the Israeli Palestinians were excluded. Now there is contact and communication. In Islamist discourse now, the Palestinian citizens of Israel are talked about as the Palestinians 'inside'. This terminology of 'inside' is very important, I think. It puts the Israeli territory as the centre. Islamic discourse has adopted the Christian and Jewish discourse of talking about this country as the 'Holy Land'. Palestinian citizens of Israel have finally got an autonomous role in the Islamic-nationalist discourse. They are the guardians of the Holy places, such as the Al Aqsa mosque, and of the holy land in general - until the modern Salad-a Din shall once more conquer the Holy Land from the Crusaders (this time, Jewish).

Needless to say, I left these encounters with the two pairs of siblings with a heavy heart. The deterioration in the situation since I left Israel does not add anything to lighten it. However, emails from friends in Israel who, in spite of the general situation, continue consistently to protest, resist and expose Israeli war crimes just add to my respect and admiration to them. This might not be enough to change the course of events, or to create a space for democratic co-existence, but globally as well as locally, we need every bit of alternative discourse we can get.

Letters from the Palestinian ghetto

8-13 March 2002

Lena Jayyusi

Lena Jayyusi *describes what it is like to live with the violence of the Israeli occupation.*

1

The principle of non-simultaneity - it is wonderful to hear children laughing down the stairs of our building. After months in which all sounds were banished from the place, save for the imagined and remembered sounds of shelling from the green-dressed army camp across the valley, the sense of normalcy creeps back, albeit only in doses. But children's laughter in the here-and-now inhabits one dimension; normalcy, the taken-for-granted and yet plannable course of quotidian life, inhabits the point at which dimensions intersect. I know this will not yet be a constituent of our compass of existence here. As the laughter trips down the staircase, at this very moment, in the refugee camp of Tulkarm, in the Aida and Dheisheh camps of Bethlehem, in the already partly destroyed neighborhoods of Rafah, children are hearing the continuous sound of heavy fire, of planes and helicopters that pierce the ceiling of their world with a ferocity of surveillance and destruction. They are not like children in the spaces over there, across the Atlantic, where the weapons are manufactured, where the master decisions and policies are made, where the new regime of domination is being secured and perfected. The principle of non-simultaneity - the existential condition which, in a world traversed by the cruelty and blindness of power, must be overcome. Solidarity.

They will come to Ramallah soon enough ... they will pass again with their gunfire close to this very place, this building. This neighbourhood lies on the route of a probable entry point for their invasion force: it will not be the prime target, but will stand as part of the landscape to be mastered. The target will be the refugee camps: Al Am'ari can be reached down the road from here. My sister asks me to go over to her in Jerusalem. But I have no wish to leave ... finally I understand the ordinary refusal to budge. My fear, which will no doubt raise its haunting head at the zero hour, is docile at present, prior to that inevitable moment; what raises its head insistently is refusal. What moves through my body is not the gut-clenching fist of dread, not yet, but the catapulting jolt of anger. And the will to simultaneity. How am I to leave? How many can leave the camps? Can I forget the shame I felt that night, months ago, when I first crouched in a corner of the middle room, with machine-gun fire battering the walls of the building, battering my ears and memory? The wild fear I felt and the shame that came with it, provoked by the thought of that much more terrible and palpable hell of Beirut during the three months of Israel's assault and siege in the summer of '82? The summer my new-born child finally came home. Then too I could only grapple with non-simultaneity, I could only choose to acknowledge and refuse it at the same time.

The Israeli Leviathan continues to exact its toll, continues to march through our lives, the small moments and the great, all marked by its imprints, the sound of its machinery. The moment of birth, the wedding, the shopping trip, the reunion with those we miss most - these were always and deeply marked, long long before Oslo, and right through the period of pseudo-grace that was Oslo, the phase when we were being dressed for the final ceremony. Everyone cheering in the gallery, while we were being gathered in the stadium. While the bounds and latitudes of the meta-colony were being drawn,

2

We are getting used to this ... this periodic assault of death at the hands of the Israeli army and its allies; this fearful stream of dying, of bodies carried on the shoulders of friends and kin. Every few years we live through an interminable age of aching, an upheaval of loss, when a smile seems a distant object, a dance an impossible dream, when our whole world is forcefully plunged, once more, into a punishment of killing by a power which demands we cease to dream, punishes us for daring to will a future of our own. We are getting used to this: patience, limping soul, stand steadfast, or these young bodies, and these old ones, broken by fire, will not release the freedom of their spirit. Patience, even as we wake up to the toll, sleep to the toll, every cell aching to fashion a new reality. 8 March 2002 ... oh, the impossible green of their banner-covered coffins, rows of them, carried by the crowds, all of them already their brothers. Already fifty today. A tumult of the collective will to live and to be. We are getting used to this.

They shoot at will. They kill civilians and say they are terrorists planning to carry out operations. They drive over ambulance cars with their tanks; shoot at the ambulances to prevent them from picking up the injured, killing the doctors and emergency personnel, and deliberately leaving the wounded to bleed slowly in the streets, in the corners where they were picked out, to bleed until they die. Their tanks storm the small corridors of the camps, shattering the frail rooms of the already dispossessed, destroying lives, gutting neighborhoods, intending to terrorize a new generation. This is a population which for 53 years now has been hounded by those who conquered their land and homes. The witness, the dispossessed, must be dissuaded from demanding restitution; must be broken so that the world is not reminded, prodded to rehabilitate ... such systematic, insistent and heavily muscled cruelty used to have a name. I still call it fascism: the entire range of military, political, economic, and mediational instrumentalities converging to crush the adversary, to penetrate, shape and master the entire range of ordinary living in the world. The fascism at the heart of all colonial order, unmasked by resistance, by an indigenous population awoken to its own rhythms.

3

The bubble of the meta-colony has been punctured. The colonial machine is at full throttle. And the silence of the many fills the great void of the sky. They have come to settle from all over the world, and now stand on all the corners of the country, at all the entry points to our lives. Tonight, after only one hour in Jebalya camp, in Gaza, eleven killed, fifty wounded. According to the report they stand with their invasion force on all the entrances to Ramallah. This small room I have prepared in the middle of the flat is a palace ... how small I feel, unable really to share and do. I declined to stay at Raji and Rose's place tonight, where earlier we had spent some hours of the evening, despite their insistence and the report of tens of tanks on their way. They would not come over to my place after tanks made their appearance on the bypass road below their home. Almost twenty of them. Khadija, who left at the same time as I did, lives right opposite Psagot, the furious settlement which belched missiles all through the recent months, at homes, school, gym in Al-Bireh. She too declined to come over. She has lived through Black September, the siege of Beirut. We laugh with each other over the phone ... if you need anything at any point I am here. But we're all in it, like everyone else. Areej, much younger than any of us, has the same feeling. We all stay put. What happens to all, happens to each. But it is not entirely true. Down there in the refugee camps, down there they will receive the fury that inhabits the fear, and animates the will to crush, that the colonizer always vents. They will receive the depleted uranium, the heavy missiles, the columns of tanks smashing though the small alleys, the army which will bore through the walls of the close bordered homes. Down there the real battle, the big toll will be had. The refugee camps. The very mark of our condition, the sign of the original deed which catapulted us all into this unending journey, the embodiment of what might have been, what was, what could be, the body which must be dismembered for so many to breathe lightly, rest back in comfort. The body within our body, the representation of our memory. The actual face of the encounter which has ceaselessly been miscast and untold over the years, but which will not stop telling itself to anyone who will look in its eyes.

The radio broadcast, the Voice of Palestine, transmitting from its new location, has suddenly stopped. I know what that means. Heavy gunfire. My heart beats fast. Who will lie bleeding tonight, ambulances prevented from reaching them? How many will die here? How many will be led away, like they were yesterday in Qalqilya, all males between the ages of fifteen and fifty rounded up, blindfolded, their arms marked. with numbers. Always the marking. Stripped, interrogated, and beaten, led away for more to the place of concentration. Like they were twenty years ago in the sports stadium in Beirut. I cannot help remembering. I cannot help remembering Santiago, as well,

Sarajevo, Srebrenica. Steps on the ladder to hell. For us who receive and resist. And yet resist after each new step. And for them who come to batter us ...

4

The tanks have surrounded the hospitals in Ramallah. They shoot at the medical staff. They shoot at the reporters. They have entered the camps. They are stationed everywhere. We cannot move. A long, very long way away, Anan talks of 'the unnecessary use of lethal force'. There is then a necessary measure of lethal force that the Israeli war machine can wreak on us in our own land? On the BBC, on CNN, anchors and reporters talk to the world of 'the cycle of violence'. Equal and equivalent. The new stack of phrases that position you endlessly on the road to nowhere, the occupation itself effectively sanitized and packaged, institutionalized and countenanced. As it was from the very first years - the 'benign occupation'. The accumulated utterances of decades of deliberate or uncaring collusion. The deeds of denial. The deeds which dovetail with the systematics of violence, of negation, and the decades-long project of undoing an entire society.

The shooting is right below us now. The building is hit. Again. At moments like these, all the solidities around you, beneath you, turn fluid. A fluidity which threatens to drown the senses. Every part of your body takes on a life of its own; your ear rushes at every sound, dizzying your hold on what immediately surrounds you. I understand what my friend meant when he said that at the moment when death hangs in the air, the only person who is not under its spell is the one who is engaged with it, actively resisting it.

The tanks have surrounded all the hospitals. In the maternity hospital, five women are waiting for help with difficult deliveries, but the doctors cannot get there. Upstairs, on the third floor, my neighbours have their young cousin staying with them. She is due in a few days. She is a breach birth. If she goes into labour now, she will not make it. A few days ago, a young woman died at the checkpoint, giving birth. And the baby. The soldiers would not let her through.

5

Occupation is violence. How is it that this truth seems to have fallen into the shadows? That, at the gateway to this heralded new century, a condition of outright corporeal oppression should be redefined through the suppression of the manifold details of daily policy, and represented merely through the foggy optic of 'the need to return to the negotiating table'? The reductive logic of an overtly-detached, secretly-invested ethic. To negotiate what? A limited measure of freedom from the limiting constraints of occupation? An occupation that persists, and increasingly insists on consuming and appropriating place and space, land, air and water. An occupation in the service of a colonial order, of a colonial will to erase, marginalize, silence, replace, and dispose at will. Colonialism is a project of violence. How is it that this knowledge is discarded, violated and inverted? Centuries of colonial experience - the small details of terror inflicted on the body in and of the everyday; that erupt with ferocity at every intersection where collective wills confront each other. What allows this historical memory to be excommunicated? Official Europe straddles the full spectrum of complicity: the acknowledging gesture empty of the act; the silence; the continued investment in the relationship with the colonial state. It has not dismantled its colonial ethos. The Arab order straddles the full spectrum of complicity. With even greater injury. It has not reconfigured its colonial psyche. The USA is on its imperial march.

The tanks surrounding the hospitals have blocked their entrances, preventing the wounded from being brought in for treatment. Their water and electricity supplies have been cut off, needed oxygen cylinders prevented from delivery. A death sentence. The doctors say they will operate on the wounded in the streets, in front of the tanks. Families in Ramallah are being prevented from burying their dead. An Israeli representative on the BBC announces that the infrastructure of terror is being destroyed. Palestinian violence has to be stopped. Arafat has been given permission to move as he wills in the Palestinian territories. There is no prodding question in return.

Perhaps on this day, when the powerful speak what they will, and the rest act as though this was the 'truth', silence would be our best companion. It is difficult to speak in the face of the consummate lie, trumpeted and reproduced in various small details across the spectrum of the institutional means of discourse: media, politicians, academics. 'The talk would talk and go so far astray … you don't want madness and the whole thing there …'

There is no constative any longer: only the pure performative. The constative, the kernel of actuality in the spine of each performative, has been vacuumed out. And the pure performative is a monstrous tool in the hands of the powerful. The performative utterance is over-determined in the age of the advanced machinery of killing, the age of concentration of financial power, translatable always into the power to starve and to assassinate. But the courage of ordinary people has no bounds.

What register does one speak in, when every register is contaminated? The concrete, the historical, the moral, the political, the quotidian, the existential ... all these are inflected with the performance of power, and the cruelty that attaches to it. All these are distorted by the machinery of power.

And yet, I carry their faces with me, their voices, over and over again, saying tell them, why don't they hear, where is everyone, just like their counterparts did in Bosnia. I carry their gestures, reaching out to beckon, their proclamations, their stories their puzzlement, their resolution. Their will to be. They are all mine. I have carried them for years through the long trek of exile. After I first discovered my mother, one spring day, secretly crying, and could not understand what her words meant, 'on this day, three years ago, they took my country from me'. It is hard to keep company with silence.

'An Englishman's home'

Reflections on the Tony Martin case

Anita Biressi and Heather Nunn

Anita Biressi *and* Heather Nunn *explore the links between English identity, property and violence.*

Commenting on the arguments surrounding the Tony Martin case last year, William Hague argued that 'there is all the difference in the world between the career criminal who sets out deliberately to burgle a house and the terrified homeowner who acts to protect himself and his home. Unless our laws reflect natural justice, then they fall into disrepute'. Central to this article is an enquiry about the nature of the concepts of home and nation that underpin this difference between forms of criminal violence - the intrusion and violation of the home, and violence enacted in the defence of the home. And, more broadly, we explore the discursive and imaginary - fantasmatic - links between violence, home and national English identity in current political and cultural discourse.

We look at two figures who have triggered debate about the powerful symbolic status of the home, and the integral links between the home, nation, rural community and English countryside. The first figure is Roger Scruton, right-wing philosopher and now experimental farmer: this article is partly a dialogue with Scruton's book *England: An Elegy* (Chatto and Windus 2000; hereafter *Elegy*), which is one of a number of recent popular publications that seek to grasp the essence of Englishness at a moment when it is perceived to be slipping away. The second figure is the fenland farmer Tony Martin, resident of the run-down, appositely named, Bleak House in Norfolk, who shot two intruders on 20 August 1999, killing one and injuring the other, thus provoking a national debate about crime, justice and protection of rural communities. The juxtaposition of these two figures is intended to encourage us to think about current defensive attempts to re-create an authentic English identity, in response to a perceived sense of social decay. The discourses and images these two very different figures articulate and provoke are concerned with preservation, safety and containment; security in the face of the changing landscape of the English countryside; and the silenced voice of the embattled rural community. The way in which we might perhaps characterise their relation is as the mannered voice of English conservative civilisation, and the rage of its discontent.

Scruton writes of the threatened and largely abandoned 'hidden order' that once underpinned English identity - what he calls 'the soulful permanence' of 'the landscape', and the habitual domestication of home (*Elegy*, pp41 and 9). For him, being civilised had involved a peculiarly English self-moderation, upheld by the apparatus of English law and fortified by 'local customs'. This elegant melancholia is one possible response to the massive structural changes that have taken place in the countryside heart of Englishness. Another is Martin's defence by shotgun, which provoked discourses of retributive vengeance against those who threaten the world of property and security, and demands for 'the full force of the law' to be brought to bear in support of beleaguered country homeowners. Arguably, this case played a role in fuelling the broader political mobilisation of the countryside that is now a feature of current politics.

The Martin case was described by journalists Tim Rayment and Dipesh Gadher (*Sunday Times*, 23.4.00) as a tale about the real England ...

> the elusive, timeless place where apples come from orchards, buildings barely change and some people end their lives a few miles from where they started them. The England where Tony Martin shot Fred Barras.

Following Martin's conviction for murder, there was a flurry of political activity on behalf of the countryside and property. A one-hundred-strong group of Labour MPs drew up a manifesto for Labour to do more to tackle concerns of voters in the countryside. A group of Conservative MPs - including Gillian Shephard, the MP for Martin's constituency - demanded that the government boost resources for rural policing, and also that it clarify the law on the defence of self and property (*Telegraph*, 25.4.00). Linked to these responses, sometimes explicitly, sometimes implicitly, were images of the 'underclass': the traveller, the petty criminal, the thug; such people, it was suggested, encroach the boundaries of the home and set off 'natural' defence mechanisms. Anne Widdecombe stated, in response to the Martin case, that householders, before being prosecuted, should be allowed greater leeway to use force against such criminal classes to protect themselves and their property. In her words: 'I think it is quite right to say, "have a go" as long as one is responsible about it' (*Telegraph*, 25.4.00).

Rural life, violence and the private sphere

Roger Scruton (*Elegy*, pp7-8) analyses 'disquiet' over cultural changes as stemming from a perceived disruption of an old experience of home - 'a loss of enchantment which made a home a place of safety and consolation' (and here he refers, among other things, to immigration). His choice and validation of the notion of 'enchantment' invites a closer look, since it evokes several other, more critical discussions of national identity. In particular, Tom Nairn (see *The Enchanted Glass: Britain and its Monarchy*, Vintage 1988/1994) has criticised the 'gilded image' of the 'enchanted glass' by which the British perceive their national identity: an image 'made up of sonorous past achievement, enviable stability, and the painted folklore of their Parliament and Monarchy' (p9); and Patrick Wright (in *On Living in an Old Country*, Verso 1985) has discussed how the 'nation' and its symbolisation work to 're-enchant a disenchanted everyday life' (p24). In contrast to these writers, Scruton seems to endorse enchantment as a positive way of recalling 'England'.

Here and elsewhere he draws on an unusual vocabulary of magic and enchantment to articulate an elusive and probably mythical 'experience' of national identity. For him, the key movements in English literature have been movements to 're-enchant the land', to discover 'a hidden order', a natural order perhaps, that would explain our presence - an order that would seem (though this is unspoken) to relate blood and soil (pp40-1). Enchantment, states Scruton (p15), is a process whereby customs, institutions and even objects are endowed with a *moral* character that invites loyalty.

This mystification of home is certainly not new, but the collision in recent years of events and symbols relating to the rural, *violence* and the private sphere have offered unique inflections of 'home'; and these have been resonant and politically mobilising for many ordinary people. Political activism and physical confrontations on a range of issues - foxhunting, GM foods, petrol prices, foot and mouth disease, policing - suggest that new strategic (and sometimes contradictory) constituencies are beginning to emerge. And within this emerging set of concerns we can see new articulations of relationships between the home, violence and a defensive individualism that seeks to reinforce the home as a fortress against the outside world.

As Scruton notes, privacy more than any other social gift has been given priority in English cultural history. He observes that the freedom to close your door is the most valuable of freedoms: 'the Englishman's home [is] not just his castle but an island of "mine" in an ocean of "yours"' (p51). Home is the bricks and mortar that seem to shore up our defence against lawlessness and disorder. It is also the homeland, and the apparent structures of feeling that underpin it; and this homeland, in both public and private discourses, often seeks to shore itself up against something less tangible - contamination perhaps. In explaining the English fear of intrusion, of physicality, and of 'spontaneous social emotion' (p14) Scruton argues: 'physical existence exposes you to danger of contamination. Strangers must remain strangers, lest they pollute you with their intimacy' (p50). Scruton's image of the English home is one of carefully constructed defensive isolation - behind gardens, shrubs and borders, which establish 'an inalienable right to possession' (p52). This retrenchment is both material and psychical - self enclosure is not only about ownership of a plot of the land but also fear of exposure.

Home can be anything from a nation to a tent, but it is always an object of intense emotion. And the privately owned home in particular is intricately bound up with notions of respectability. The private world of the home has become symbolically central to public discourses of law and order, disciplinarity and national identity. And politically, home *ownership* is coupled with moral concepts of self-reliance and civic responsibility. In Conservative political discourse, home ownership has been traditionally held as an emblem of patrilineal obligation, an exemplar of social stability, through the inheritance of property and wealth across generations. Scruton interrelates the countryside, property and the litigious nature of the English (an alleged legacy of their Anglo Saxon roots), to produce a national sense of 'trusteeship'. This is a Burkean idea of society as a contract between generations: property, land and law infuse the 'national consciousness' and are emblems of the contract between generations - the dead, the living and those not yet born (*Elegy*, p119).

To be 'homeless' can thus come to be seen as existing in a condition of failure and immorality. The vagrant is severed from the past and gives nothing to the future. And a renting tenant on a run-down sink estate must constantly negotiate those long-held distinctions between the rough and the respectable; the notion of the 'underclass' underlines the difference between the worthy and unworthy poor. Furthermore, all homelands are not equal. Recent populist debates about asylum-seekers place them as both homeless and fraudulent, thereby erasing their own particular homeland histories.

The search for security

Though we started this essay with a quotation from William Hague, it should be emphasised that these particular discourses are not the exclusive property of the Conservative Party. Jack Straw's 'Zero Tolerance' initiative as Shadow Home Secretary in 1997 conjured up the spectacle of the decent citizen beset by squeegee merchants, winos, drug addicts and beggars. Here he was enunciating a neoliberal concept of individual empowerment, linking it to the right to security from crime, the right to consume and the right to choose - an approach which became hegemonic in the Thatcherism of the 1980s.

Personal responsibility for risk avoidance was also frequently presented as a model of good citizenship in Thatcherite discourse: one obligation of home ownership was the defence of property and the consumer goods within it. Law and order involved the individual's eternal vigilance. Anita Biressi has discussed elsewhere the rising tide of home security manuals that sprang up during the 1980s, along with Neighbourhood Watch and Crimestoppers initiatives (in *Crime, Fear and the Law in True Crime Stories*, Palgrave 2001). One manual for householders published in 1984 noted:

> Security is really an attitude of mind and the techniques now available to translate that attitude into physical protection can be effectively deployed only if *all* the risks are recognised ... to form part of a total security plan.[1]

It is this 'attitude of mind' that needs to be interrogated: the political articulation of a fear of crime and violence, in what is, in fact, a relatively safe society; and the fortress mentality in which the good citizen walks with purpose, or keeps 'em peeled, preparing their mind as well as their home against attack or invasion - in Scruton's terms, patrolling the boundaries between what is 'mine' and 'yours'.

The language of home security is essentially urban or suburban - Crimestoppers, *Crimewatch* and Neighbourhood Watch are about homeowners in the metropolis, the town or the outskirts of big cities. Indeed the encroachment of the urban on the rural, on the parochial small town, has itself been described as a threat to an ideal of home security. The liminal space where the city (and its connotations of dirt and disorder) meets the countryside is especially fraught with anxiety. As Wilmott and Young noted in *Family and Class in a London Suburb* (1960), the interwar ideal of the suburb as 'the country in the city' had collapsed under the pressure of postwar resettlement by the 1960s. Thus responses by suburban dwellers in Woodford, Essex to a perceived influx of former East-Enders revealed a violent resistance on their part to any invasion by the human overspill from the city's slums. The older residents spoke of their home as 'a fairyland', now defiled by those who, in their class difference, had breached the suburb's boundaries, bringing noise, chaos and litter.[2] There is a sense of estrangement here, not only from the new inhabitants of Woodford and their language, manners and behaviour, but also from the safety of suburban home itself.

The Tony Martin case has a political resonance that is related to the world of the urban home defender, but it is weighted differently. For the rural homeowner has arguably been excluded from the language of law and order until relatively recently. This is in spite of the fact that the figure of the farmer has been central to notions of English national identity: the farmer guards not only the domestic home but also the home-land, and as such is an

1. R. Traini, *Home Security and Protection*, Willow Books, London 1994, p8.
2. See V. Lebeau, 'The worst of all possible worlds?', in R. Silverstone (ed), *Visions of Suburbia*, Routledge, London 1997.

avatar of Englishness. But since the eruption in the press of the BSE crisis in 1996, the farmer has been at the nexus of contradictory discourses concerned with the preservation of the land and the collapse of rural livelihoods. A populist environmental discourse about threatened health and 'unnatural' farming practices, and political incompetence or cover-up, has been criss-crossed with economic discourses about the collapse of farming and consequently the collapse of the nation's economy and international standing in general. In recent coverage of foot and mouth disease the *farm* has figured as an object of nostalgia and of panic. It has been the symbol of a politically ignored rural community, and the focus of fears about the maintenance and crossing of thresholds - food and non food, human and animal, safe and unsafe country. These themes have appeared in displaced form in the recurring press images of defilement: the burning pyres of animal carcasses on the green fields of England.

Tony Martin: living in fear

The country as unsafe was at the core of media attention to the Tony Martin case. Martin was convicted of murder on 19 April 2000. The jury heard police evidence that Martin did not call the police when he realised that therc were intruders. Instead Barras was fired at with an illegal pump-action shotgun, being hit three times, twice in the legs and once in the back. The burglary ringleader Brendon Fearon received serious leg injuries. No warning shot had been fired. The case generated huge coverage. Martin was described as a tabloid hero, having received support from almost 300,000 *Sun* newspaper readers. He was even credited with briefly reinvigorating William Hague's political standing (P. Holland, *Guardian*, 4.9.00). The comment made by a resident of the nearby town of Wisbech seemed to sum up local feeling: 'I'd have done exactly the same thing, but worse. I'd have made sure I shot them both. A man's home is supposed to be his castle'. This comment was published in a *Telegraph* newspaper article called 'Everyone in this town is living in fear' (*Telegraph* 22.4.00) - a title that indicates the generic fearfulness and lawlessness that was identified as the condition of the town and of rural life more generally. What's more, Barras was a repeat offender from a family of travellers, and much of the concern articulated in the article was focused on the travelling community. Thus notions of the fecklessness and immorality of the homeless/ the traveller/ the nomad were once more brought into play. The travellers' difference certainly made them conspicuous in a small town. One *Telegraph* interviewee commented:

> Travellers can be really scary. A lot of people really hate them. They just go round stealing things. But they are a bit the butt-end of blame. They talk differently, they don't talk like normal people, they've got their own codes, they just sound like idiots.

Here a fear of homelessness is linked to abnormality, and used to express fears about policing and crime which extend beyond first-hand experience to a more general image of the dangerous and dissolute.

The 'Tony Martin Support Group' presented him as an emblem of the deep divisions in British society between the 'urban-minded government and rural folk'.[3] They suggested that he stood for the rural values of 'self-help, hard work, respect for authority, the family and the Crown as symbol and totem of the nation'. Of his rough justice they added, 'Not all country people have the same defeatist attitude to crime as our metropolitan elite'.

Martin was known as an eccentric to local police, and slept at Bleak House fully clothed with his boots on. He was obsessed with idea of being burgled. Three months before the murder, thieves had stolen furniture packed with irreplaceable family mementoes. Not long before that a grandfather clock had been stolen. He had informed friends that he had been the victim of at least six other break-ins in ten years although he did not report them and police cannot be sure they occurred. When the jury visited Bleak House they saw the booby traps he had laid out for burglars; they were not told that he had had guns removed two years before after incidents of shooting at someone stealing apples, or that in an argument with his brother he had shot out a window. He had harboured violent fantasies about the travellers he employed to pick fruit, and had talked of putting them in a field, surrounding it with barbed wire and machine gunning them.

The law exists to protect us from crime. But, it has been argued that it is also there to protect us from ourselves (see Tim Rayment and Dipesh Gadher's article in the *Sunday Times*, cited earlier). It is there to deter the primitive emotions and violent excesses to which we could be provoked if,

3. Tonymartinsupportgroup.org/pages/tandc.htm accessed 08.02.2001.

as with Martin, the home became for us a site of fear, a prison. In this sense it failed to deter Martin from his dangerous irrationality. As Rayment and Gadher wrote: 'After so many burglaries, real or imagined, he felt he could not trust the state to protect him, and grew so irrational that he was dangerous'. Martin's fears thus not only provoked debate about rural policing and its inadequacies, but also highlighted the fact that in some rural areas fear of crime was endemic. In their article Rayment and Gadher also recalled Freud's 'uncanny', as one of the prevalent metaphors through which we explore the contradiction between our desire for the familiar, the homely, and for a stable coherent community, and the fissuring of that image by the unspeakable, the terrifying, the alien or unknown. Freud's essay famously begins by noting the convergence of two apparently polar words, heimlich (familiar or close to home) and unheimlich (unfamiliar, strange), around a sense of 'something hidden and dangerous' (Pelican Freud Library, Vol.14, p340). He described the uncanny propensity of the familiar place to turn on its owner and become defamiliarised. In the case of Tony Martin, his nostalgic childhood memories were ruptured by fears of invasion and death, which fractured the safety of his fortified farm.

When Patrick Holland interviewed Martin for a TV documentary, he visited Bleak House and noted the thicket of trees that surrounded it. Martin described this 'mantle of trees' as a rainforest he had created for wildlife; it signified for him naturalness and isolation but also a moat-like protection from the dangers of the contemporary countryside (*Guardian*, 4.9.00). While awaiting trial in a 'safe house', Martin appeared unrepentant about the shootings, seeing them as the appropriate response to fear: 'We are supposed to live in a civilised society, but it is not the way I have been treated. People are not aware of what it's like in the countryside: criminals prevail - it cannot be right. It's not right that people should live in fear' (*Telegraph*, 20.4.00:1).[4]

4. In a speech made to the Labour Party Conference one month after the murder in September 1999, Home Secretary Jack Straw listed the five evils that Beveridge had aimed to tackle: idleness, ignorance, want, squalor, disease. To this he added another evil, which his 'crusade against crime' would tackle: 'the evil of fear'. Inevitably, his speech conjured up the spectre of social chaos and violent crime at the very moment he was purporting to alleviate fear of such scenes (news.bbc.co.uk/hi/english/uk_461000/461967.stm accessed 29.05.2001).

British exceptionalism

Andrew Stevens

Andrew Stevens *looks at the Blair government's lack of enthusiasm for a thoroughgoing modernisation of the British constitution.*

In 1997, American political scientist S.M. Lipsett expounded upon the theory of 'American Exceptionalism' in his book of the same name. For Lipsett, the term is predicated on the narcissistic belief in a vulgar dogma of 'Americanism' (as an ideological basis above all others), and on the constitution worship that permeates the American political system, history and popular culture. The term is by no means new: similar arguments were presented by Werner Sombart in his 1906 classic *Why Is There No Socialism In the United States?*; and legendary US pundit extraordinaire Gore Vidal has argued that the Democrats and the Republicans are just two wings of the same 'America Party'.

Around the same time as Lipsett wrote his book, former Charter 88 Director Anthony Barnett made more or less the same claim about 'British Exceptionalism' in *This Time*, the first of a series of analyses of the prospects of constitutional reform that has recently rattled off the word processors of liberal left commentators. At a basic level, British Exceptionalism can be taken to mean the defence and continuation of the hereditary principle in the House of Lords, Dicey's notion of the sovereignty of Parliament, the lack of a Bill of Rights or codified constitution, the establishment of Protestantism at the heart of government, antipathy towards the European Union (both its institutions and other member states), a hopelessly antiquated honours system ... and so on and so on: an onlooker might observe that, within this 'Western liberal democracy', there still remains in place an amalgam of some of the worst elements of Middle Eastern, tribal and pre-enlightenment practices. The term 'exceptionalism' here should be taken to refer not just to an assumed sense of superiority or of being a political system *par excellence*, but also a particularly close-minded smug mentality of dismissiveness. Another version of British Exceptionalism manifests itself in the version of British history that is often taken to define our national character - the assertion springs to mind that English philosophy has always eschewed abstract thought and is grounded in empiricism - though this conveniently ignores the writings of Thomas Paine and Thomas More, William Hazlitt and William Morris, in favour of Shakespeare, Burke and Bagehot. British Exceptionalism has long been the abiding domain of *The Spectator* and what passes for an intelligentsia on the right, and it manifests itself more recognisably in the 'stiff upper lip' attitudes and concerns of Scruton-esque *Telegraph* readers in Berks and Oxon. If anyone needed further persuading of its existence, they could do no better than to consider Lord Levene's defence of the feudal and anachronistic City of London Corporation in an edition of the *Wall Street Journal*: 'It is a British system. It may seem odd but it does work.'

Whiners, whingers and wankers

Given New Labour's commitments to modernise the constitution under the aegis of democratic renewal, and what is perceived as a general lack of reverence for the relics of Britain's imperial past on the part of the left, it could be assumed that British Exceptionalism would now be at least on the wane, if not at an end. However, things are not that straightforward. Like the many people who remain convinced that the discussion of constitutional reform is best left to the likes of Lord St John of Fawsley or the chattering classes of Hampstead, the Labour Party has traditionally shied away from radical thought on the constitution. This is for two reasons.

Firstly, the party has long sought to assuage the fears of the establishment and its representatives in Fleet Street over its intentions for the British state, both at home and abroad. After the debacle of 1924 and the Zinoviev letter, the party has historically sought to portray itself as a moderate force for the amelioration of the living standards of its core supporters. Indeed, the Attlee government, noted for its economic and social reforms, was altogether silent on the issue of the constitution, despite a burgeoning home rule movement in Scotland at the time; it even went so far as to appoint a particularly right-wing Lord Chief Justice in order to preserve its reputation as a 'responsible government'. During the second world war, George Orwell had the foresight to realise that a Labour Party with a Parliamentary majority would never stray too far from its accepted terrain: 'It will abolish the House of Lords, but probably will not abolish the monarchy. It will leave anachronisms and loose ends everywhere…' (*The Lion and the Unicorn*, 1941).

Secondly, the Labour Party, throughout its history, has never possessed a coherent strategy for the management of the state or its reform, and has always preferred expediency to any kind of principled stand. Within the administrative socialism of the Fabians, such a state reform strategy was viewed as either a distraction or a falsehood, since the British state, like any beast, could always be tamed and turned to use for their ends. To this day, this remains a popular argument within the Labour Party. Only recently, newly elected Labour MP and 'old right' stalwart Tom Watson could argue in the Blairite house magazine *Progress* that Labour shouldn't 'meddle with the constitution'. Such an attitude typifies the unsophisticated thinking that continues to foster the notion of 'British Exceptionalism' on the left and more widely.

Another worrying symptom is the Blair government's commitment to seek the extension of religious involvement in governmental affairs; it proposes an increase in the number of religious state schools, and pan-religious representation in a reformed House of Lords: 'But it will never lose touch with the tradition of compromise … It will retain a vague reverence for the Christian moral code and from time to time will refer to England as a "Christian country"' (*The Lion and the Unicorn* again).

There does exist, however, a more sophisticated view on the party's progressive wing, a small vanguard of which is firmly ensconced in think tanks, and in Ministers' offices as special advisers, and which is well-represented on the party's National Policy Forum; as leadership loyalists in all other respects, on this issue they transcend the formal division between Labour and the Liberal Democrats on the centre-left, in pressing for a more radical line on issues such as Lords reform and PR. They are unlikely to be successful on these issues, however.

These radicals flourished in the mid 1990s, as constitutional reform began to seem a real possibility, in the early heady days of New Labour and its rhetoric of a 'Young Country'; reformers were no longer dismissed as the 'whiners, whingers and wankers' of Neil Kinnock's era. Proponents of politics as usual, and the bread-and-butter politicians hanging around the old right of the Labour Party, became unfashionable. Previously overlooked blueprints offered by ginger groups such as the Labour Co-ordinating Committee were seen as lending force to the reforms proposed by the late Labour Leader John Smith in the name of doing the decent thing. Old politics was swept aside as Gordon Brown pondered 'how much of Will Hutton's book to put into practice'; and liberal opinion-formers such as Anthony Barnett wrote optimistically in the pre-Geoffrey-Robinson-era *New Statesman* about New Labour's new-found willingness to embrace radical constitutional change. Charter 88 had Tony Blair and Tom Nairn nodding in unison, while Andrew Marr and David Marquand claimed that the constitutional landscape would be changed beyond recognition once New Labour was in power.

But this progressive coalition was clearly in for a shock. Still intoxicated by the rhetoric of modernisation, it had to look on as the Prime Minister's (apparently republican) Press Secretary denounced constitutional reform as 'crap'. As events unfolded, the chattering classes began to smell betrayal. Some commentators remained sanguine, but writers such as Anthony Barnett and Tom Nairn went on the offensive, with terms such as 'corporate populism' being bandied around. Some glimmers of hope and confidence manifested themselves, as Scotland's first Parliament in three hundred years opened its doors for business. And Jonathan Freedland, having added himself to the ranks of polemicists in 1998 with *Bring Home the Revolution*, managed to gain an appreciative audience in Downing Street for his Yankophile writings, albeit for the wrong reasons (citizenship ceremonies, etc). But the introduction of the multi-arena politics of devolution had been thwarted by the 'cynical machine politics' that forbid anything remotely unacceptable to the centre. Things still remained very British.

To the seasoned constitutional observer, the claim that 1 May 1997 represented some kind of 'velvet revolution' seemed worthy of no more than a guffaw. Expectation had been built on the rhetoric of opposition; and, aside from what was promised in the manifesto, it would have been naive to imagine that Labour in government would do any more than bolt a few overdue and expedient reforms on the back of the 1688 constitutional settlement. By 2001 the constitution was about where it should have been when the Tories took power in 1979, had it not been for long-term government neglect from both parties when in office.

Stuart Bell MP, addressing an audience drawn from the then politically fashionable Christian Socialist Movement in 1998, stated that disestablishment of the Church of England (a chattering class reform not without its proponents on the left) would not happen under a Labour government. The Prime Minister saw the Church, along with Parliament and the Monarchy, as one of the three vital pillars of British society. It seemed that the 'Young Country' was going to have to rely on 'Cool Britannia' to deliver the goods

Though it means risking pariah status in New Labour circles, it is worth pointing out that an efficient framework for capitalism requires a democratic infrastructure other than what is currently in place. Ironically, so far this realisation has only found its way into the programmes for government of two parties, the Socialist Alliance and the Socialist Labour Party of Arthur Scargill fame, both of which are unlikely ever to form a government and certainly not a capitalist one. Letting daylight in on magic, to utilise Bagehot's famous phrase, would probably do us the world of good. The proponents of progressive thought in the business community, such as Charles Handy and George Soros, appreciate the need for capitalism to operate within open and codified surroundings, as opposed to the veritable dog's breakfast we currently possess. Neal Ascherson, among others, has argued that British management has been so inefficient since the second world war not because of economic factors but because of problems in the operation of the state. Turning on its head the notion that constitutional reform is of little or no practical significance, he argues against the 'common' and 'comfortable' view that there is nothing wrong with British institutions, that they are 'the finest in the world', and that they are not working because the economy is in such a bad state. In his view, the reason why the British economy does not work is that 'British institutions are in terminal decay' (*Games with Shadows*, 1998).

Harold Laski, another proponent of constitutional change, said that the rationale behind his desire for Parliamentary reform lay in the fact that society had changed more during his lifetime that in the period between the 'Glorious Revolution' of 1688 and the Liberal victory of 1906. Constitutional modernisation is not keeping pace with history.

But what would 'a nation at ease with itself' resemble? How will the era of 'new politics' be defined in an age when, as Blair himself has claimed, the 'new generation has come on that doesn't have the outdated attitudes of the past'?

The second term

The continuation of British Exceptionalism hinges on a number of factors, and the ball is squarely in New Labour's court. Firstly, the nature of English national identity, one of the most salient components of the concept of our 'exceptionalism', needs to be addressed. This was brought into the centre of debate by devolution to Scotland and Wales, and remained there throughout Labour's first term. Debates concerned both the question of Englishness, and the case for regional devolution.

Devolution was a constitutional reform based on expediency, and one which Blair would have dropped at the outset were it not for the affection in which party members still held the late Labour Leader John Smith (its chief proponent). Its aim was to stop Celtic-fringe nationalism at the ballot box - such is Labour's dependency on Scottish and Welsh seats under the First-Past-The-Post electoral system. The government does not appear to have realised that this reform, already uncongenial to those subscribing to the party's centralist culture, would have the effect of sparking off more debates and demands for reform. And it doesn't appear to have a strategy to respond to these.

Since Labour's conversion to the devolutionist cause, it was widely expected that Scottish and Welsh devolution would be followed by devolution to the English regions. One of the key strong points of the alliance of Scottish, Welsh and English anti-devolutionists in the 1970s had been the pro-devolutionists' lack of plans for England; but a strong regional lobby, particularly in the party's hinterland in the Northeast, had ensured that Labour in opposition, under both John Smith and Tony Blair, did not repeat this mistake. Calls for English regional assemblies became a recurring theme amongst the party membership, after a considerable period of Conservative government in which many parts of the country had suffered badly at the expense of London and the Southeast. Once in government, however, New Labour did not see the need to pander to its regional interests, and this reform was one of those conveniently slid onto the backburner by a sceptical Civil Service, occasionally being reheated by the promise of a Green Paper as a tantalising motivator for grassroots activists. Labour managed to duck the issue of the English Question (which became Westminster parlance for the erstwhile West Lothian Question) throughout the first term, with Home Secretary Jack Straw claiming that England's 'violent' past meant the issue shouldn't be raised, lest we ignite some Braveheart nationalism of our own, whilst the bread-and-butter Commons leader Margaret Beckett offered an English Grand Committee as an answer (akin to the Scottish Grand Committee revived by Tory Scottish Secretary Michael Forsyth in the run-up to the 1997 general election). If England had its equivalent of the Stone of Scone then this would have surely been returned from Westminster to its rightful home as an easy placatory gesture!

English regional government may strike some as the panacea to deprivation in the North and Southwest, but even if it were instituted there would still remain the question of Westminster's legislative deficit after Scottish devolution. So far devolution has had to be accommodated by the familiar resort to British Exceptionalism. Meanwhile, though cut from Westminster's apron strings to some extent, the Welsh Assembly remains a toothless talking shop. (It is seemingly a myth peddled by English politicians that the Welsh did not want devolution - perhaps the small margin of victory in the 1997 referendum had more to do with a Welsh rejection of an assembly with so little power.)

A second collection of issues concerns the nature and role of the British Parliament; here, New Labour's commitment to reform will be a litmus test for the survival of British Exceptionalism.

In spite of a general insouciance about all things relating to constitutional reform, the role of Parliament was seldom out of the headlines during Labour's first term; it became a political football between Labour and the Tories (and arguably between Labour's backbenchers and its leadership), and was the *leitmotiv* of Blair's premiership insofar as the aggrandisement of the executive was concerned. The erosion of the powers of Parliament in favour of a stronger executive was lamented throughout the twentieth century. Some see the pressure to modernise as an extension of this erosion - arguing, for example, that sensible working hours are designed to keep MPs out of the chamber. However, one only has to look at the way in which Michael Martin was elected as Speaker, or see MPs trudging through the division lobbies, to see where a healthy dose of modernity would come in useful. But people become suspicious of the language of modernisation if it seems to be linked with the continual increase of executive power.

The top hat used in Parliamentary debates may now be gone but much remains of that era, particularly in the House of Lords. Since the late nineteenth century, the House of Lords has evolved into the lesser chamber of Parliament, with its members largely owing their existence to birthright, judicial or ecclesiastical office, or patronage in recognition of service to the nation. Reform of this second chamber is one of Labour's most longstanding and popular commitments, and its abolition has remained a firm favourite of party members. As with regional devolution, however, the government is well on course to disappoint or even upset. Labour's Lord Chancellor Derry Irvine is arguably one of the most conservative holders of the office in recent times, and this has been borne out by his refusal to countenance anything but a largely unreformed house. Circumstances and policies are still constantly changing on this issue, however, and there have recently been some signs that the Government may be shifting its position. But they are clearly reluctant to undertake radical reform. It seems that a small ministerial turf war is taking place between the (elected) Leader of the House of Commons and the (unelected) Lord Chancellor - with Robin Cook under pressure from his own backbenchers to rethink the reform proposals.

There have at times been some signs of holistic thinking on this question. Meg Russell, one of Cook's special advisers, argued before the 2001 General Election that Commons and Lords reform should be packaged together, 'as distinct elements in a coherent constitutional package.'[1] In terms of actual reforms, however, there are few signs that a coherent package is being assembled, as some previously proposed reforms are shelved, and others, such

1. M. Russell, 'Democracy', in *Transforming Britain: Labour's Second Term*, Fabian Society 2001.

as the Freedom of Information Act, are watered down.

Proportional representation for the House of Commons (having been introduced in Scotland, Wales, Northern Ireland and London) is another reform that could command popular support amongst the electorate, but it is one more area where the government is reluctant to institute change. It is deeply embarrassed by its 1997 manifesto commitment to hold a referendum on the issue. This pledge, another part of John Smith's legacy, was conveniently dismissed in the face of evidence that Labour, on course to win a second term, was likely to have a third in the bag as well. Opinion polling amongst the electorate has, over the last twenty years, shown a healthy majority in favour of some kind of PR for the Commons. But this is an area where support from the Labour Party's active membership, and its elected members in council chambers and Parliament, remains pitifully low - and its proponents remain divided on the exact kind of PR required, to boot. The forces of conservatism on this issue are well organised amongst the key players in the trade unions and the Labour Party's decision-making structures.

The Secretary of the First Past The Post Campaign, Tom Watson, obviously sees some need to address the issue in his advocacy of compulsory voting. Compulsory voting is presented as a panacea for all kinds of electoral ills, ranging from low turnout to the deficiencies of the First Past The Post system. Watson and his colleague Mark Tami, another recently elected Labour MP of the old right, dismiss opposition to this proposal on the basis of its threat to civil liberties as a concern of the 'libertarian right'.[2] For them, British Exceptionalism, seemingly acceptable for other facets of the constitution is no longer *de rigueur* as far as this argument is concerned: 'As an observation, this is fair enough. Using this observation as an argument, though, is facile in the extreme.' Proposals for compulsory voting, and for other piecemeal reforms such as the direct election of mayors in local government, are knee-jerk reactions to some of the deeper problems of our democracy, whose effect would be to graft a managerialist culture onto yet another facet of our national life, and to further the trend towards the installation of the party manager into the democratic process on a more formal footing.

---

2. T. Watson and M. Tami, *Votes for All*, Fabian Society 2000.

In their introduction to *Beyond 2002*, one of a glut of books debating 'signposts' for policies in the second term, Martin Linton, Katherine Raymond and Alan Whitehead write:

> Our constitutional model still assumes a hierarchy from monarch, through the nobility, to the commoner. Our social system no longer reflects that. Most people nowadays would regard a duke or a marquess as a social equal, not a social superior. It is important to bring the constitution in line with society, not just by ending the political power of the peerage, but by bringing an end to all conventions based on deference and re-anchoring the constitution in the concept of citizenship.[3]

This would suggest that there is some consensus within the Labour Party in favour of ending the bi-partisan acceptance of British Exceptionalism. Indeed they go further:

> Deference breeds not only submissiveness but social irresponsibility. If people think of themselves as socially 'inferior', they find it easier to accept that they are 'unemployable' or 'welfare dependent'. If they think of themselves as citizens, on the other hand, they are more prepared to accept the responsibilities that come with their rights.

As steeped in Blair-Brown-Straw or Etzionian thinking as this is, they have a point. However, 'ending the political power of the peerage' suggests its retention for other purposes. When faced with demands to abolish the feudal office of the Lord Lieutenancy, Blair's banal response was to (unsuccessfully) pressure Buckingham Palace to appoint more people from ethnic minorities to the post. Similarly, those who heralded Blair's arrival as a reformer would have naturally expected New Labour to modernise the honours system, yet it is still based on an Empire that now only consists of a few scattered islands too small to govern themselves. Faced with ever-dwindling congregations, many in the Church of England feel that disestablishment would give it the freedom to work with other Protestant

3. M. Linton, K. Raymond and A. Whitehead, *Beyond 2002*, 1999.

churches, yet the organised religious lobby in the Parliamentary Labour Party remains fiercely opposed to this.

The cracks have been appearing on the face of British Exceptionalism for several decades now. The question is: when we will run out of paper to cover them up with?

The economic policies of Gordon Brown and the treasury

Stability for what?

John Grieve Smith
and G. C. Harcourt

The authors look at the principles underlying Gordon Brown's policies.

Gordon Brown is almost unique among Chancellors in the pains he has taken to set out the basic principles on which he believes economic policy should be conducted, and the rules which should govern the Treasury's budgetary policy. He did this most succinctly in his lecture to the Royal Economic Society's Millennium Conference in July 2000;[1] and more recently the Treasury have covered the same ground in more detail in a 350 page handbook on economic policy, *Reforming Britain's Economic and Financial policy: Towards Greater Economic Stability*.[2] These guidelines, which faithfully reflect the prevailing neo-liberal

1. Gordon Brown, 'The Conditions for High and Stable Growth and Employment', *Economic Journal*, Vol. III, May 2001, ppC30-C44.
2. H.M. Treasury, *Reforming Britain's Economic and Financial Policy: Towards Greater Economic Stability*, Palgrave 2002.

orthodoxy, deserve more critical attention than they have so far received.

The Thatcherite revolution in the1980s replaced full employment by price stability as the primary objective of economic policy. This remains the key feature of New Labour policy, despite its recent reaffirmation of 'full employment' as a key objective. The basic principle is now that unemployment should not be allowed to fall below a level that threatens price stability. The Bank of England's remit, in particular, is couched entirely in terms of an inflation target. Government responsibility for the state of the economy should be limited by making monetary policy the responsibility of an independent Bank of England and eschewing any active role for fiscal policy in maintaining a stable level of demand. The power of financial markets, particularly in a global context, must be acknowledged and propitiated.

Demand management

Gordon Brown's familiar keynote is 'stability'. It has not always been clear, however, what is to be held stable. Left to its own devices, the economy is unstable: demand and activity tend to fluctuate, and the rate of inflation varies. If greater stability in output and employment is to be achieved, measures must be taken to stabilise demand. In other words demand management is essential. That means that whoever is in control of economic policy must be free to vary whatever instruments are available to affect demand, i.e. tax rates, public expenditure or interest rates, in a counter-cyclical manner. This may seem obvious, but at one time Mr Brown and his advisers seemed to be treating 'stability' as referring also to stability in such instruments (i.e. tax rates, interest rates, etc). In the event, he has maintained this position on budgetary policy, and ruled out counter-cyclical variations in taxes or public expenditure, but he supports the active use of monetary policy to help stabilise demand. Although the current doctrine is that 'fine tuning' is dead, the Treasury have initiated a system under which interest rates are fine-tuned to a degree never hitherto imagined, with the Monetary Policy Committee agonising monthly whether to change interest rates by ¼ per cent!

Monetary policy is to be directed to one simple objective – 'price stability', the common misnomer for a steady rate of inflation. It is not altogether clear whether the inflation target is the sole objective of monetary policy in the belief that this will also optimise the stated objectives of high and stable growth and employment, or whether they believe that low inflation should be the over-riding objective for its own sake – which was the position effectively adopted in the Thatcherite revolution, in response to the inflation crises of the 1970s. Given, however, their reiterated statement that there is no 'trade off between inflation and unemployment', it is difficult to see why inflation should be the only variable targeted. The emphasis on the 'symmetrical' inflation target highlights the point. If inflation falls to 1½ per cent, why should the Bank of England try to get it up to 2½ per cent again, unless a relaxation in interest rates would be good for employment?

The use of the phrase 'trade-off' confuses the causal relation. There can be little doubt that low unemployment and strong demand make it more difficult to curb inflation; and, conversely, higher unemployment and weak demand, other things being equal, tend to keep down the rate of inflation. On the other hand, nobody has ever believed that higher inflation will in itself be a cause of lower unemployment. Certainly at no time during the post-war period did the Treasury deliberately go for higher inflation, as Gordon Brown and his advisers so often seem to suggest.

The Golden Rule

The worry today is that monetary policy on its own is unlikely to be sufficient to counter any threat of a serious recession. In that event a more expansionary fiscal policy would be essential. So far, however, the Treasury have shown no willingness to adopt any 'discretionary' budgetary measures, such as temporary tax cuts or increases in public expenditure, to increase demand. The Pre-Budget Report did indicate that by maintaining existing tax and expenditure plans, the Treasury would allow the 'automatic stabilisers' to take effect (i.e. lower tax revenue and higher social security payments). But there was no suggestion that they would be prepared to go any further and take any deliberate measures to expand demand. To do so would conflict with the Chancellor's Golden Rule that the current budget should be balanced over the business cycle.

It is intriguing that although the Chancellor is happy with 'discretion' in the case of monetary policy, he favours 'rules' for fiscal policy with almost religious fervour. The distinction appears to be based on the idea that a group of economists can be trusted to make decisions in the public interest, but a Cabinet minister cannot. This is very flattering to the economics profession, but hardly very democratic – are we to leave foreign policy to the diplomats and defence policy to the military? There is no particular sanctity in the rule that the current account budget should balance over the cycle, and government borrowing should equal public investment; it is purely arbitrary. In economic terms the government's net claim on resources reflects the overall balance between (a) current and capital expenditure and (b) revenue. Therefore in terms of its effect on demand the rule implicitly suggests that the Treasury's contribution to expanding or contracting demand will depend solely on variations in public investment – back to early Keynesianism! In social terms (or inter-generational accounting), a few moments' reflection will suggest that there is no inevitable validity in the idea that current expenditure solely benefits *current* taxpayers and capital expenditure benefits *future* taxpayers – so that it is all right to borrow for the latter, but not the former. Just as current expenditure on winning the second world war benefited future generations, so today's expenditure on education or health may have benefits for many years to come.

There is in reality no economic or social justification for the Chancellor's Golden Rule – much as financial markets may like it. Moreover, though the Chancellor has committed himself (properly in our view) to planning public expenditure in the light of the medium to longer term needs of the economy, he has not coupled this with the necessary corollary that variations in taxation will be needed from time to time to maintain macro-economic stability. Indeed, given the multiplicity of tax changes over the last three years it would be strange if the need to vary the fiscal stance were not a factor involved. Financial commentators frequently raise the question of whether the current 'fiscal stance' is appropriate to the state of the economy, and the Treasury assure us it is. But by 'appropriate', they virtually always mean tight enough to curb inflation, rather than loose enough to stimulate flagging demand.

Full employment

The most fundamental revolution in recent years has not been in the use of the tools of demand management; the change lies more in the purpose and direction of such use. Whereas after 1945 the prime objective was to maintain full employment, that is no longer so today. During the 1970s the prime objective became to reduce the rate of inflation, whatever the cost in terms of unemployment. Since then, maintaining a sufficient pool of unemployed (i.e. the NAIRU – 'non-accelerating rate of unemployment') to limit inflation has remained the over-riding objective. That this remains so has been made quite clear in the Treasury's Budget Reports during Gordon Brown's Chancellorship. This emphasis most obviously reflects the general tendency to refight the last war, in economic as in military strategy. But in political terms, Mrs Thatcher's election victories at a time when unemployment was at a previously unthinkably high level of over 3 million made it plain that for the majority of the electorate mass unemployment had become acceptable as an anti-inflationary weapon. This in turn reflected the fact that the shift in power away from employees and trade unions consequent upon the abandonment of full employment suited the powerful echelons of society whose views tend to dominate the media.

On both a national and international plane, the key characteristic of current approaches to fiscal and monetary policy is their contractionary basis. This is characteristic both of Gordon Brown's 'prudent' fiscal policies and the EU Stability and Growth Pact. The latter puts strong limits on the freedom of member countries to run budget deficits, and hinders the use of expansionary measures in a recession, such as Europe faces today.

How does this square with New Labour's readoption of 'full employment' as a major objective in the face of the decline in unemployment during their first term in office? The Government's approach to the unemployment problem has been particularly confusing. Ministers tend to speak as though it can all be put right by supply side measures, such as Welfare to Work etc. In other words the jobs are there, if only the unemployed were willing or capable of taking them. This is clearly not the case, particularly in parts of the country hit by the decline in traditional industries, like coal and steel. The more sophisticated version peeps out of the back pages of the Budget Report, and is now explicitly stated in the Chancellor's article: Layard's thesis that by increasing the competition for jobs, such measures can make it possible to have lower unemployment without sparking off higher inflation, i.e. they reduce the NAIRU. The tacit implication is that the present Government would like to see 'full employment' – in the sense of lower unemployment than the present 1½ million ILO unemployed – provided it does not upset the balance of power between unions and employers established by the Thatcherite revolution – in other words without a return to the more egalitarian society associated with post-war full employment, and with no need to work in harmony with trade unions and employers to achieve non-inflationary wage settlements.

International

On the international side, the Chancellor's credo has little new to contribute. As regards the EU he has stated that 'we are challenging the old claim ... that tax harmonisation and a federal superstate run by the European Commission are the next stage after monetary union'. But apart from the fact that a federal state would be run by an elected government not by the Commission, tax *harmonisation* is an intergovernmental not a federal issue – a federal government would levy uniform European taxes in its revenue raising fields, not harmonise national taxes. Tax harmonisation is a key issue not only in Europe, but also on a wider international context. There are a growing number of instances where effective taxation makes international co-operation and harmonisation of rules and rates essential. This will soon be true of taxes on financial transactions which can take place anywhere on the internet, for example the stamp duty on share transactions. It applies to many of the dealings of the mobile rich and their use of tax havens. It is strange that a Labour Chancellor should be 'putting the case for tax competition and against tax harmonisation'. The corollary would be a gradual reduction of taxes on the rich and companies, and an increasing burden on Middle England and the lower paid. (To look on the bright side, however, perhaps this means that he will reduce taxes on wines and spirits in the next Budget!)

On the wider question of reforming the global financial system, the Treasury has said little beyond renewing the call for greater transparency and better surveillance. Despite the Chancellor's affirmation of the 'high ideals and public purposes' of Bretton Woods, he has so far shown no awareness of the need for *fundamental* reform of the global financial system. Like other finance ministers and most financial commentators in this field, he sees the problems as lying between one or more countries in difficulty and the IMF (or World Bank), rather than as a matter of the mutual interaction of debtors and creditors, or those with strong currencies and those with weak ones. A fundamental point in Keynes's and White's approach to Bretton Woods was to try to establish some symmetry between deficit and surplus countries, with obligations on both sides in the process of readjustment. Creditor countries had an obligation to move back into balance as well as those in deficit. Although Keynes's original proposals to penalise persistent creditors were not embodied in the final Agreement, it did include the Scarce Currency Clause permitting discriminatory restrictions against imports from a persistent creditor. Given the fact that the country most likely to be hit by this was the US, it was a remarkable sign of the spirit of the times that the original proposal came from White and was accepted by the American negotiators. Today it is more important than ever to recognise that the strong, as much as the weak, have a role to play in financial crises.

The Asian Crisis was not solely a matter of over-borrowing by participants in the *Asian Miracle*. It was also a matter of over-lending by financial institutions in the West. Similarly, in the field of exchange rates the EU cannot raise the level of the euro on its own; it can only be done in conjunction with the authorities responsible for the dollar and the yen. Joint action is the key to tackling such problems. What is missing in the global field at present is any concept of combined action to stabilise financial markets and exchange rates. This is partly due to the large number of countries involved – although that does not stop the more powerful ones getting together for defence purposes. There are more encouraging signs of regional economic co-operation – not only in Europe, but also to a lesser extent in Asia and the Americas – where more manageable numbers of countries are involved. The Treasury's minimalist efforts towards greater co-operation to tame global financial markets contrast embarrassingly with the grand designs of its wartime predecessors. It is to be hoped that the greater emphasis on international co-operation sparked off by the terrorist attacks in New York and Washington will lead to new efforts to reform the global financial system.

When Brown was red

Fraser MacDonald and Andy Cumbers

Fraser MacDonald and *Andy Cumbers* revisit Gordon Brown's classic socialist text, *The Red Paper on Scotland.*

Every few months it seems that the media rediscover - in the manner of a freshly revealed conspiracy - that Gordon Brown, along with a disproportionate number of his front bench colleagues, is Scottish. There usually follows a crude typology of national traits among which dourness, canny-ness, thrift ('prudence') and Presbyterianism figure prominently. It is as boring as it is predictable: a half-baked political caricature of the eighteenth century served up hot for the chattering classes of the twenty-first. It must irritate him terribly, and yet, with all his talk of being 'locked into fiscal tightening', the Kirkcaldy money-counter cannot help indulging the hacks in their portrait. Although his other fellow travellers from the old days - Robin Cook and George Robertson - have deftly sidestepped these stereotypes, it is notable that all three have devoted much attention to softening their accents. This tactical flattening of vowels represents a peculiarly Scottish neurosis: that one wants to be Scottish but not *too* Scottish. The significance of this is rarely understood. It is an absurd and depressing paradox of the 'new' Scotland, that many regional dialects still carry the freight of diminished status in terms of class, education and professionalism. It is the political distance accompanying these vocal transformations that is our concern here, for the demise of the brogue parallels the demise of an important radical commentary.

Our story starts in 1975 at the inception of Gordon Brown's impressive career. A first class history student, Brown was not only studying for a PhD, but was student rector of Edinburgh University, an elected position of no little influence in the educational establishment. Not that the ambitious young politician needed such authority to ripple the still waters of the Scottish labour movement. But this he certainly did, by marshalling some of the foremost intellectual voices on the left to contribute to what has become an important if neglected memoir of socialist thought: *The Red Paper on Scotland.*[1] According to Neal Ascherson, the significance of the book sits oddly with its status as the *unread* paper. While many know of its existence, comparatively few have ventured inside its angry red covers and squinted at its tiny font. It is a long read: in true dialectical fashion, its sheer volume invokes the struggle aspect of class struggle. Stories abound of Brown being unable to resist 'just one more' contributor, squeezing in one chapter after another by reducing the typeface to a mere six points, and thus cleverly avoiding expensive additional pages. Such typographical prudence gives the book an unmistakably austere appearance, unwittingly mimicking the mass-production-chic of the Soviet presses. This authenticity of form was easily matched by the calibre of its contributors. The book's twenty-eight chapters included offerings from a young Robin Cook; Tom Nairn, already a well known commentator on nationalism; Vincent Cable, presently Liberal Democrat MP for Twickenham; the writer David Craig; the playwright John McGrath; and the literary critic, Owen Dudley Edwards.

Although the *Red Paper* represents something of Brown's own political energies, few have acknowledged the extent to which he was building upon an earlier radical legacy. If the title 'Red Paper' suggests a suitably militant (one might even say communist) heritage, the credit must, to Brown's certain relief, go elsewhere. His book was in fact the second, and as it turned out the last, in a series initiated by Robert Cuddihy who compiled *The Red Paper on Education* as a progressive antidote to Rhodes Boyson's infamous 'Black Papers'. But if the redness of *The Red Paper on Scotland* was almost incidental, its content positively bristled with the theory and rhetoric of socialism even if, like its editor, it was dressed in the peculiar fashions of the 1970s. Unmistakably

1. G. Brown (ed), *Red Paper on Scotland*, Edinburgh University Student Publication Board, Edinburgh 1975.

a product of its time, the *Red Paper*'s vision of socialism was concerned with seizing the levers of state power for the workers; with 'the planned control of our economy'; and 'the organisation of alternative production to meet social

The front cover of the Red Paper on Scotland

needs'. It can also be seen as part of a wider critique of the failure, not just of post-war social democracy but, perhaps paradoxically, of state socialism itself, for its centralising, bureaucratic and non-participatory politics.

Twenty-seven years on, as Chancellor of the Exchequer, Brown symbolises the journey made by many on the left in coming to terms with the hegemony of the right over the past two decades. The acceptance of the politics of TINA (there is no alternative to free market capitalism), in response to the crisis of social democracy and the pressures of globalisation, has characterised both New Labour and the centre-left throughout Western Europe. Brown's ascent to the international stage reveals his shrewd, one might also say cynical, tendency to don his radical garb when it suits him. Like the cartoon character Mr Benn who visits a costume shop in his lunch break, swapping clothes and his pedestrian identity for that of a zoo-keeper or a spaceman, so Brown adopts a socialist alter ego by wearing his old Labour attire. No magic is necessary. Simply a skilled oratory as the occasion calls, replete with the lexicon of social justice and fairness for the TUC, competitiveness and tax-relief for the CBI. That there is this measure of political schizophrenia about Brown has not gone unnoticed, as the recent portraits of 'Good Gordon' and 'Bad Gordon' (Andrew Rawnsley) and 'Old Gordon' and 'New Gordon' (Iain MacWhirter) testify. Perhaps it has always been this way for the more ambitious Labour politicians, but there are few who can match Brown's record at using his legitimacy as a closet socialist to pursue an aggressive programme of market liberalisation, deregulation and privatisation.

As many journalists have already told us, the story that Brown used to be red is no longer interesting. *The Red Paper* is perhaps worth revisiting for other reasons; less for its sneer potential against its now city-friendly editor, but because it contained some imaginative and workable ideas. We argue that its vision of a democratic and community-based socialism, as an alternative to the growing power of multinational capital, resonates with contemporary concerns about the consequences of neo-liberal policies at a global level. Moreover, that Brown - an architect of the neo-liberal world order - still lays claim to the militant tradition of Keir Hardie and Jimmy Maxton demands of us a rescue operation in historiography. We want, then, to reclaim the *Red Paper* and the Scottish socialist tradition of which it is a part, from both the glib dismissals ('Stalinist guff': George Kerevan) of the free-marketeers and the soothing patronage of the 'modernising' centre-left. We believe that the *Red Paper*'s emphases on community democracy and workers' control can reinvigorate the left project and, with it, an alternative politics of globalisation.

The *Red Paper* and its antecedents

The *Red Paper* was clearly written at a specific historical juncture and addresses the immediacy of its own time and place. During the 1970s a broad left discontent was directed at the failures of post-war social democracy, particularly in the context of an emerging crisis of accumulation. Scotland's own political and economic transformations were also important: the resurgence of nationalism, the implications of the discovery of North Sea oil and the growth of external control of the Scottish economy by foreign multinationals were all key themes in the *Red Paper*. At the same time, many of its contributors were part of a growing movement within the Labour Party to try to democratise its structures and broaden participation. Intellectually, the book's inspiration was very much that of the New Left, with its dissatisfaction with a dominant Western European style of socialism that prioritised a politics of redistribution over one of greater empowerment and participation. In its advocacy of workers' control of production, greater community involvement in economic planning and a general call for more decentralisation of political and economic decision-making, the *Red Paper* carried with it echoes of a much broader agenda, which rejected the failed policies of Keynesian demand management and Morrisonian nationalisation. The book was certainly not confined to a narrow Marxist concern with historical materialism and political economy. The influence of Gramsci (whose political notebooks had just been translated into English for the first time) and his concerns with the importance of cultural difference and the role of civil society in forging political consciousness is readily apparent. Most notably, the contribution by Tom Nairn, himself a key figure in the emerging New Left, draws heavily upon Gramscian ideas in understanding the role of the British state and the resurgence of Scottish nationalism.

There was, as one might expect, a distinctively Scottish flavour to the *Red Paper*'s radicalism. The early 1970s had witnessed an upsurge in industrial unrest across Scotland as the consequences of the British state's economic modernisation programme unravelled. Growing unemployment levels in both the traditional industries of coal, steel, shipbuilding and heavy engineering, and in the post-war growth sectors such as car manufacturing, revealed the inadequacies of industrial and regional development strategy. The *Red Paper* laid the blame for this recession at the door of post-war Labour administrations as much as it did Conservative ones. The 'accumulative failures of successive Labour Governments' was held to account for containing a growing working-class consciousness; there was criticism of a Labourism that over time had grown tepid, interested only in developing 'a scheme for compensating the least fortunate in an unequal society'. The top-down reactive modernisation pursued by successive governments could be contrasted with a new militancy among the grassroots, signalled by the work-in at the Upper Clyde Shipbuilders (UCS) yard in Glasgow in June 1971, an action that forced a U-turn by the then Conservative government to shelve its closure plans. For what had seemed a local dispute, the UCS strike - which at its peak attracted support from another 200,000 workers in Glasgow - was successful in generating a national debate about the right to work and the manner and direction of industrial policy. The symbolism of this was certainly not lost on Brown, who used a photograph of the UCS workers - hundreds of arms raised in reaffirmation of the strike - on the front cover of the book (see pxx). It was an iconic image that spoke of workers' power, community democracy and the importance of solidarity.

But if the *Red Paper* was a emphatic rejection of the conservatism that had precipitated the strike, it was also a rejoinder to the Scottish National Party, which by October 1974 had achieved an historic 30 per cent of the vote with 11 seats in Parliament. Countering the claims being made by the SNP about the prospects for an independent Scotland bolstered by massive North Sea oil revenues, the *Red Paper* puts the case for radical socialism over economic nationalism. For Brown, greater democratic participation in decision-making and working-class control over the means of production was preferable to an identity politics that would replace the British corporate state with a Scottish version, whilst leaving the mass inequalities arising out of uneven development intact. A forceful attack on Scottish nationalism would have been considered mandatory for a Labour activist of the time and yet it is surprising how restrained Brown is in this regard. Indeed, he delegates the chore of Nat-hammering to another contributor, Ray Burnett, and uses his introduction to strike a different chord, arguing that the purpose of the *Red Paper* is to 'transcend the false and sterile antithesis which has been manufactured between the nationalism of the SNP and the anti-nationalism of the Unionist parties'. Brown at least acknowledged the 'oil-fired expectations' of the Scottish people that had propelled the SNP to a position of credible political standing, and even gave one contributor, Bob Tait, a platform to amplify socialist currents within the SNP.

The most extraordinary move in the *Red Paper* - and perhaps its most notable achievement - was to consider devolved government for Scotland, not just as a possibility but as a socialist priority. It is difficult to emphasise how heretical this would have sounded to the gnarled old Left in Glasgow, and even the sleekit new Left in Edinburgh. Prominent factions in both mafias opposed devolution, like nationalism, on the grounds that what they saw as the politics of ethnicity divided the attention of the workers from the structural causes of inequality. The Labour Party had rejected devolution as a policy in 1974, and the spectre of 'tartan Toryism' lurked in the shadows for those even willing to consider a dialogue with the SNP. Two decades later, Brown has received considerable recognition for his commitment to devolution, a version of which was eventually delivered by a Labour government with the opening of the Scottish Parliament on 1 July 1999. But the detail of Brown's vision has been overlooked. His model cannot be reduced to mere 'Assemblyism': it recommended the transfer of power to units of political organisation much smaller than a Scottish Parliament. For Brown, 'the question [was] not how men and women can be fitted to the needs of the system - but how the system can be fitted to the needs of men and women'.

The restructuring of local government was a central part of this strategy, aimed at making democracy more accountable and its instruments more accessible to workers. Brown might argue that this idea has been carried forward in current proposals for regional assemblies, but this would be to overlook the fact that his own budgetary constraints have undermined the functionality of local government. Even the Scottish Parliament enjoys only the thinnest veneer of fiscal autonomy from Westminster; it is capable of raising a puny 3 pence tax in the pound, or around £700 million out of £20 billion budget. The difference between the kind of devolution delivered by New Labour and that conceived by the young Gordon Brown is therefore sufficiently wide to challenge the validity of his status as one of its early architects. Certainly, if we are to recognise the courage of Brown's stance on devolution in the *Red Paper*, we must also concede that the transfer in power he envisaged in 1975 has not been delivered by the Scotland Act 1998.

As a Scottish labour historian, no one was more aware than Brown that to acknowledge the heroic antecedents of the socialist movement is, in some sense, to place oneself among them. He was careful to locate the *Red Paper* firmly within the venerable tradition of the Scottish left, from the origins of the Independent Labour Party to Red Clydeside and beyond. None of this is allowed to be lost in the small print. Indeed, one doesn't need even to open the book to be made aware of its place in the annals of socialism: the iconography of the cover could not be described as ambiguous. If the UCS picture on the front had a contemporary force, the rear cover photograph of the 1913 Leith dockers' strike had the weight and authority of history. Sandwiched between these images, between past and present, is the book itself, heralding its succession as the rightful political heir to the movement. Brown consciously aligns the policy and critique in the *Red Paper* with that of the Scottish socialist 'pioneers' such as Keir Hardie, James Maxton, John MacLean, Willie Gallacher and John Wheatley. Of these notables, it was Maxton who became a political hero for Brown, who finally published his substantial biography of the Labour leader in 1986. It is an interesting echo from history that Maxton fashioned his own version of the Third Way in the 1920s, albeit a radically different one from its current Giddensian rendering. The 'Third Alternative' was a practical socialist politics, as Brown himself puts it, 'a third way between Labour gradualism and communism'.[2] Amongst other demands, it called for the nationalisation of the banking industry, the introduction of a 'Living Wage', and a programme of public investment that could be seen as foreshadowing Keynesianism. During the late 1920s, Maxton and his friend and collaborator John Wheatley (architect of Glasgow's first mass slum clearance and public housing building programme) railed against the rightward drift of the first Labour government under Prime Minister Ramsay MacDonald and his Chancellor Philip Snowden. There is little doubt, in reading Brown's biography of Maxton, where his sympathies lie: he clearly supports Maxton's vision of achieving a parliamentary socialist transformation. It is also

'the most extraordinary move in the *Red Paper* was to consider devolved government as a socialist priority'

2. G. Brown, *Maxton*, Mainstream Publishing, Edinburgh 1986, p192.

the view expressed in the *Red Paper*, where Brown acknowledges the necessity of what fellow historian E. P. Thomson called 'a peaceful revolutionary transition to an alternative socialist logic'. One might argue that this is the primary theme of the book: that democracy can be harnessed to devolve economic power to the workers.

The *Red Paper* further draws upon the legacy of the earlier 'pioneers' in its acceptance of a pluralist socialist vision. Like the Red Clydesiders, who were made up of a disparate assortment of communists, parliamentary socialists and anarcho-syndicalists, the contributors to the *Red Paper* represent a broad spectrum of left opinion. In contrast to the assiduous and tyrannical 'consensus building' approach of New Labour, in his role as editor Brown gave voice to the full range of political groupings that were active in the 1970s. Furthermore, writers were selected not merely from the aspiring political elite (Robin Cook, Jim Sillars, Vincent Cable) but also from journalists (David Gow), trade unionists (Alex Ferry), community activists (Colin Kirkwood, Richard Bryant) and writers (Tom Nairn, David Craig, John McGrath), the remainder being made up largely of academics. One might argue that it would be a hard task to enlist such a broad representation of left opinion from current Scottish civil society in support of Brown's New Labour. It is certainly the case that a new generation of Scottish writers - James Kelman, Alistair Gray, Tom Leonard and Iain Banks - have all signalled their support for the Scottish Socialist Party, which more closely resembles the politics of Gordon Brown circa 1975. But that it is to get ahead of our story.

New shades of Brown

The *Red Paper*'s openness to a diverse socialist vision contrasts sharply with the model of New Labour under the direction of Blair and Brown. Even within an ideology as ostensibly open as social democracy, New Labour has, through effective suppression of dissent and debate, fostered a managerialist politics whose singular focus is upon achieving and retaining parliamentary power.[3] As Mouffe and Rustin have both noted, despite the proclaimed consensus between

3. See M. Rustin, 'Editorial: A Third Way with Teeth', *Soundings* 11, 1999; and 'The New Labour ethic and the spirit of capitalism', *Soundings* 14, 2000; also C. Mouffe, 'The Radical Centre: a Politics Without Adversary', *Soundings* 9, 1998.

left and right that underpins the 'Third Way', New Labour's authoritarianism has stifled attempts to imagine a political alternative to neo-liberalism. Rather than revitalising social democracy, as centre-left commentators like Will Hutton, David Marquand and Andrew Gamble had originally hoped, New Labour's real achievement has been, as Rustin has suggested, in cementing the Thatcherite legacy and ensuring its survival. This realignment has proved so successful that even *The Economist,* not known for its endorsements of the Labour Party, felt moved to write: 'our instincts remain closer to William Hague's: for lower taxes, a smaller state, individual freedoms. But he has failed to make a credible case either against Labour or for his own party. Tony Blair is the only credible conservative currently available '(6.2.01).

Countenancing alternative political platforms and projects which might rival the dominant neo-liberal discourse is avowedly not part of the New Labour agenda. Starting with Neil Kinnock's 'modernisation' drive of the 1980s, a determined effort has been made to marginalise anti-capitalist alternatives in response to what was seen as the electoral logic of Thatcherism. If the party was to become electable, so the argument went, the expulsion of Militant and the ditching of Clause Four were the immediate fronts in the wider battle for the heart of the Labour Party. But alongside this very public contest, a more subtle initiative by Brown, Blair and other authors of New Labour was undertaken, to exclude the traditional diversity of the labour movement. At the very heart of the distinction between (old) Labour and New Labour was a sly rhetorical manoeuvre: that all the vote-losing baggage was now in the past, and thus the past itself, with its traditional openness to various currents of left and centre-left thought, was no great loss. And so a point of rupture (old/New) was invented, to secure control for one specific group within the Party, to the exclusion of everyone else - the Militant Tendency, the Campaign group of MPs, those involved in the GLC of the 1980s, even supporters of the centralist social democracy of the Wilson and Callaghan governments. It is remarkable that Brown, who only a few years before was preaching outright socialism, could become one of the central figures in establishing this new narrative for a new party. Several commentators have argued that he has always been more comfortable with his socialist past than some of his front bench colleagues. Perhaps this confirms the sharpness of Brown's political skill, that he has avoided any detailed public scrutiny of his own political transformation. It also speaks of his ability to make imaginative use of his past in a way which none of his contemporaries - who are either in outright denial of their previous convictions, or who travelled light in the first place - can match.

From the *Red Paper* to his PhD thesis on the Labour Party in the 1920s, to his biography of Maxton, Brown has built a strong reputation for himself within the Scottish labour movement as someone in tune with its radical traditions. A large part of his legitimacy within the Labour Party, in contradistinction to Blair, stems from his reputation as in touch with its core constituency, which from time to time requires an affirmation of the movement's radical traditions. Unlike Blair, whose instincts are more liberal than collectivist, Brown continues to use the s-word if it seems expedient to do so.[4] Writing as recently as 1999 in a pamphlet in the wake of the post-devolution settlement, Brown and Douglas Alexander return to the *Red Paper*'s position on nationalism and once again resurrect Maxton:

> In 1941 the Clydeside socialist James Maxton wrote of the SNP: 'They came to us who were international socialists and asked us to give up our internationalism in favour of nationalism. That I was not prepared to do.' And so it is today. Our aim should be not just to build a better country, but to build a better world and to recognise that, in the age of economic interdependence, to build a better country we need to build a better world.[5]

Poor Maxton. In this instance he is enlisted to attack what Brown and Alexander perceive as the economic nationalism of the SNP, which would erect - as they see it - costly new barriers to trade. But, reflecting Brown's attachment to orthodox economics, the evidence he offers in support of this argument is taken from the Cecchini report, a neo-classical modelling exercise designed to justify the European Single Market.[6] And so, although the 'internationalism' of Maxton is a clear euphemism for international solidarity among workers, Brown invokes it in resigned recognition of the interdependence of free trade and international

---

4. See for example his *Fair is Efficient: a Socialist Agenda for Fairness*, Fabian Pamphlet 563, 1994.
5. G. Brown and D. Alexander, *New Scotland New Britain*, The Smith Institute, London 1999, p3.
6. P. Cecchini, *The European Challenge 1992: the Benefits of a Single Market*, Gower, Aldershot 1988.

competition. Despite protestations that his economic policy is a form of supply-side socialism, the limits of market intervention are carefully respected by Brown. His surrender of monetary policy to the Bank of England, his adherence to tight spending limits, and his highly personalised backing for the Private Finance Initiative, all amount to an implicit endorsement of the market as a regulator of social life. It is a familiar paradox of the free market that, while Brown envisions a leaner state which is more reluctant to 'intervene' in the allocation of market goods, he has also has strengthened the state through re-centralising economic decision-making. In a move which might be seen as consolidating his own power base within the Cabinet (we might speculate on his Prime Ministerial ambitions), Brown's Treasury has assumed a new control over every area of fiscal expenditure, particularly through its system of service contracts. Thus, 'neo-liberal', like the term 'Labour Party', is one of the more successful misnomers of our time.

Remembering the *Red Paper*

We do not claim here that the *Red Paper* had any seismic impact on the Scottish political scene. It did not transform the electoral landscape, usher Scotland into a new socialist utopia or even convict many doubters about the need for a radical reorientation of national wealth. If anything, the reception, and certainly the appreciation, of the book have been slow and measured. Of the many myths of origin that it has generated, one story recounts that in the dusty recesses of the publisher (Edinburgh University Student Publications Board), there was a cupboard full of unsold copies of the *Red Paper*. Over the years, copies slipped away until - oh the poignancy! - the cupboard was bare. One supposes that such a fable is intended to emphasise that the book's impact must be assessed over the long term. And for this reason we arranged a conference on 1 December 2000 at Aberdeen University, to mark the twenty-fifth anniversary of the *Red Paper*, inviting (of course) Gordon Brown, Robin Cook and all other contributors to examine what, if any, relevance the book may have for a new political age. Brown, predictably, did not accept our invitation. While we cannot pretend that his blunt refusal would have caused him any embarrassment, the unfolding of his political diary gave him a fairly concrete excuse. Indeed, on the very day of the conference, he addressed the farewell rally of the debt campaign coalition *Jubilee 2000*, announcing that Britain would, within the end-of-year deadline of the campaigners, renounce its right to interest payments on £1 billion owed by developing countries. Aside from the coincidence of its timing, Brown's address to the debt campaign is a good illustration of the general pattern we identify in this paper: with consummate political skill, Brown is seen pledging to tackle the crippling consequences of debt, while continuing to support the free trade model of the World Bank and the IMF.

Although many *Jubilee 2000* campaigners point to the essentially superficial efforts that the G8 have made in relation to debt relief, the development of Brown's international sense of social justice is a welcome departure from the emphasis in the *Red Paper*. Of the many legitimate criticisms that can be levelled at the book, one of the most valid is the nearness of its political horizon. As Neal Ascherson has already remarked, its vision was very much of socialism in one country, with little reference to Europe or other units of sub-national or international governance, or even links to other socialist movements across the world. The *Red Paper*'s intensely local concept of solidarity must surely be made global if it is to have meaning for our own time. And yet, in the current climate, when it is conventional to talk glibly about being beyond 'old certainties' (class), it is hard not to feel depressed that an everyday class-consciousness within Scottish political culture is being subsumed by the illusory politics of consensus. This impression, however, is more evident within the media than among the grass roots. Indeed, beneath the quiescent culture of party politics in Scotland lie the stirrings of dissent. From the Trident Ploughshares protests at Faslane to the occupation of a Govanhill swimming pool - a rare amenity in one of the poorest constituencies in Scotland, earmarked for closure by the Labour-run council - currents of localised radicalism recall the spirit of community democracy that we find in the *Red Paper*. More significantly, the presence of organic and autonomous protest movements across Scotland reveals that socialist politics have found new vehicles of expression outside the often inhospitable structures of political parties and trade unions. That these groups have become internationalised, routinely making connections with global anti-capitalist movements from Pollock to Palestine, could hardly have been anticipated in 1975.

The young Brown is more accurate in identifying the structural causes of inequality, which have only consolidated their grip in the intervening quarter century. The hypermobility of finance capital, the growing power of multinational corporations and the increasingly dependent position of the Scottish economy within the international division of labour are all anticipated in the *Red Paper*. Brown's solutions of the time (wholesale renationalisation of the banking and energy industries) might seem a little distant from his own Government which, when faced with the financial collapse of the national rail system and overwhelming public support for public ownership, still insists on the role of the private sector. New Labour have even resisted the most workable intervention in the circuits of global capital, the introduction of a Tobin Tax on international currency transactions, which would not only stabilise financial markets, but could also raise an annual $250 billion dollars for health and education initiatives across the developing world.

The regressive aspects of the *Red Paper* are not confined to its occasionally parochial vision. Of its 28 contributors, all are white men. The absence from the *Red Paper* not only of a gender politics, but also of any female voice, cannot be lightly dismissed as merely another feature of its time. Not only would this be to occlude the significant remodelling of the socialist project by feminists, which was well underway by the early 1970s, certainly within the political circles in which Brown moved: it would also be to fail to challenge the familiar patriarchal association of labour, masculinity and Scottish national identity. Front and back covers feature hundreds of men: women simply do not exist. Other commentators have observed this situation as if it were some minor oversight, easily corrected by the addition of a 'bolt-on' feminism to a pre-existing socialist politics. We insistently reject this view, and the systematic exclusion and denial that it represents.

Aside from the *Red Paper*'s general success in promoting a form of socialist vision that transcended the then stale arguments about devolution and nationalism, we can also point to specific conceptual achievements. One chapter by Frank Stephen prophetically outlines the need for, and describes the remit of, a new Scottish Development Agency: an institution with the same name and similar goals was set up the following year. Two chapters by Jim Sillars and John McEwen make the case for a far-reaching programme of land reform, one which would entail a profound reorganisation of resources to finally defeat the power of Highland landlordism and open up land for the small farmer and crofter. Remarkably, Scotland still has the most concentrated pattern of private landownership in the world, a fact that the current Draft Land Reform (Scotland) Bill has approached with considerable timidity. It is true that even having a Parliament through which to pilot such a Bill would have been a distant goal in 1975. But the gratitude of those who waited expectantly on a Labour government to deliver these and other basic reforms must surely be tempered by the rapid realisation of their finitude.

The *Red Paper*, in short, is worth remembering. At a time when New Labour have invested so much political capital in the renewal of social democracy, the figure of the young Gordon Brown gravely points to the failure of previous Labour governments to tackle the extent of material inequality. The limits of social democracy in our own context, as in earlier ones, are becoming increasingly evident. The concern with income redistribution through a system of welfare benefits, for instance, is being replaced by calls for a guaranteed minimum income and the redistribution of working time. The latter has of course already been adopted in part by Jospin's Socialist Administration in France with its policy on the 35-hour week. The contrast with Blair and Brown's fixation with American-style employment flexibility and the contested welfare-to-work programmes could not be more apparent. In this, as in other policy areas, the departure from the *Red Paper* script is fundamental rather than tactical. Gordon Brown, more than anyone, needs to revisit *The Red Paper on Scotland*. Occasionally there are moments in his public oration when he can speak the language of social justice and sound convincing. The funeral of the late Donald Dewar was one such instance, when in airing the late First Minister's core values, it almost seemed as if he was trying to remember his own. To re-inspect those early ideals is to acknowledge that the socialism of Brown's youth has not so much lost the argument but been dropped from the political question.

Four poems

In the Evening after the Morning

In the evening after the morning
of your departure the weather broke.
A high wind rolled clouds over the sun,
which turned moon-pale, went under,
then briefly lit the slate roofs.

When the train slammed into the station,
our faces touched. Walking away,
I went on talking, taking both parts,
confounded what we had,
and what we might have, said.

That evening I said: what will it matter,
in the end, when the sun swallows the earth,
that tonight I lie untangled, straight
as a plank, say '*you, you*' into the dark,
not expecting an answer?

Susanne Ehrhardt

Knowing

You've planted your Encyclopaedia of European Flora
as if to staunch this flood of grasses, bore me,
pin down this troupe of Woodbines? Vetch? Wind-flowers?
Whatever … dancing us along their path this early summer.

I never seem to learn the name of flowers and trees
anymore than of history I remember its triumphal days,
its ultimatums; I let things drift and drifting
with them see white bells, white Bluebells? … Windflowers?

Whatever … flare their nostrils, blow trumpets pianissimo
as we pass. 'To know their names is to really know, as no
mind awash with kitsch knows, you say'. You're right!
Only I remember once, by the sea, waiting imprisoned

While you frowned down the index for Scilla Marittima …
frowned at my gushing over a clump of them:
silky majorettes with yellow batons crowding
the thick black stem; and your finger pausing:

'A common name for this type is the Seashore Onion:
fat red bulb, pyriform, six petals joined by a long
raceme petiole, to be found in coastal zones';
and me lying low, holed up in the regime of your truth.

But it never lasts. It's summer again and we've come
to this field of yellow flowers – okay, what's the name!
Buttercups? Tormentil? Hoary Cinquefoil? Sickle Medick?
Let's leave them nameless as the smelted gold this field's
become.

Judy Gahagan

Children of 'The Revival'

1.
Some of the days we wake up
and something both arresting and violent
in us despises history.

Desire is not even spoken of
in such days; we watch the sky instead.

2.
We waited weeks for it to open.
We raided our hearts - ransacking our imagination -
drank the flickers off the sea and searched
each other's clothes and pockets for meaning
or even a sign.

Our mothers do not comfort anymore,
our fathers are not here. All we've got are women -
we are surrounded with aunties and wives -
but everyone is silent,
dream stricken.

Hisham Matar

Carole Richardson

I'm talking with this woman
In the empty Away seats at
Watford Football Club about
The Guildford 4 and how she
Went to the same school as
Carole, but in a different
Year, while our respective
Sons run around the pitch
As part of pre-season training
And the harsh afternoon heat
Blisters the fresh yellow paint
Even before it dries. A man in
A suit opposite has brought his
Boys over from Ireland. The coach
Has just called 2 minutes and 1.

Meaning two minutes more
At the steady pre-season pace
And then a final lap sprint:

Where it matters and they all run
As though they are being pursued.

Suddenly the woman who went
To the same school as Carole
Squints into the raw sunlight
And says unexpectedly,

like Tupperware:

It must be nice, having beliefs.

Steven Taylor

[Carole was one of the four innocent people charged and convicted of the Guildford pub bombings in 1975. Carole, Paul Hill, Paddy Armstrong and Gerry Conlon were finally released in 1989.]

Journeys to the motherland

Sasha Miller

Naomi Wolf, *Misconceptions*, Chatto & Windus £12.99
Rachel Cusk, *A Life's Work*, Fourth Estate, £12.99

Sometimes it is only when a person arrives that you realise they have been missing. Much has, of course, been written about pregnancy and motherhood. To find it, as Rachel Cusk describes, you must 'pass nearly everything, the civilised world of fiction and poetry, the suburbs of dictionaries and textbooks ... books about how to mend your motorbike or plant begonias and books about doing your tax return. Childcare manuals are situated at the far end of recorded experience, just past diet books and just before astrology.' And yet women - real, thinking women with lives and feelings and friends and jobs - are strangely missing. For the most part, mothers are not people. They are carriers of babies and they are the bodies from which the babies are delivered. They are the night-waking providers of milk and changers of nappies. They have concerns about what equipment they should buy or how their child is developing. But real people whose lives are inevitably and permanently altered by the arrival of their first child? Not according to the textbooks.

What both Rachel Cusk and Naomi Wolf successfully do, in *A Life's Work* and *Misconceptions* respectively, is put the woman centre stage in the drama that becoming a mother necessarily entails. Each writer recounts her own experiences of pregnancy and motherhood and - though both women share a desire to expose the grim reality behind the more saccharine and sterile accounts of motherhood that are widely disseminated - here the similarity between the books ends. Rachel Cusk's journey is an intensely personal one. Battling with conflicting emotions she hopelessly tries to hang on to the vestiges of her life under the irrational and unreasonable reign of her newborn 'tetchy monarch'.

Wolf takes an altogether more political stance. For her the blame for the hardships of modern motherhood lies with the medical profession who have dehumanised the birthing process, turning it into a brutally industrial one, and with a society that has sent the status of mothers into freefall, no matter what they have achieved in their prepartum lives.

Wolf's analysis of the birthing industry is useful. Motivated by the traumatic birth of her daughter - she underwent 24 hours of largely unsupported labour before being wheeled into theatre for an emergency Caesarian - Wolf takes on the medical professions with the same zeal with which she approached the beauty industry in her best-selling book *The Beauty Myth*. She describes the two totally distinct doors open to women as they start on their journey to childbirth. One is marked 'conventional', the other 'natural'. Neither, Wolf argues, offers women the best care, although most of her vitriol is, perhaps understandably, directed at the 'technicians' who stand behind the 'conventional' door. Challenging the arguments behind standard hospital procedures such as foetal monitoring and recumbent birthing positions, she paints a picture of labour wards organised like conveyor belts for the convenience and efficiency of the doctors who run them, with little or no consideration of the needs and choices of the women who labour in them. Yet the 'natural childbirth' movement also has its faults, principally the ideological slant that tends 'to romanticize the truly difficult aspects of natural childbirth in a way that makes thoughtful women of today sceptical of their otherwise important and accurate claims'.

The answer, suggests Wolf, is that those behind each of these doors share their skills.

> Women deserve a birth culture that unites the best of these worlds without ideologues at the two extremes, who do not take the needs of individual women into account, tampering with the agenda. Women deserve honest brokers and true advocates who will inform them about all risks and options available, who will explore what pain can be and what it might not have to be; who will make a concerted effort to eliminate unnecessary interventions and who will stop romanticizing either the controlled nature of high-tech mechanized labour or the culture of alternative birth.

It is when Wolf returns home with her new baby that her story becomes less compelling. Struggling to cope with a post-natal depression that she attributes at once to a bio-chemical crash - 'an entirely foreseeable crisis', she suggests, given the stress of the birth and the brief time allowed for recovery before being left to care for her baby alone - and to the 'acute sense of demotion that came with motherhood', she apparently sees the world through new eyes. The couples 'who were living in different social classes' because the man is in paid work while his wife stays home to look after the baby. The women who still took on the lion's share of the domestic duties despite both partners being in paid work. How no one wants to talk to you at a party if your day has been spent caring for children. The lack of money spent on public facilities to make looking after children easier and more pleasurable. All these are valid issues. But they are also the bread and butter of feminism and are hardly breaking new ground. For such a celebrated feminist as Naomi Wolf to pounce on them with such indignation simply because she is now experiencing them for herself leaves the reader more irritated than enlightened.

In her conclusion to the book Wolf advocates a new 'Motherhood Feminism' to campaign for everything from paid parental leave and woman-centred birthing procedures to community play centres with toys and activities for the children and newspapers, coffee and internet access for their carers. This is not a Utopian vision, she insists. Goodness, fifty years ago who would have thought a space filled with exercise machines would have been a viable commercial proposition? Yet such a vision will require revolution in the value we attach to motherhood, and on the evidence of this book one can only feel pessimistic. Half way through her pregnancy Wolf, in a moment of epiphany, suddenly sees the role of mothers in the world around her. 'It was something that had always been invisible to me before, or so unvalued as to be beneath noticing: the *motheredness* of the world.' If Wolf couldn't see it in her pre-motherhood days, what hope is there of her convincing the rest of non-mothering society.

One can't imagine novelist Rachel Cusk would attend one of Wolf's community play-centres, with its artistic daytime activities and pot-luck dinners by night, even if one was built on the corner of her street. While Wolf's narrative is interwoven with the voices of others - we are continually told of the experiences of Tessa, an editor, or Sarah, a travel agent - the canvas of Cusk's *A Life's Work* - her first piece of non-fiction - is a startlingly empty one. True, she discusses books that she reads or recalls during this period of her life, books whose insights 'seem to me to give voice to my theme'. These books include Edith Wharton's 1905 novel, *The House of Mirth*, which 'asks the question of what a woman is if she is not a wife, a mother, a daughter?'. When trying to teach her baby to sleep through the night she recalls Charlotte Bronte's Jane Eyre for whom, 'the lesson of sleep is a lesson in loneliness'. But on the rare occasion Cusk introduces real rather than literary characters into the narrative - the well-meaning health visitor; the demonic child minder - the encounters are largely fleeting and unsatisfying. The effect is to tune out the outside world, leaving only herself and her daughter as they negotiate the first year of their life together. It is an intense place to be and a potentially claustrophobic one. As the baby learns to crawl, Cusk finds herself confined to the kitchen, the only room in which she feels safe. 'Time hangs heavy on us and I find that I am waiting, waiting for her days to pass, trying to meet the bare qualification of life which is for her to have existed in time. In this lonely place I am indeed not free: the kitchen is a cell, a place of no possibility. I have given up my membership of the world I used to live in. Sometimes I listen to music or read, and it is like a ray of light coming in from outside, bright and painful, making me screw up my eyes.'

Cusk's evocation of motherhood is a series of complex contradictions. She is split in two, the 'person' and the 'mother', two entirely separate entities, but at the same time she is conjoined into the single unit of 'motherbaby'. She longs for freedom, yet when she achieves it, she spends her expensive time hovering at the door of the study listening for signs of her daughter's distress. She describes vividly her fierce and painful love for her daughter, but when another new mother reminds her 'you mustn't forget the good things', in response to her tirade against the tyranny of babies, she has to stop herself from retorting that there aren't any good things.

What ameliorates the bleakness of this vision is Cusk's humour, a wickedly unsentimental wit that forces you to laugh even at moments more normally treated with hushed reverence. For example, when the midwife encourages her to suckle her baby for the first time: 'I put her to the breast. The word "natural" appears in a sort of cartoon bubble in my head. I do not, it is true, feel entirely natural. I feel as though somebody is sucking my breast in public.' Shocked by her baby's apparent competence in the business of sucking, Cusk then embarks on a flight of bizarre fancy in which she views the baby as an alien interloper who has been issued with these instructions. 'The milk will be in the breast. The midwife will give the signal. You must take the milk every three hours otherwise the supply will dry up. Our agents will be in touch shortly. They will come to the house calling themselves "health visitors".'

Where Wolf concludes with a Mother's Manifesto, for Cusk, time provides its own solution to the mothering meltdown that occurs in embryonic families. Just as we fail to see babies until we are mothers, so when we become mothers it is easy to forget that our children will not be babies, utterly helpless and dependent, forever. As mother and daughter separate, Cusk begins to catch glimpses of herself, the person. 'Brief pauses appear in the score of motherhood, silences like the silences between album tracks, surrounded by sound but silences nonetheless ...Increasingly, motherhood comes to seem to me not a condition but a job, the work of certain periods, which begin and end and outside of which I am free.' And where once she viewed her child as the cause of her confinement, now she is part her freedom, 'something new that is being added, drop by daily drop, to the sum of what I am.'

Perhaps Cusk has had an easy ride. In the introduction to *A Life's Work* she informs us, with wry irony, that her husband has given up work to look after the children, allowing her to write a book about looking after the children. (This information was a warped mirror image of my own situation, as I failed to look after my children, so engrossed was I in Cusk's account of looking after her children.) Cusk accepts, if gloomily, that a book about motherhood is only of real interest to other mothers, which perhaps is why it is hard to imagine the seeds of Wolf's manifesto taking root. As a mother, the confirmation that one day my life will be returned to me, changed for certain, but mine to do with what I will, offers more hope than any Utopian vision. It is for that reason, and for the laughter, that it is to Cusk I will turn should I need reminding of the journey we make to reach the motherland.

Cultural politics

Gregor McLennan

Timothy Bewes and Jeremy Gilbert (eds), *Cultural Capitalism: Politics After New Labour*, Lawrence and Wishart 2000

This is an engaging and serious volume which stands fittingly in the Lawrence and Wishart tradition of trying to give recent academic debates and methods of understanding a definite purchase for concrete analysis and political motivation in the 'present situation'. Of course, if there are echoes in this of the various texts produced in the wake of the 'Communist University of London' and related forums of earlier days, there are symptomatic differences too. The collection is conceived as a response to circumstances of 'total defeat' for the left, and reflects pervasive anxiety about what constitutes progressive thought and action in ever-newer 'new times'. It also concentrates overwhelmingly on the idea and politics of 'culture', at the expense of other dimensions of social structure and political struggle. Or rather, it falls into line with the true but tautological and not always productive 'insight' that because there is nothing outside culture, all politics is cultural politics. Beyond this, the editors' admirable aim is to try to get more explicit forms of leftist politics back into the business of thinking and acting culturally.

The implication here is that the politics has somehow leaked out of thinking about culture, and with this in mind the book forefronts a series of chapters addressing the dilemmas and prospects of 'cultural studies' as an intellectual project. Though these 'interrogations' are able enough, the book's title and subtitle come to seem quite misleading as a result of this ordering. There *is* material about cultural capitalism and New Labour, but not enough to take centre stage; and so, overall, the different registers of aspirant academicism on the one hand and moral and political exhortation on the other compete rather than coalesce.

One of the principal contentions on the ostensibly political side is that New Labour, contrary to the complaint that it represents no hegemonic project, constitutes an impressive and systematic refiguring of political action and subjectivity. This works by presenting the needs of a managerialist, conformist, and work-centred ethos in moralised and culturalised terms. Jeremy Gilbert insistently takes this up at a general level, arguing that there is little to be gained from just bemoaning this cultural *mores*, nor even from trying to improve or correct it. Instead, we must develop a fully alternative approach, featuring the idea of radical democratisation at its core, and a commitment to nurturing the kinds of cultural spaces - evident in some dance and music subcultures - where better practices and values have emerged. Various chapters on particular aspects of New Labour discourse provide ammunition along these lines, notably a good analysis by Alan Finlayson of the Blairite culture of governance, with a range of more sporadically useful observations by others on such things as the Dome model of the creative economy; the holistic 'missions' of business organisations and corporate identities; and the way in which cultural phenomena like the Young British Artists 'fit' the logic of the Blair project.

The argument that New Labour discourse shows distinctive substance and novelty is convincing and important. Its immediate plausibility is seen as receiving deeper support in Timothy Bewes's contention that any analysis of innovation conducted in terms of the denunciation of 'spin' is unappreciative of the logic of mediation. Be that as it may, the political alternative that is presented remains questionable. For example, Gilbert barely signals just what he means by true 'democratisation', and does not give reasons why people might find this a more fulfilling political medium for the organisation of their lives than other governing ideas. He also continually invokes the thoughts of Laclau and his associates on questions of hegemony and democracy, though it has been plain for many years now that under Laclau's formalistic understanding of the democratic imaginary as abstract 'antagonism', no substantive social arrangements, or moral collectivity, can be singled out as embodying it. Thirdly, hedonistic subcultures are praised for their *creative* alternative to the dour working virtues of Prudence. But there are difficult questions here: some elements of hedonism are clearly *anti*-political, and it is not merely puritan to see *any* viable politics as requiring dutiful commitment to the collective endeavour, including the production of wealth.

Finally, there is at times an almost Giddens-like discounting of 'old left' understandings, though The Third Way is otherwise cogently critiqued.

Thus, the possibility that the common situation of being *workers* in postmodern capitalism remains crucial for politics is quickly binned. Yet Gilbert paints a picture in which millions of supposedly 'middle-class' types are over-monitored, over-ranked, performance-indicated, under-valued, and under-utilised. Even the managerial class, we are told, is insecure and facing social redundancy. Well, if our shared experience as alienated and exploited workers can hardly be *sufficient* for a positive social alternative to arise, it is still arguable, and perhaps increasingly plausible, to see this as a *necessary* basis for societal evaluation and collective action. Generally, the book lacks *explicit* reference to class and exploitation in the depiction of contemporary capitalism, however 'cultural' it may be.

Turning to the book's engagements with(in) cultural studies: Paul Smith gives notice that he is going to be pursuing the recovery of Marxism in this domain, whilst Jeremy Gilbert sticks up for 'discourse analysis'. The others weave their way in between these two stances in a way that broadly reflects the state of play in other recent collections; solutions to the question of culture are conducted in the commentary mode, with obligatory nods in the direction of Hegel, Adorno, Benjamin, Hannah Arendt and, of course, Laclau and Mouffe, rather than by way of independent conceptual crafting. Thus, some read Williams (or Hall) this way, some read him that way. Some see cultural studies as a project, others as a field, or a new discipline, or a meeting point, and a still-evolving nexus. The politics/culture interface is explored, moving towards less decisive conclusions than the prose sometimes suggests. None of these discussions is uninteresting, but the rather typecast handling of 'debates', and the concluding thought that diversity of opinion is a positive end in itself, reflects what cultural studies now fully shares with many traditional academic discourses, as a result of its massification and disciplinisation. This is not necessarily something to be regretted; it probably just is. Yet it would at least be good in a 'reflexive' kind of way if spokespersons for cultural studies stopped inflating the radicality and distinctiveness of their, and its, contributions. Strangely enough, that kind of deflationism could also be the way to its productive renewal.

A lifelong market pessimist

Peter Howells

G. C. Harcourt, *50 Years a Keynesian and Other Essays*; and *Selected Essays on Economic Policy*, both Palgrave 2001

When Geoff Harcourt retired from his full-time position in the Cambridge Faculty of Economics in 1998, English-speaking economics lost one of its most consistent and courageous carriers of the Keynesian flag. However Harcourt remains Emeritus Reader and Emeritus Fellow at Cambridge and Emeritus Professor at Adelaide, and the prompt appearance of these two volumes (of 24 essays each), and his continued work on the intellectual history of Joan Robinson and her circle, suggest that there is more to come.

Like many students of economics, Geoff Harcourt originally took to the dismal science to make things better: hence the emphasis upon policy throughout these two books. The unifying theme in this avalanche of recommendations is the corpus of thought now known as Post-Keynesianism, by which is meant a recognition of certain fundamental principles that were often submerged in popular post-war interpretations (the 'Bastard Keynesianism' referred to in I/1).[1] Among these principles are the dominant role of demand and spending in determining the level of output and employment; the absence of any automatic mechanism to ensure that the level of output warranted by demand coincides with full employment; the presence of intractable uncertainty (ignorance which cannot be eased aside by appealing to probability distributions); a view of dynamics as characterised by cumulative causation (rather than feedback mechanisms tending to restore the initial equilibrium); and the desire for a more equal distribution of income, wealth and life's opportunities generally.

This is a specific version of a wider set of economic ideas best described as 'market pessimism'. This broader heading embraces Marxists, socialists and

1. For the purposes of this review, 'I' refers to the volume *50 Years a Keynesian* while 'II' refers to *Selected Essays on Economic Policy*. Arabic numerals refer to the number of the essay in the volume.

institutionalists, to whose work Harcourt has often been sympathetic. Harcourt's general radicalism and specific Post-Keynesianism are shown to good effect throughout this collection. The two matching volumes are produced to a high quality and the publishers deserve special commendation for troubling to provide a good index with each.

In *50 Years a Keynesian* we are given 24 recent essays, 23 of them organised into six groups. These include a group of four devoted to reflections on Keynes and the continued relevance of his work. The first, 'Is Keynes Dead?' (I/2), shows that the 'real' Keynes, of the *The General Theory of Employment, Interest and Money* (1936) had much to say that would have permitted a perfectly coherent analysis of the stagflation of the 1970s - a phenomenon which is often said to have shown the inadequacy of Keynesian ideas, and has been widely used to repudiate them. The problem, Harcourt argues, was the way in which the Keynes of the *General Theory* came to be synthesised and popularised after 1945. The essay is particularly hard on the US economists Paul Samuelson and Robert Solow who, claiming a Keynesian inheritance, falsely grafted the Phillips Curve on to the *General Theory*. When the relationship between inflation and unemployment proposed by the Phillips Curve broke down under the pressure of events in the 1970s, and the model's reputation sank, Keynes's name sank with it - guilty by association.

There is also an interesting passage about what might have been. Lorie Tarshis, a Canadian graduate student doing his PhD at Cambridge in the 1930s, attended a number of Keynes's lectures and expounded a very lucid version of Keynes's *General Theory* in the book he published after the war.[2] In Tarshis's version, Keynes would have had no problem in coping with stagflation. But Tarshis fell victim to the American Right, which campaigned, with some success, to have the book removed from university reading lists. This paved the way for Samuelson (and many others) to use the IS-LM model of the macroeconomy as the basis for a convenient exegesis of Keynes's ideas, and gave at least one generation of economics students the impression that supply conditions did not matter. This was something Keynes would never have suggested.

The ideology of economics surfaces in another essay in this group (I/3), where

---

2. L. Tarshis [1947], *The Elements of Economics. An Introduction to the Theory of Price and Employment*, Houghton Mifflin, Boston, 2e 1966.

Harcourt describes the ambitious and entertaining project to publish a 'second edition' of the *General Theory*, in which a selection of Keynesian scholars were asked to imagine what Keynes would have said about the ideas in the *General Theory* some years on. When it appeared it was subjected to a range of reviews including some which wilfully misrepresented it.[3]

Other groups of essays include 'Intellectual Biographies' (Joan and Austin Robinson, Tarshis, Keynes and Marx); 'Tributes', which includes an excellent essay on George Shackle and a reflection on the capital theory controversy that, though little understood by onlookers, divided the Cambridge Faculty in the 1960s. Probably Harcourt's best-known and most frequently cited piece of work was a heroic attempt to clarify the issues in a survey paper published in the *Journal of Economic Literature*.[4]

The remaining essays are 'Review Articles' (Nicholas Kaldor and more on Joan Robinson); 'General Essays' (including 'The Cambridge Contribution to Economics'); and a 'Survey', a single paper on Post-Keynesian Thought (I/19), which goes to some lengths to explain the history of these ideas and their links with others - with Sraffa and Kalecki in particular. It also contains a valuable section on 'method', and contrasts, with obvious approval, the Post-Keynesian practice of starting from what *is* (even if what is is so complex that it has to be rendered as stylised facts), rather than with a set of axioms in the style of neoclassical economics. It also finds room to explain the importance of the endogeneity of money in Post-Keynesian thinking, though Harcourt skirts around some controversies within Post-Keynesian thinking where money is concerned. (Maybe this is inevitable coming from a man who, in 1974, when sounded out about the possibility of taking the post of Governor of the Reserve Bank of Australia, declined, saying 'You know me Jim. I'm a real man, not a money man' (II/1)). That said, it is hard to think of a better place to look for a brief exposition of Post-Keynesianism.

The second volume is devoted to essays on economic policy. These span a much longer period, the earliest ('The Quantitative Effect of Basing Company Taxation on Replacement Costs') dating from 1958. Again there are 24 in total,

3. G. C. Harcourt and P. Riach (eds), A *'Second Edition' of the General Theory*, 2 vols, Routledge, London 1997.
4. G. C. Harcourt, 'Some Cambridge Controversies in the Theory of Capital', *Journal of Economic Literature*, 7, 1969, pp369-405.

23 of which are grouped under the headings 'Background to Policy Recommendations', 'Taxation Reform and Investment Incentives', 'Accounting Conventions and Policy', 'Package Deals' and 'General Essays'.

The first group tells us quite a lot about the author and his outlook. Here we see the basis for Harcourt's agreement with Keynes that, when it comes to awkward policy choices, it is better to disappoint the rentier than the worker. Given a collection of nearly fifty essays it seems mean to complain about omissions, but an excellent paper which could have been included here, 'Why I am not an Economic Rationalist', gives a succinct account of the basis of Harcourt's market pessimism.[5]

Readers unfamiliar with Harcourt's early work may be surprised at the amount of advice to business he has offered. Four papers that first appeared between 1959 and 1968 share a concern with the promotion of investment. They range from the appropriate design of investment allowances (II/6) to the choice of investment decision-making criteria (II/9). Programmes to raise the rate of economic growth and labour productivity in particular were popular during the 1960s (*vide* such initiatives as the 1966 Labour Government's 'National Plan') but Harcourt's interest in these issues stemmed at least as much from his PhD work and his interest in accumulation.

'Accounting Conventions and Policy' also contains recommendations for business. The first (II/10) is concerned with what happens if, for taxation purposes, company profits are calculated using replacement rather than historic cost. The answer is not as obvious as it might seem. In 1950 and 1951, some firms would have paid more tax on this basis, and others less. The paper shows that the outcome depends on the company's expenditure on durable assets, and factors over which they have less control, such as the rate of stock appreciation and the rise in prices of their durable assets. What must have seemed a bit arcane to fellow students at Sraffa's postgraduate seminar in 1956 was to become a crucial issue in the early 1970s.

The 'Package Deals' section contains a number of policy recommendations for the general good, charting the various crises that have faced developed economies over the past 25 years. These range from proposals to counter inflation

5. Harcourt G C (1999) 'Why I am not an Economic Rationalist', *Queensland Economic Review*, 2.

INTRODUCTION

Regimes of Emotion

Pam Smith

This second special *Soundings* issue on the theme of emotions is a testimony to the interest and debate fuelled by the first special issue published in Spring 1999. The original idea came as a result of the debate in the 1990s about care and its invisible function in propping up a failing welfare state. We were coming to the end of the nightmare Thatcher years and we were hopeful that things could only get better under New Labour. Our issue on emotional labour looked particularly at the relationship between emotions and care, using Arlie Hochschild's analysis of emotional labour in the service sector. Her description of how flight attendants and debt collectors managed their emotions to influence the feelings of others showed the commercial power of emotional labour in extracting profits from passengers and payment from debtors. She also described the importance of gender in defining the nature of emotional labour both in the work place and in the home, concluding that because it is traditionally associated with women's work it often remains invisible, unrecognised and undervalued.

Hochschild also tested her emotional labour analysis within the domestic sphere, finding that, despite the rhetoric of gender equality, working women in two-job couples with children were still the main carers when it came to child and home care.

Why is emotional labour so compelling a concept? We concluded that the great power of Arlie Hochschild's analysis was that, at a time when service-sector and people-orientated work is replacing heavy and manufacturing industries, she has provided a language through which to describe the nature of relationship work, whether paid or unpaid, public or private (and frequently-taken-for-granted).

In the Spring 1999 issue we used the language of emotional labour to track these issues in looking at the changing contexts and cultures of care in eastern and western Europe, and in trying to understand how immigrant communities managed the emotional as well as the territorial boundaries between home and host country. An emotional labour logbook tracked a range of emotional labourers - pilots, politicians, air traffic controllers, ambulance crews, actors and nurses. The contract culture, particularly in the public sector, was on the ascendant, and set a harsh and demanding emotional tone, which resulted in deteriorating work conditions, low pay and fragmented work processes. Elsewhere we looked at the politics of emotions, detecting in the ideology and language of the 'Third Way' a number of contradictions and tensions: between care and control; liberalism and equality of opportunity; capitalist economics and socialist politics. It was argued that marketised and spin-doctored emotions should be replaced with the construction of emotional democracy. The final piece examined the learning required to prepare nurses to acquire the skills to manage their emotions in complex caring situations.

The interest and debate generated by the first issue led to the organisation of two conferences and workshops to explore the theoretical and practical dimensions of emotion work, and to examine the political and policy implications. In this second collection of writing from these debates, Steve Smith charts our collective journey in his *Manifesto for Feelings*; an important point in this journey was Arlie Hochschild's public lecture post 11 September, in which she talked about *Emotion Management in an Age of Global Terrorism*, which we also publish here. Arlie introduced the notion of the *emotional regimes* which have been opened up and laid bare by 11 September. She further suggests that these *emotional regimes or regimes of emotion* (the title chosen for this special issue) set out feeling rules, which in turn are part of a set of framing rules for how we should both see and feel reality. These regimes, Arlie says, require us to do emotion work in trying to live up to them.

In this issue we have extended our examination of emotional labour and begun to explore the notion of emotional regimes. Two articles, by Fiona Douglas and Maria Lorentzon respectively, juxtapose employment and unemployment, in looking at the work of careers counsellors during the 1970s, when full employment was the norm, and, contrastingly, the hopelessness of the unemployment which dominated the 1980s and early 1990s. Unemployment is again becoming an issue - especially in the airline and associated industries. Perhaps the catastrophe of the twin towers has been used as a convenient smoke screen to hide the fact there was already a serious downturn in the economy prior to the events of 11 September.

Articles by Gay Lee on cancer nursing, Del Loewenthal on involvement, and David Newbold on the links between emotions, therapeutic nursing and economics, re-examine the usefulness of emotional labour for understanding the complexities of care. As a practitioner, Gay has some reservations as to whether emotional labour is useful or whether it is merely a fascinating idea. As an academic, Del is concerned to use emotional labour alongside his data to critically reflect on nurses' involvement with patients, and the individual costs and benefits of institutional life and socialisation processes. David sees a paradigm clash between health technology and emotional labour, and explores the potential of economics to provide the link between the two by identifying the therapeutic contribution of nursing.

Bridget Towers discusses the disappearance of convalescence, and with it the caring context that enables the definition of illness and recovery. Hochschild's classifications of 'cold-modern' care and 'systematic neglect' appropriately describe this phenomenon.

Stuart Nairn's descriptions of heroism and horror in narrating emergency take on a new significance post 11 September. In recent months it has become fashionable to abbreviate the date to '911', the emergency telephone number in the USA.

Rick Rattue and Nelarine Cornelius re-examine the gender dimension of emotional labour in focusing on front-line male-dominated police work. Officers try not to let emotions get in the way of their work, but at the same time they develop ways of looking after each other when 'off the beat'. The ways in which they do this are not always beneficial, and Rick and Nelarine argue that the concept of emotional labour could be a really useful tool of analysis for improving a number of crucial aspects of police work - both for the police themselves and for the public.

Under some regimes, however, the police may be implicated in creating a sense of threat and uncertainty among refugees, and in some instances they may actually be the torturers. Some of the emotional regimes experienced by refugees are described by Ian Robbins, who works as a clinical psychologist in the Traumatic Stress clinic of an NHS hospital. The article is illustrative of the bleak prospects for refugees who come to Britain alone, without the emotional safety nets created by family and friends.

Finally Marjorie Mayo, Trudi James and Pam Smith explore the emotional labour associated with the changing face of regeneration in the Broadwater Farm Estate, Tottenham. The authors comment on a portfolio of photographs and newspaper clippings, which evoke a range of powerful emotions - from rural harmony in the late nineteenth century, to the riot-torn community of the 1980s, and finally the transformation of the estate into a 'happy and secure' place.

We have been mindful in both *Soundings* special issues of the importance of the pictorial and poetic representation of emotional labour. Our cover picture conveys the intensity of the emergency - in this case experienced by a young St John's ambulance volunteer. The four images of nurses included in the issue update Dympna Casey's photo-essay in the earlier collection. These are images of nurses engaged in the extremes of high-tech and hands-on care, with babies, an older person and a cardiac monitor. They aptly convey the messages contained in the articles by Gay, Del and David about involvement, and emotional and technical labour in the delivery of patient care.

Although care- and people-work continues to be central to the emotional labour debate, new and urgent issues have emerged since the last issue in spring 1999. Emotional labour has taken on a new meaning, and the debates have been expanded. We have tried to address some of these issues here: global terrorism and the management of our responses to it; the managing of emergencies more widely; the refugee experience; and regeneration and urban renewal. As Stephen Smith argues in his article in this issue, in an age when our emotions are increasingly managed for us, there is acute danger in *not* trying to produce a democratic manifesto for the emotions - there will always be others only too willing to step in to fill the gap.

Towards a manifesto for feelings

Stephen Lloyd Smith

Feelings are political. A manifesto for feelings begins to make sense inasmuch as our emotions are already not strictly of our own making. But what should a manifesto for feelings cover? Steve Smith *looks back on presentations made at recent conferences and workshops on Emotional Labour in an attempt to start to get a sense of what such a manifesto should include.*

The idea that anyone should write a manifesto for feelings will strike many not just as odd, but as deeply and disturbingly *wrong*. Feelings might be seen as too private, personal, internal, cherished, natural, precious or sacred to be determined by 'some damn group or other'. Feelings are 'close to the heart' and therefore, perhaps, entirely one's 'own business'.

One reason for this kind of reaction is that we are a liberal society infused with Christian dogma. We live with the idea that feelings are 'inner' (associated with a metaphorical 'heart-soul') and 'integral to our individuality'; and that we are responsible for ourselves (and our souls). The outcome is that we think of ourselves as being responsible for our feelings, and for guarding them as our feelings - and not anyone else's. The idea of self-determination and mastery is essential to liberalism, and personal responsibility is essential to Christian ethics.

But what we feel 'inside' is affected by others whether near or far from us. A manifesto for feelings begins to make sense to the extent that our emotions are already not strictly of our own making, and that we live under what Arlie Hochschild calls *emotion regimes*, governed by *feeling rules* - rules that are being made and remade all the time by many agencies. Emotions are sensations-in-relation-to-people-and-events-through-feeling-rules. Feeling rules shape what we feel at weddings and funerals, welcomes and goodbyes, on holiday and beside the sickbed. These rules are fought over in *feeling-politics*. That is partly why 2002 'feels different' to 1968 or 1948, why 2008 will feel very different to 1668 - and why 10 September felt different from any day since. If our feelings are already partly-prescribed for us, then we should examine who is prescribing them and ask ourselves, 'why do we let them do this to us?'.

Hochschild argued in her public address of 4 October - reproduced in this edition of *Soundings* - that in times of crisis we look to authority figures to find out 'what I should feel'. She is intrigued by why we do this. Why do we *ask* them, indeed *expect* them to help us define our feelings? She suspects that in crisis we treat prime ministers and presidents 'like parents', acting as if we were small children. For all the talk of liberal autonomy and mastery, when it comes to looking catastrophe in the face, we often respond as dependent children, rather than as adults. There are surely dangers in treating our leaders as our mothers - and dangers in leaders who infantilise their citizens.

Our manifesto might question the tendency to look to others who act in the place of parents - in order to make us feel safe, to tell us to when it is 'time to mourn' and when it is 'time to get back on the horse' (to quote Arlie Hochschild again); it also might query the tendency to require leaders to talk reassuringly to make us feel secure, while glossing over their (sometimes honourable) failures to address problems that contribute a serious - but often improbable - danger to us as individuals.

In the post-11-September crisis - which, I think significantly, was followed immediately not by *feelings* but by *numbness* - what Bush and Blair were apparently feeling was taken as a parental cue for the masses. Indeed, their political performance was measured by the extent to which they managed to cue our feelings. Blair seemed 'better than Bush', especially in the first few days when the president's stumbling attempts to devise feeling rules made for excruciating television viewing. My feeling was 'Hell's teeth! If the President is not brave enough to rush to stand on the wreckage of the Twin Towers as fast as he damn well can - and to hell with his security advisors' whisperings about the "credible threat" of an assassination attempt - how should he expect the rest of the world to feel about that?!'

Yet the president is neither 'my father' nor 'mother', so why the expectation that he be fatherly and demonstrate at least a minimum standard of bravery? I am not keen on 'God as my father', and I was especially provoked recently to hear a politician insist that 'The Queen *is* our Mother'. But the idea that the prime minister is our 'father' should be almost as problematic and offensive. Why welcome being worked on by the feeling rulers?

Tony Blair was praised for having shown a 'fatherly' touch around the Death of Diana, and more recently in relation to the death of the Queen Mother, in a way that evoked a palpable and I think infantile shift towards greater support for the Windsors. How should I feel about the death of the Queen Mum? The BBC's court correspondent Jenny Bond opined that it was really awful news, a tragedy, a terrible national loss. Hundreds of thousands took to the streets and queued all night because it was 'the least thing' they could do. The feeling rule was: 'be "happy-sad" for the life that was led and the life that is over'.

The emotions that surrounded the death of the Queen's sister, which arguably better justified the language of personal tragedy, was also subject to effective feeling management, this time aimed at maintaining a low key response. This kept the masses off the streets and drew a veil over the more dysfunctional attributes of the family Windsor. The feeling-rule was 'it is sad, but it is over'; that it was consolation enough that her 'suffering was ended', it was 'not unexpected'. The death was managed in such a way that few people came forward to sign the books of condolence.

Similarly, emotion arbiters jumped to pronounce on the murder of TV personality Jill Dando, treating it as the emotional equivalent of the assassination of a minister of state. In the meantime the murders of 'nobodies' merit only a brief mention in the main news most days, often only making it onto regional news programmes, particularly if the victims are neither elderly nor children. And it took several months of courageous campaigning from outside the class of emotion leaders before the mishandling of the investigation of Stephen Lawrence's murder was eventually promoted to the status of a national disgrace. We will not forget it.

Emotion contributes to *order*, but it is also integral to *dis*order. Within the last two years rioters have taken to the streets in a small number of British cities, in very public examples of collective emotion work; but legitimate-feeling-rule-writers have struggled, and failed, to come up with very much in the way of a credible response. There is acute danger in not writing emotion-manifestos in areas where fascists are only too willing to step in to fill the gap. Poppy Day is a reminder, above all else, that in the past century imperial and then fascist emotional mobilisation cost somewhere over fifty million lives.

The rules are powerful and matter very much. So it is hard to see why we should treat city, regional or international feeling regimes much differently from workplace and household feeling regimes. It is *easy* to see that we are affected by other members of our household or work group, and that what is experienced as a normal emotion regime in one household or workplace might seem weird in other households or workplaces. (So too with different classes, countries and periods in history.) Workers leave to find new employers and partners leave to find other partners. We contribute towards and experience domestic and workplace feeling-rules each day.

It is unlikely, however, that *global* feeling regimes exist, experienced similarly in all countries. Linguists and anthropologists find that many of the worlds' peoples *feel* in a different way from Westerners. For example, in some cultures people may refer to feelings not as internal, 'heart-felt' sensations, but as external qualities flowing from relationships. Thus instead of 'I feel angry', it is possible to feel that, 'There is annoyance present'. Instead of 'getting a grip on oneself', there might be a call for 'more ritual', to clear 'bad feeling'. It is also found that there are many varieties of love.

I am arguing that if you do not have a manifesto for feelings, you can be sure that others will already be at work imposing theirs on you, and that this can happen unobtrusively - for example it can produce the crushing experience of romantic love in teenagers.

But what should the manifesto cover? Manifestos usually place 'liberty, equality and fraternity' in some order of priority. But how much *liberty of feeling*, what *equality of feeling*, what *solidarity of feeling* and in what order of priority? On the basis of what evidence and on what kinds of analysis should the manifesto be written?

Since the last special edition of *Soundings* devoted to emotional labour (Issue 11, Spring 1999), we have convened as practitioners and academics at two conferences and through a continuing workshop series.[1] The specialist articles found in this edition of *Soundings* are an outcome of the discussions we have had. But they are also touched by 11 September, and Arlie Hochschild's response to it. Can a manifesto be discerned in what was said?

At the *Emotional Labour 2000* and *2001* conferences, we enjoyed discussion among practitioners in emotional labour from many professions and disciplines. Delegates were drawn from nursing, language translation, psychology, psychoanalysis, psychiatry, neuro-physiology, sociology, economics, geography, photography, poetry and political science. It strikes me that the many issues raised were well encompassed by Mike Rustin's keynote question: 'After broadly having achieved the emancipation of manual and mental labour, what is required for the emancipation of emotional labour…?' After the impact of 11 September we must add to this the need to investigate the way in which the good features of the emotional regime that existed on 10 September have been placed at risk - with threats to an open society, to the valuing of many kinds of diversity, and to mutual confidence, trust and liking.

The tone of contributions to this debate has varied between optimism and pessimism, partly because the issues are so complex. A general feature of effective manifestos is that they are *optimistic*. The feeling rules of calls-to-action require something to feel bad about and a solution to feel good about. Do we have to be pessimistic about what capitalist social relations do for the emotions? And what changes would we feel happy about? There have also been differences on the relationship between the market and regimes of feeling, and whether or not the measuring and valuing of emotions is possible. In what follows I want to sketch out some of the most interesting ideas that have come out of our discussions so far, in an effort to tease out some of the elements that might make up a future manifesto.

Discussing the emotions: emotion and history

At *Emotional Labour 2000* I argued that it seemed that the 'founding fathers' of sociology had 'got it wrong'. Capitalism had *not* eliminated 'passion and emotion' (Marx) in favour of 'reason and rationality' (Weber); nor is urban life only a set

1. Many excellent and helpful contributions to our discussion were made at these seminars, many of which we have not been able to acknowledge in this short introduction. We thank those whose views are quoted here.

of 'superficial, impersonal' roles (Simmel). The twentieth century was the century of the passions, both lethal and virtuous. Being there was anything but a 'mechanical' experience.

On the contrary, the expression and perhaps even the capacity to feel was enlarged over time in 'emotion regime struggles'. Innovations like rock and roll sensibility, 'jazz cool', rave culture, pay-and-pray television, shock-jocks, gay pride, shopping, evangelical sales techniques, ideological arousal, new forms of comedy, horror films, total war and enduring peace, were forged by the activity of individuals, political parties, interest groups, corporations, musicians, charismatics, comedians, drug dealers, genders, classes, age cohorts, armies and diplomats, pursuing various interests; often beset with failure.

Complaints about 'alienation', 'urbanism' and 'estrangement', and the desire for 'self actualisation', are enabled by unprecedented living standards that sustain *more* emotion. Perhaps we should drop the sentimental association between emotions, the heart, the soul and the past, and give a positive, this-worldly welcome to the commodification of emotion. Capitalism is an effective over-producer of commodities. If emotions are commercialised, there may be gross inequalities in the ability to buy them, but there is unlikely to be shortage in the total volume.

In Europe, the most numbing experiences are associated with the early- or pre-capitalist world, particularly the dulling effect of having to live with high infant mortality. Lawrence Stone has argued that our capacity for 'affective individualism' - to be feeling-full, expressive, needy and romantic persons - has developed only slowly since the late seventeenth century (see *The Family, Sex and Marriage 1500-1800*). In the seventeenth century, romantic ties were weaker and family bonds quite different from those of today. *Household*, *lineage* and *neighbourhood* mattered; individuality much less so. Indifference was shown towards infants, whose survival rates were low, most of those who survived leaving home at around the age of 12. Two-thirds of householders contained non-kin members. Feelings between spouses were quite cool - and therefore domestic murders were rarer than today. Heads of household were more calculating than caring, and life outside the household was extraordinarily instrumental, explosive and murderously violent. That is, feelings have not always been felt the way we feel them now. Only gradually did the social importance of children and spouses grow stronger, and with this grew stronger feelings. Stone thinks that 'capitalism' is only part of the explanation. Affective individualism was a partly-accidental side effect of Puritanism, the regulation of marriage contracts, changes in educational theory, the weakening power of the Crown and the growing authority of the state; but above all, it was the result of better health and longer life expectancy.

After reading Stone it is hard to look in quite the same way as before at modern assumptions about the passion for self-actualisation through paid work, acceptance of the 'long hours culture' and the attenuation of 'home life'. The contemporary mania for work is driven by a new emotion regime, with new costs and new inequalities. Does more love of work mean less love elsewhere? Individual liberty, which has grown alongside feeling-full self-possession, seems to be compromising solidarity at home. As Hochschild puts it, given a choice between more work and more home, Americans are choosing more work, because, as they tell it, work is 'warm' and where friendships are made, while home is 'cold' and 'stressful'. That is, workplace acquaintance is in the ascendant and home-place attachments weakening. There is no reason to suppose that the historical changes Stone describes have reached any kind of stable equilibrium. Currently the care deficit in work-rich families tends to be met by immigrant care-workers - maids, nannies and residential nurses, who are often treated as our least welcome and least cared for guests.

All emotion-regimes contain contradiction and discontentment. It is unlikely that we can sustain our current dominant feeling regime - liberalism and passion for work - without a profound increase in solidarity with migrants, in processes of inclusion, and a more open society. A manifesto for feelings must address the new imbalances, mindful of the contradictions in the emotion regimes they replaced. This is a major task, but what is clear enough is that those who experienced childhood in the 1990s will not feel the same as those who experienced it in the 1950s, and that further shifts in the nature of feelings, new feeling-rules and new institutional arrangements will be forthcoming. Because capitalism has a genius for commodity production, it seems likely that *private enthusiasms* and *absorbing things* will provide an increasingly important source of consolation outside work. This may partly explain youthful passions for mobile phones and virtual friendships.

It may even be that the viability and direct consequences of the inner-heart-soul model should be re-examined.

Debating the contradictions of emotional discourse

Many - but not all - of our conference delegates would resist this last proposal. 'Don't go there!', one whispered loudly in a recent workshop, as if to underline that to ask this question was to enter a sacred and forbidden zone. Emotions are experienced as real enough, but many argued that they are elusive, not easy to measure and even, perhaps, that they should neither be captured nor measured.

For example, in discussing the management of emotions, Rob Briner argued that the *ambition* of management theory and practice in this field had altered with the transition from managing manufactures to managing services; but workplace emotion, though certainly palpable in the ebb and flow of organisational life, was at least as elusive a thing to manage as the much-discussed 'management of organisational knowledge'. Though there are practitioners who claim to have measured the emotional labour output of service organisations, and others who have quantified 'emotional intelligence', the possibility of managers being able to manage emotion in others remains doubtful, as does their ability to commodify and capitalise on 'emotional intelligence'. He and Steve Fineman felt that it was probably a good thing that the measurement and management of emotion were difficult. But my worry was that this makes it harder to make sure that it is paid for at its value. I say measure and pay.

Jan Savage argued that it was the elusive that mattered most. For example, reading a verbatim transcript of a conversation often does not convey the emotionally-led collective insight experienced and reported by participants in the conversation. Talkers could experience breakthroughs in conversations that looked dry and uninteresting when written down on paper. *Something* is exchanged in verbal discussion; but it is only partly in the words. This hinted at the existence of an unwritten emotional language among groups with a common purpose.

The 'ethical basis of emotional labour' was discussed by Del Loewenthal. For him, 'autonomy' is not the best basis for offering care, because autonomy is bound to mean putting the self first *as a good thing*. He argues that an ethic of 'heteronomy' - an ethic of 'putting the other first' - would take much of the aversion out of emotional labour. Autonomy, he thinks, is a Greek notion; while heteronomy is a Jewish one.

Loewenthal's analysis certainly reinforces the importance of understanding the ways in which ethical (including theological) principles inhabit our taken-for-granted-assumptions about what day-to-day life should be like. But I wonder whether a this-worldly ethic cannot grow from a this-worldly life, and whether autonomy, rather than heteronomy, might not be best at ensuring that the carer at least gets employed (and paid) in a way that will provide them with adequate resources and rest. You can't 'put the other first' indefinitely, unless others are going to put *you* first just as often. What guarantees reciprocity?

Anne Marie Rafferty was interested in another contradiction. She felt that the link between professional carer and patient was peculiar. 'Was it not odd', she asked, 'that we become *professional* [which implies dispassion or emotional indifference] in order to be close to the patient'. She also argued that life was becoming increasingly confessional, and that these features of contemporary life were driving an emotional speed-up. These were not independent processes. Being well-practised in emotional reflection may indeed help the speed-up of emotional encounters. It is easier and more efficient to get to the emotional point *fast*. These elements - confessional living (not rectitude), emotional fluency (not privacy), and speed-up - could be beginning to look like what Hochschild would call a new 'emotional regime'. Would a regime based on emotional efficiency be a bad thing? Perhaps it would be to-the-good, especially if we contrast it to regimes that could be characterised as 'Edwardian', aristocratic or managerial 'stiff-upper-lip'. The feeling-rule 'keep it buttoned' can serve the powers that be very well.

Maureen Mackintosh, in an approach which contrasted with some of those quoted above, argued that emotional deficits were both real and explicit. Social structures of inequality were remarkably robust and not to be under-estimated. Through the marketisation of care, inequality had remade itself: 'Though there is some reluctance to discuss inequality, it is foolish not to. Why is "emotional intelligence" so much better paid ... than emotional labour? ... because emotional intelligence is the emotional labour of the *well paid and powerful*.'

Markets work partly by allocating the doing of emotional labour to the low paid, while the better-paid are better paid for *containing* their emotions, not for expressing them - something which Rattue and Cornelius comment on in this edition of *Soundings*. Mackintosh argues that this is partly the result of the operational practices of large organisations that hire labour:

> The literature on contracting focuses on emotion among purchasers and providers as the problem of trust in partnerships and alliances. The dominant theory is that good quality *relationships* are needed between contractors. If the emotions of contractors are good, then relationships between contracting organisations will work well ... But this emphasis on emotional wellbeing - which reflects a middle-class fight-back against marketisation - is absent from their treatment of the care workers they are managing.

Thus there is both an interaction and a divergence between the market and the ethical evaluation of emotion. Contracting means counting outcomes, but working-class emotional outcomes are counted *last*, if at all.

This has increased the inequality between nursing staff and non-trained carers, for example in the devaluation of the skills of skilled carers in home care service. Care has been shifted to the patient as 'self-care', supported by low skilled, rushed, badly paid and untrained 'amateur nursing'. David Newbold, in his contribution, also discussed the contradictory relationship between therapeutic nursing, emotional labour and economic exchange. The clear implication for our manifesto is that New Labour should press ahead with undoing the marketisation of health.

Pam Smith described the emancipating difference a ward sister could make. Individuals can transform the wider organisation - for better and for worse. It was clear from her research that good clinical leadership was essential to the maintenance of care through emotional labour. For her the term emotional labour remained the most valuable way of capturing differences between one clinical setting and the next. Senior nurses can emancipate or wreck the individual student nurse's experience of the organisation - and make or ruin the patient's stay. Only partly does this have to do with the maintenance of resources such as bed linen. It is also a result of the senior nurse's capacity to create a good interface between the unit and the larger organisation. The effective nurse emerges as an emancipated, politically astute emotional labourer and clinical leader. The emotional labour of care is elicited in good learning laboratories, where exploration, innovation, reflection and practice change is enabled.

Mike Rustin was among the optimists, arguing that recognition of anxiety in nursing had 'feminised the policy agenda', and that infantilisation was not necessarily a bad thing. Infantilisation could be useful, for example as a means of managing anxiety in air-travellers. Anxiety was also present in teaching and learning, and universities should realise that marks awarded to students reflected the adequacy with which anxiety was handled in relationships, by personal tutors (or impersonal tutors) and by counselling services. He argued that respect for the whole person and authentic recognition of emotional needs was called for.

Much of this agenda was 'double-edged', though, as for instance with sexual liberation and emancipation in relation to pornography. Similarly, self-analysis techniques and questionnaires in glossy magazines, Seven-Step Improvement groups, Relationship and Sex Counselling and many other services promise 'spiritual' enlargement, but can be deforming.

Danny Kelly thought that Cancer Charity Advertising too could be double-edged, and in particular it could be at variance with what clinicians were trying to do. Cancer adverts appealed to donors' understandings of cancer in a way that was comforting, and which certainly 'got the money in'. But they made carers' work harder in many ways, because patients, their relatives and carers needed a more realistic understanding of disease and care than what was presented by the adverts: they should expect care, treatment and some degree of disease control; not miracle cures. If the treatment of cancer is thought of as a simple *fight*, then in most cases patients and carers would lose. Better to foreground *caring* care not just *medical* care.

At *Emotional Labour 2002*, Sue Himmelweit recounted the many economic theories that are supposed to explain why care work gets allocated to women. But, as she argued, economics could not provide an adequate vocabulary to describe the regimes that exist.

The vocabulary of emotional labour

How do these presentations fit into a manifesto for feelings? One striking thing about them is that they all allude to *puzzles* and *contradictions*, and usually to contradictions that hint at solutions. In all cases the vocabulary of emotional labour seemed not simply helpful, but to offer an exciting way forward.

Thinking about the deficits and inequalities that Maureen Mackintosh described, for example: if we somehow managed to stop picturing emotion in terms of the heart, with think-work as 'what the head does', and manual labour as what 'hands' do, would the strange divergence between the moral and market evaluations of emotional labour begin to disappear? Would the allocation of care work change?

Since Marx, many have argued that 'hand' and 'brain' should be 'reunited' through the reintroduction of skilful craft-work. Why does the distance between 'brain' and 'heart' seem so much greater - more of a *cosmological gulf* - than the simple problem of co-ordination between hand and brain? In writing my manifesto, I would want to explore the possibility of different, non-magical models of human-being. Can we still be thought of as precious if we discard our heart-souls? Is there an alternative metaphor for preciousness? As one delegate asked of Arlie Hochschild in a workshop last October, 'What is the "it" which is so precious in us anyway?' What is that inner part that needs protecting and preserving against the demands of *soul-prostituting* employers and *soul-stealing* customers?

Thinking more about Mike Rustin's comments, it strikes me that we can and should aspire to educate the emotions and explore how this can be done. Explicit and systematic training in emotional labour is mostly confined to theatre and sales work. Implicit and indirect training is more common. Disciplinary control in soldiers and fire fighters begins with behavioural training on command, leading to simulations, tests and debriefings. The capacity for courage and comradeship develops both directly and incidentally with the habits of close communal association. But no instruction in the emotional labour of cross-examination is given to barristers.

Would all emotional labourers be better served by explicit emotion-training? Should emotion be automated and choreographed through participation in infectious, public, familiar and comforting *rituals* like the 2002 Arsenal Cup Double? Or should it be more deliberating, self-managed, reasoned, dyadic and communicative? The complex issues involved in education and emotion are being discussed in our current round of workshops.

The idea of democratising care-regimes by increasing the power of nurses and patients and perhaps, from there, remaking feeling-rules, appeals to me. Another good place to look for popular feeling manifestos might be poems and popular songs, especially pop anthems, often written as feeling manifestos.

It is a feature of songs and poems that their impact is fleeting. In the case of typical popular songs, the sentiment might be limited to three and a half minutes, with an emotional half-life of maybe as little as thirty seconds, with that feeling halved again for every half minute after that. In this way we carry a great number of rather minute traces of popular sentiment. Short half-lives are not as much of a limitation for feeling-rulers as they might seem, however, because manifestos can be switched back on or revived and recast in astonishingly short periods. Songs have simple choruses which reactivate the feeling very fast: 'It's coming-home; it's coming-home; foot-ball's coming home...' Similarly, in times of crisis the emotion regime may need to provoke rapid social redeployment under a manifesto call, for example in mass-mobilisation for war. Interestingly, it is during such times that John Lennon's *Imagine* tends to get banned by the BBC, as 'inappropriate'. This suggests that popular music is not at all ephemeral, but can be central to feeling regimes. These are areas that need further exploration.

The long-lasting nature of emotional half-lives can contribute to some of society's biggest problems, particularly the half-life of the feeling-rules of righteous hate and victimisation, which contaminate life in Northern Ireland, Israel/ Palestine, and many other places. Here the need for new feeling manifestos is most urgent.

Measures of democratisation and movement are found in many places. For example, employees whose lives are made miserable can sue their managers for 'constructive dismissal'. The search for well-being, happiness and 'self actualisation' at work represents a long-term tendency to which enlightened managers should respond - regardless of trends in relation to the home.

The pursuit of love and affection - often beset with failure - is dramatised each week in several hours of TV soaps, which attract mass audiences; and it is idealised through *Hello* magazine coverage of the households such as that of the Beckhams. The right to happiness (enshrined in the American constitution), self-care, enhancement and intimacy, both at home and at work is detectable in brightly coloured breakfast TV studios with their soft domestic seating, reaction shots and homely chat to camera. *Richard and Judy* are always coming back to TV by popular demand, as people-like-us for millions. Is it fair to cringe?

Maybe - because Peronist tendencies are also present, for example in the sheer daftness of treating celebrities such as Princess Diana as adult 'imaginary friends'. This is another area where more analysis is needed.

Inequality is a severe worry rather than something to cringe about: debt collectors, credit controllers, prison wardens, immigration officers, doorstep security staff and police officers provide the coercive emotional backdrop to a 'service economy' which contains persistent inequalities, misery and crime. Finally, we might need to look at mood-shifting by extortionists, terrorists, traffickers, prostitutes, protection racketeers, rude-boys and drug-dealers, who perform emotional labour in the shadows of the night-time economy and who connect every neighbourhood to illicit world trade.

'the sheer daftness of treating celebrities, such as Princess Diana, as adult "imaginary friends"'

While we have indicated the scope which a manifesto for feelings might cover, there are bound to be several emotion ideologies. I want to broadly indicate what these might be.

A *social-democratic* manifesto for feelings would always call into question whether the right balance exists between liberty of feeling, equality of feeling and solidarity of feeling. While social democrats, even left-social democrats, would generally place Liberty, Equality and Fraternity in that order of priority, they sense that these ideals cannot be optimised, because the pursuit of one usually has negative consequences for another. They also look for theories and evidence.

Libertarians would welcome liberty of expression, individuality, and that free movement of carers that may yet meet the home-care deficit which Hochschild describes.

Socialists would place equality of feeling first, from each to each according to need on the basis of ability. On the face of it, equal treatment might flow from treating all selves as having a common 'outer/ inner' structure, and therefore a common basis for comradeship regardless of class (as an *ideal*, if not a fact). One basis for objecting to current regimes is that managers, even owners, find their authentic selves threatened and compromised. (The Young Marx might have talked of damage to their 'species-being'.) But the idea of the anxious executive, frightened of exposure, does not sit well with the notions of the *passion for work* and the *care deficit at home* which white-collar Americans seem happy to tolerate. There also seems to be an inconsistency in the tendency within the left to welcome a re-uniting of hand and brain, yet remain uneasy about skilful emotional labour done for large corporations like Delta Airlines.

Why should Marxists see the commercialisation of emotions as more problematic than the commercialisation of other kinds of labour - unless they ascribe special existential qualities to the 'heart'?

A *conservative* feeling manifesto would put well-ordered emotions, solidarity of sentiment, the sacred, the soul and all matters mystical first, and stand against the tide of emotional regime-change, especially 'change from below'.

Can you identify which of these I subscribe to? And can you also identify the feeling manifesto that you already carry with you?

Emotion management in an age of global terrorism

Arlie Russell Hochschild

This is a slightly edited version of a public lecture at Brunel University, 4 October 2001.

On the morning of 11 September mothers packed their children's school lunches. Busy executives worried that a button might come off a suit coat. People worried they couldn't finish their reports on time. Most Americans were 'bracketing' such issues as the establishment of US military bases in Saudi Arabia, the plight of the Palestinians, or even the offence that others could take at brash American culture itself - bracketing such issues to get through a 'normal' day in the 'normal' modern world. By the end of the day on 11 September, as we all know, scores of executives, secretaries, restaurant workers, were leaping from flaming offices on the top floors of the World Trade Centre and landing a quarter of a mile below in fragments. Instantly, the nation and world saw and knew. The iconic targets - the World Trade Centre and the Pentagon - the nerve centres of global capitalism - were revealed as shockingly vulnerable. If those who once seemed the safest people in the world could be wiped out in an instant, well, the idea began to dawn, why couldn't that happen to you and me? And if it could happen to you and me, at any time, we need to emotionally absorb the idea of 'danger'. And whether we respond to the idea of danger through detachment (as expressed in denial or fatalism) or attachment (as expressed in alarm, depression or anger), it is to a sense of danger that we are now responding.

But this all happens in stages. After the first moment of attempting to grasp the reality, there was for me - and I think for many - a crisis of relevance. Given the enormity of the disaster, how can what I had planned to do matter? Do I just continue to do what until just now I had assumed was important? Isn't continuing as if nothing had occurred a form of sacrilege? A betrayal? An absence of participation, a diminishment of honour owed the victims? I myself had a crisis of relevance directly related to the subject of this talk. Am I going to talk about the 'Commercialisation of Intimate Life'? [the topic I had planned to talk about]. I care a great deal about this topic. I see it as part of a far broader growth of a 'market orientation' to life, which I think is developing as more human activities move from the realm of use to exchange value. I see an emotional market paradigm emerging, to go with the 'systems world' we're entering. I think it's important.

But the topic I had planned was based on the premise that we'll all be alive to experience the problem. After 11 September, that premise was shaken. So today I'll try to put together some initial thoughts about what 11 September has exposed to view - the structure of an entire *emotional regime*.

This emotional regime includes a set of taken-for-granted feeling rules (rules about how we imagine we should feel) and framing rules (rules about the way we think we should see and think). Together these rules shape how we see and feel about everyday reality.

This emotional regime, as I'm calling it, is also tacitly associated with the smooth functioning of the *nation state system, its monopolisation of the means of violence and the pre-eminence of its leaders as makers of the emotion-rules.* After 11 September, it has become clear that ordinary people, outside the state apparatus, can do state-size harm. Previously it has generally been nation-states which have done the most *massive and anonymous* harm to civilian populations. Auschwitz, Hiroshima, Dresden and Karaganda - the largest of Stalin's gulags - all these have been the result of state organised terror. In this light, 11 September - the work of a well co-ordinated global gang, not a nation state - is a departure.

And while media depictions of Osama Ben Laden as a person, an image, seemed to be an attempt to make him seem as large and ominous as a state, he is not a state. But the counter-challenge of 11 September has, paradoxically, strengthened the American nation-state, and it is to its (ill equipped) leaders that many now emotionally regressed American citizens turn for guidance about how afraid, angry or trusting to feel.

Laying bare the structure of an emotional regime

Human beings always live within the boundaries of emotional regimes. But seldom do we see - as in an illuminating flash of lightning - how it is that we do so.

A whole set of factors maintains our normal emotional regimes. And this set of factors determines an entire range of ways in which we experience reality. In the first instance, at least at the beginning, it determines the degree to which we *acknowledge* an event ('did this event really happen?'). It also shapes the degree to which we *identify with* the victims or perpetrators of it. (Did this happen to *me* or mine, or did I or people I identify with do it?) Our emotional regime also dictates the timing of moving in and out of 'emergency mode' (When is it okay to go back to trying to live life as usual?), and the setting of new feeling rules concerning fear, suspicion, blame and fear of being blamed. (Are Americans victims or world villains? Should we be angry at the terrorists (right-wing response) or guilty for the damage to the world we've done to which they are a possible response (mixed left-wing response)?) The events of 11 September led most Americans to feel momentarily regressed, in need of protection, and to turn to national authority figures for guidance about what we ought to feel. At the same time, this new need raises questions precisely about the feelings followers have toward leaders.

Did it really happen?

In the first hours of 11 September, the question arose: did this really happen? One is tempted to assume that people intuitively *know* when they or people with whom they identify are in danger, but history tells us otherwise. Many assimilated Jews in Germany couldn't bring themselves to leave in time. And many Americans who are not, in fact, in danger feel that they are. While the crime rate in America has actually fallen in recent years, for example, the fear of crime has risen.

Thus, the perception of reality can quite obviously depart from reality, through denial, projection, reaction formation and other mechanisms of ego defence, which the culture can encourage.

We get our picture of reality from television or from what people we trust see on television. It is often noted that small children who watch television have difficulty telling fantasy from reality. Parents are often put in the position of telling children, 'no, that scary man who shot 13 people in a bar room is a television actor, and the blood is really catsup'. Now we face the reverse: something frightening on the television actually *is* true. And it is not simply children who have a hard time grasping this fact.

A word more about television as a mediator of our reality. With the decline of participation in civic and community affairs, and the parallel rise in television-viewing - so well documented by Robert Putnam in *Bowling Alone* - critics have argued that many people are substituting TV for a 'real life', and make a case that the average TV-absorbed couch-potato should 'get a life'. In response, I think, the American television industry created 'reality TV', as if to say 'TV *is* life'. So viewers now watch 'real' people who are 'really' roughing it the Australian outback, or facing sexual temptation on a Hawaiian island. So again fiction and reality seem mixed. In his excellent book, *The End of Victory Culture*, Tom Engelhardt argues intriguingly that reality and fiction are really intertwined. We had World War One, World War Two, Vietnam. Then, he argues, when there was a lull and we were at a loss for nation-building heroes, our emotional cravings led the emotional-barometer-reading artists of Hollywood to invent *Star Wars*. In other words, he argues, our emotional needs lead Hollywood to respond to reality - with a 'reality' of its own. The dream makers read history for emotional voids. And then they fill them. This, then, was the weird 'make-believe-real-make-believe' cultural world into which the real bad news of 11 September intruded.

How does this affect me?

Not only do we need to understand how it is people grasp the reality of a disaster, we need to understand how a person understands who - emotionally speaking - the disaster happened *to*? To us? Or to them? On 11 September, I happened to be living in a small town in Maine and taking care of my 90-year-old aunt, who keeps her television on 16 hours a day. The TV reported that in one small town after another throughout the US, stores closed, and churches opened. Strangers held candle-lit vigils in small towns across the nation, including one nearby. Blood donations doubled. In other words, people felt - as the TV reported it -

this had happened 'to us and to me'. There were some reports that crime fell and that a sense of spontaneous community increased across all divides.

But this 'team-formation' had limits. I talked with a Afghan taxi driver in New York on my way to London and asked what 11 September meant to him and he said, 'I'm worried that the American government is going to bomb my country, and the reason I'm here is that I left with the Russian invasion, and this looks like another invasion and I'm worried.' He identified (and this was before the US invaded Afghanistan) with the future Afghan victims of American adventurism - with another 'us'.

Regression and the leaders as feeling legislators

When a crisis arises, part of us becomes child-like and we look to leaders - to authority - to guide our feelings. That is, we regress and look to authorities *as parents*. For in times of crisis, leaders provide what the psychoanalytic theorist Donald Winnicott calls a 'facilitating environment' or 'holding environment', which offers us a sense of being in an atmosphere of safety and trust. This is important because it is precisely trust in our environment that disappears in moments of crisis. So we do not turn to leaders simply for comfort. We turn to them for a sense that we live in an environment where things make sense.

Among the authority figures to whom people turned was the newly installed - and by many liberals including myself, strongly disdained - President George W. Bush, fresh from a highly controversial election, along with Secretary of Defence Ronald Rumsfeld, and Secretary of State Colin Powell. Their words were, in turn, passed on to the public through the medium of the personalities of TV network newscasters - the compassionate Peter Jennings, the stolid Dan Rather, the imperturbable Tom Browkaw - whose personalities during this time of stress became objects of intense scrutiny - and news - themselves. The loyal court jester of TV, David Letterman, lightly ridiculed the vague but urgent and authoritative edicts to 'be prepared for a second attack' but 'we can't say where or when'. Meanwhile, with probably little practical function, low-level gun-toting national guardsmen in the nation's airports functioned as local security blankets to the nation.

Timing: when to return to nervous normal

From 11 September through to 17 September President Bush told Americans, 'It is time to grieve'. Then after a week, as if ending a prayer in church, Bush said, in effect, 'It's time to get back on the horse'. It would be 'letting Osama Ben Laden win' to stop work, become depressed, or 'grieve too much'. We needed to show the world what Americans are made of.

In the days following 11 September the 5:00 PM newscasters in Lewiston, Maine had some very interesting interviews with footballers. After the 11th, all football games were cancelled in deference to the victims of 11 September. After a week, the games resumed. The TV sportscasters on several channels were featured interviewing footballers, asking them, 'How do you feel about getting back on the field of play?' One soldierly footballer replied, 'We have to get back on the horse. I think it is my patriotic duty to get back to the game'. Another football player answered the same question in a more therapeutic vein: 'Getting back to the game helps me deal with my shock at this'.

But the boundaries between grieving time and normal time had to be accepted, and with them ambivalence about the placement of them. A recent commemorative issue of *Newsweek*, read:

> Americans will have to put up with the spectacle of David Letterman, the nation's ironist, on the verge of tears [a leading TV comedian, Letterman was seen on television crying about 11 September]. This is not to say that Letterman's emotions were not genuine, or that he was wrong to strike a note of compassion at a delicate moment when his program returned to the air. But it would be a sad distinction of National Normalcy if he and his fellow comics were now expected to emote regularly on the tube. That it also serves to help us laugh at him. The entertainment industry in general seems to be groping for the correct response to September 11th, fearful of any sign of insensitivity. This led to some strange comic occurrences: Hollywood was anxiously re-editing new movies to delete any shots of the Twin Towers, as street vendors in New York did a booming business in paintings, photographs and tee-shirts depicting … the Towers.

So the *Newsweek* article was saying 'OK, grieving time is over. We should be able to laugh again. On the other hand, we don't want to see reminders of what we've lost: we still need our "holding environment"'.

Who has a right to lead the laughter, and in what way, was still being worked out, however, in the current pages of London's *Time Out*. There one can find an article about an Iranian comic ... who plays the part of a short fat Arab, 'who continues to have fun throwing himself around the stage channelling new characters like some comic medium - the Indian Bingo-Caller, the Over-Analytic Comic...' So the Iranian comedian has to decide, 'What am I going to be doing? Am I going to continue as usual? Am I going to cancel?' Tacitly at issue here, perhaps, is whether an Iranian - and possibly a Muslim - comic has rights to the same emotional territory as an American white man. What viewers view or readers read, then, are pioneers moving about in emotional territory, defining the edges of it, and establishing changes in an emotional regime.

An emotional catch 22

On the one hand, authorities have closed a period of 'appropriate' mourning, and established that Americans should put on their old emotional armour and face their normal workdays. On the other hand, whole new closets of terrifying information have opened up. There was news of crop-dusting planes that terrorists were planning to use to spray deadly poisons over urban areas, of plague germs, smallpox germs, or e-coli added to our water supply. Yesterday I heard a discussion on television of Taliban sympathisers in the Pakistan military, who might have access to Pakistan's atom bomb, which could be used on the US and its allies.

We have lived with the idea of fearful possibilities before. But our emotional regime has kept the idea fairly *closeted*. Now we are introduced to the feeling rule that we should 'Get back on the horse' while at the same time the horse may have to pass through a nuclear holocaust. To resolve this contradiction, this catch 22, we are now being asked to do a great deal of emotion work ... On the one hand it's reasonable to think twice about airplanes, bridges, water supplies, nuclear reactors. A new level of paranoia is now 'normal'. On the other hand, we're being asked to manage our apprehension and get on with our day.

Underneath this emotion work, especially for those closest to the disaster, people are working through what Freud called a *repetition compulsion*. In an attempt to heal and master a trauma, and to deal with unbidden images, the individual repeatedly goes over and over the traumatising event in his or her mind. In addition, some individuals may even - and this seems at first counter-intuitive - unconsciously do harm to themselves in some way so as to experience becoming the *author* rather than the *victim* of the frightening event. We can think of this as one version of 'working through' a trauma. According to some reports, about a third of those who lost a loved one have experienced some aspect of this post-traumatic stress syndrome.

In sum, because it is just now newly re-instated, a whole emotional regime is revealed before our eyes. It addresses issues ranging from the very acknowledgement of a newly revealed danger, to our identification with the victims and perpetrators, to the extent to which we are supposed to be desperate, scared, depressed, angry or hopeful about them.

In crisis, certain emotion-masters emerge. We had Theodore Roosevelt and Winston Churchill during World War II. Alas, we are now saddled with George W. Bush, who treats the world like a back street of Texas posted with signs marked 'Wanted Dead or Alive'. Still, his ratings remain high because our need for reassurance is great. This 'emotional regime' is open for viewing any time we turn on the television, open a magazine or talk to someone. It's being worked out as we speak.

Our emotional regime is geared to the leadership of the *nation-state*, its monopoly of the means of violence and the protection it can afford us. As the cultural sociologist Ann Swidler has argued, our cultural ideas 'face out' to the social structures available to us - ideas of love face out to the family, and ideas about danger, safety and violence face out to the nation-state. Cultures orient us.

Insofar as feeling rules and emotion work describe the deep part of culture, they orient us, in part, to institutions - and in this case to the nation-state.

Our new emotional regime orients us to a situation not unlike an earlier period in which the state was weak. As Steve Smith has noted (in his preparatory materials for this event and elsewhere), in the Middle Ages, a person stepping outside the walls of his courtyard might encounter a bandit who slit his throat, and left him to die. No policeman would chase the bandit. No court would try him. No ambulance would rescue him. Public life was dangerous.

Today, too, the state can offer us little protection from the new source of danger. But here we face a paradox. Just as we have begun to move to a new post-nation-state model of global networks, the need for protection is buttressing the old nation-state. In *Empire*, Michael Hardt and Antonio Negri argue that we are moving toward the end of the nation-state, and the rise of a network of micro-modules or networks - of which Al Quaeda is an aberrant example. As

President Bush beats the drum for war, little children ask the pertinent question: 'War against what?' 'War against whom?' For this isn't the work of a nation as much as of a network which weaves in and out of many nations. With the old nation-state system, one was either at war, or not at war. There was an on-off time for terror, generally gauged by failures in international diplomacy. Military structures were on permanent alert against surprise attacks, while civilian populations could more or less rest easy within the borders protected by a nation's military. Vigilantes didn't have to protect themselves. The FBI, the national guard, the army, the local police, did it for us. Now - though this remains to be seen - military structures can protect us less; and civilian populations feel themselves more on the alert.

In taking on this task of self-policing, I fear that some civilians will lash out at perceived danger in the form of young men of colour. This will create, in turn, a new form of fear - fear of being mistaken for the enemy. As a young, immigrant society, the United States has prided itself on a relatively high degree of openness and tolerance. The ideal, at least, of an open society has been that the search for security should not compromise basic social trust and civility among a highly diverse population.

The new emotional regime reorders suspicion. It sets up a new emotional stratification system: the haves are those above suspicion, the have-nots are those who are obvious objects of it. There is more suspicion in the air altogether - so few of us get by without arousing some - at least at airport security check-points. Coming to London by air, I passed through the Portland airport, the same airport which two of the suicide bombers used before getting on the plane from Boston to New York and hitting the World Trade Centre. Normally I would sit down, open a newspaper, make some slight eye-contact, slight-smile, as women often unconsciously do, to signal reassurance, 'no harm here'. This time, passengers looked furtively at various pieces of baggage, and scanned faces rapidly. When conversation did break out it was in great blocks of excited talk, as if people felt they had passed over to the other side of a strong barrier of distrust. We are each our own policeman, each in a less trusting society.

But not all people in the airport were, emotionally speaking, equal. A new emotional 'stratification system' had emerged. The 'haves' were mostly free of glances of hostility and suspicion. The have-nots were often - or felt they might now often be - the objects of hostility and suspicion. The 'haves' were white.

The have-nots were Mexicans, Puerto-Ricans, Guatemalans, and people who looked like they might be of Middle-Eastern descent. It has been remarked that anti-Semitism remains; only the Muslims have now replaced the Jews as objects of it. One 9-year-old Muslim schoolgirl who wore a headscarf (reported on in a programme for the BBC) told a newscaster that she felt a strong compassion for the victims of 11 September. But the looks of her schoolmates told her, she said, that they imagined that her head scarf meant that she must sympathise with Osama Ben Laden and be 'on the other side'. So clothes now send new emotional signals.

In the end, what the terrorists really bombed was not so much a building but a set of social premises - ones I highly treasure - about the virtue of diversity and integration. One of the real challenges ahead of us is to be architects of a set of feeling rules which prevent people of colour from becoming the scapegoats of 9-11. For as the American nation rears its ugly head in righteous anger, as a besieged population polarises into lone-star leaders and meek followers, it becomes ever more important to defend what remains truly great about American civic culture - its trust in diversity - and to reflect on the politics that so forcefully flow through the new post-9/11 emotional regime.

If you love your work, do you thank a careers counsellor?

Fiona Douglas with
Stephen Lloyd Smith

The authors argue that emotional labour - for a long time an unrecognised part of career guidance, and then squeezed out of the system by managerialism - is now once more being recognised as crucial to this area of work.

'If you can read this, thank a teacher!' qualifies as one of the best car-stickers ever devised. The slogan *works* on us because it is a reminder of an obvious truth: it is clear that teachers make a difference. Many readers will remember teachers who cared enough to 'really get through to them'. Perhaps they communicated their enthusiasm in a way that awakened and developed your sense of excitement, confidence and efficacy. Of course there were also fearful and dangerous teachers along the way, expert in the emotional labour of abuse.

The way teachers 'transform the feelings of others' qualifies them as 'emotional labourers', and if they do this well they can elicit and develop skills that will last their students a life-time. But their cumulative effects on pupils' life-chances take such a long time to show up that many teachers will be a long time dead before the value of their work becomes clear. In any case, what concerns governments is making changes to the institutional regime under which teaching and learning takes place in a way that can demonstrate readily measurable improvements in performance, which can be measured in the short term ... services are ruled by KPIs (Key Performance Indicators).

Can similar things be said about career counsellors as about teachers? And what has been happening to the institutional framework within which career guidance takes place? Have we been making more or less of a difference?

Although we spend less time with clients than teachers spend with their pupils, our sessions are 'one-to-one-intensives' and last much longer than, say, the fleeting encounters between flight attendants and air travellers.[1] Our sessions last at least as long - and usually longer - than encounters between nurses and patients. The ideal is that career-guidance encounters can transform the life-chances of the client, particularly in raising the confidence of the dispossessed or damaged, or of those who are struggling to identify a place in the world which they can occupy happily.

In this piece I want to look back and take stock of the changes I experienced as a careers counsellor; of work that can seem nebulous to politicians, senior civil servants and 'middle-dog' service administrators. Of course there is the danger of being nostalgic and writing only of the losses which have taken place. But some of what is being said today about career guidance, especially about inclusion, offers hopeful indications that our service can be retrieved.

I first entered the Careers Service in 1976, as a probationary careers adviser, having completed a first degree and the professional Diploma in Careers Guidance. I worked for a small North London borough in a socially deprived area; it was mostly working-class, with pockets middle-class prosperity. It had a significant and diverse ethnic minority population, and pupils went to 'their' local school.

When I began, service administration was straightforward: schools were allocated a day a week, and careers *officers* (as we were known) had freedom to negotiate the use of that time with the school to meet the best interests of the pupils. This was not always ideal because schools' expectations and attitudes sometimes conflicted with those held by the guidance practitioner. For example,

1. For her commentary on the emotional labour of flight attendants and others, see A. R. Hochschild, *The Managed Heart: the Commercialisation of Human Feeling*, University of California Press 1983.

one school would 'threaten' pupils with an interview with the careers officer 'if they didn't try harder with school work'.

In another school, however, a creative and memorable approach to the work was developed. Collaboration with a 'remedial' teacher lead to a tailor-made programme for pupils with learning problems who were leaving school at the end of the academic year. Each pupil participated in a programme of career education and personal interviews, and was coached in job application processes, including mock job-interviews; and there were specific training programmes for those most in need. All of this was planned with the teacher, but delivered by me, drawing on my education and training, and my knowledge of the local labour market. On reflection, the process had a strong emotional component. We could sense the difference we were making and in return we responded to their rising sense of good cheer and hopefulness. Working with young people has a reward all of its own and it is hard not to see their charm, even in truculent would-be rogues and angry rebels.

Indeed, in the mid- to late 1970s our Careers Service employed an outreach worker to find those hard-to-reach young people who were determined not to participate in the school system. We also came into contact with them through their entitlement to 'the dole'. The outreach worker could work with disengaged young people, offering support and ready access to the service when they needed it.

As a matter of course, we networked with the youth service, social services, the community interpreter, colleges, and many other agencies. Young people in distress appeared sufficiently confident in their relationship with the service to ask for help on issues that were in some respects beyond career guidance, but at the same time affected by it. How can career guidance begin when young lives were affected by homelessness, pregnancy or emotional turbulence? I even counselled a highly traumatised youth who had been held hostage at gunpoint during a siege and who had been unable to think about anything else. Another broke down pleading for help because his uncle was sexually abusing him.

The process began through emotional labour, in listening to young people, involving them in thinking about their situation and identifying who might be able to help them. It was hard not to respond to the diverse individuals who sat in front of me; the shy, the awkward, the roguish, the angry and often those with all of these qualities presented together. Only once the young person *felt* like it could we begin to look forward. Career guidance was not about getting a young person into the first available job, but a holistic process: it was about guiding them through many stages of life not just the next alighting point. (I have since discovered that the holistic approach was taken in New Zealand as early as 1914, through YMCA involvement in designing the service.)

Whilst there is no doubt that the service was managed in the traditional local authority bureaucratic way, day-to day delivery was based around micro-local needs determined by the practitioners and their extensive networks. Practitioners felt themselves to be 'professionals' working in an extended team of other professionals, able to find creative and customised solutions. We did well without being 'target-driven'. Light administrative control and a sense of social justice gave licence to an emotionally competent, socially and personally responsive service. This enabled us to *engage* with our clients through what has since become identified as emotional labour. Frankly, it was pleasing work and we felt sure that as well as the immediate modest effects on life chances, we would make a difference some day, somehow, somewhere that we would probably not see.

Eventually, new management practices provided us with a formula to allocate our time to schools according to school size, thus distributing time equally according to school population, not social need. This was the beginning of managerial control, imposed to meet the ever-changing demands of restless Conservative governments, which sought to break the careers advisers' advocacy role, perhaps in order to break our modest professional power of the time. The notion that a profession should have guardianship of its standards is offensive to the managerial urge of governmentalism.

Anti-professional resentment was encapsulated in the accusation by Peter Morrison the then Employment Minister, in 1983, that the Careers Service was concerned with 'social engineering' - a newly fashionable sneer - and should respond more to the 'needs of employers'. 'Employers are operating in the real world ... the Careers Service must respond positively to the indications employers give about the sort of youngsters they want.'

Although I had always felt there was something very 'real-world', demanding, important and immediate about working in a youth-offender unit, the service was duly rationalised and become demonstrably 'more efficient and effective'.

Managerialism became our driving force. Targets were set and monitored. Whilst we still strove to maintain our work with juvenile justice departments, voluntary networks and other previous partners, other work had to go 'underground' because it was not seen as part of the 'core business' for which we were funded. These unseen spaces in our commitment received no funding and were quickly constrained. Our taken-for-granted emotional labour - which no one had ever counted - soon became one of those items which we did not get paid to do. We also cut guidance to adults unless they paid for the service. Schools outside of the LEA were deemed to be outside of our remit, and pressure was exerted from central management to minimise service provision.

'career guidance was not about getting a young person into a job, but a holistic process'

I now became a manager, struggling to defend and maintain the earlier ideal, but with insufficient staff, recruitment freezes and the loss of juniors to less expensive areas of the country.

I was in a position to see that most services in the South East were up against similar pressures, because I worked across different services, involved in many networks. I was on a committee with other agencies to set up a counselling service for young people. These agencies included the local tertiary college, medical services, social services, youth and community groups. The intention was to hold a 'roving' surgery, taking the service out into the local communities rather than expecting young people to find their way through traditional formal channels. Another venture started a 'drop-in' information, advice and guidance service to adults, operating from the local library and staffed voluntarily by the participating services.

Even under this transitional regime, somewhere between 'professionalism' and 'managerialism', it was still possible that in the course of one week a careers adviser could be working in mainstream and special schools, liasing with 'Records of Achievement', working with Project Trident, a young offenders' centre or local prison, staffing the local drop-in centre, attending case conferences with medical services, social services, youth services and educational welfare, and still finding time to work closely with the juvenile justice department. We also visited local firms, training providers and HE and FE institutions to understand the local labour, education and training markets.

At one Youth Treatment Centre we worked with very damaged young people whose needs could not be met elsewhere in the child care system; some of them had committed grave offences and were held under Section 53 of the Children and Young Persons Act, 1933. However, over time we were compromised by the growing prevalence of a 'hit and run' approach to guidance, in which engagement was done in a hurry and evidence of a measurable outcome concocted as best we could. There was no possibility of spending a lot of time building up trust and relationships with staff and young people in the centre, in order to develop a careers education and guidance programme that felt *substantively*, rather than merely 'formally' effective. This would have conflicted with the increasingly output-driven approach in the lead-up to service privatisation, which now dictated a speeded-up and 'surface acted', fleeting service, closer to the airline model.

Decisive changes for the Careers Service occurred in 1991. Proposals to 'contract out' the service from the LEA through competitive tendering were contained within a White Paper produced jointly by the DES and the Employment Department, which challenged the Careers Service's links with education. The White Paper stated that the Careers Service would be brought '*closer to employers*'.[2] The service was wrested from local authority control by competitive tendering; and in line with the Government's desire to meet the perceived needs of employers, those bidding for the services were forced to form coalitions between private industry, local authorities and other interested parties to create the limited companies to deliver the service. The nature of these companies lay somewhere between public service provider and self-determining agent.

Privatisation of the Careers Services began in 1993. Companies contracted with the Government Office to deliver work defined and quantified by Whitehall in return for finance. Failure to deliver on targets lead to penalties. Work became measured by 'action plans', on the assumption that just *one* interview with a 'careers adviser' or 'careers counsellor' would lead to a *stable, concrete career decision* - which of course, we 'extracted' from the client. By recording 'career decisions' our 'effectivenesss' could be demonstrated, even if the 'hard' measure was not that meaningful. The early contracts paid for work with pupils in year

2. DES and Education Department, *Education and Training in the 21st Century*; HMSO, London 1991, p44.

11 (those aged 15-16). Careers services had previously worked with pupils from year 9 to year 13 (i.e. from their third year at secondary school level), but what was not in the contract could not be delivered. It did not occur to policy makers that emotional labour or 'care' should be in the contract. Gradually, amendments to the contracts, and shifts in policies on entitlement after the 1997 Education Act, have meant that many categories of school children have been stripped of career guidance.

The switch to the market as a means of control was in keeping with an economic characterisation of the service as a whole. Quasi-privatisation resulted in service coalitions of various strengths, leading to a complex round of take-overs, which continue to this day. Using this 'economic' approach, White and Watts in their 1992 study assessed the cost of occupational mismatch, based on a conservative estimate that this contributed 10 per cent to the unemployment figures; they calculated that if effective careers guidance made only a 1 per cent impact, this would be worth £10 million to the exchequer. On the face of it this should have helped the service because it implied that it would get the funding it needed.

But even now there are marketised providers that are very hard-pressed financially, and the status of the service is still unresolved. It still straddles employment and education and is beset with crises of identity and function, compounded by continuous upsets in government policy. We have become an anxious profession uncertain of our place, existing somewhere between 'social good' and 'economic reality'. I quit the service in 1995, to become a lecturer in higher education, but care enough for it to maintain contact through research.

I am finding that many experienced careers guidance practitioners with in-depth specialist experience also left, feeling unable to conform to joyless action-plans. The new managers do not seem to miss them. I am told: 'There is definitely less place for an individualistic person; those who had specialisms have more difficulty in coping with this. Individualistic people find it difficult to work with others, and do not muck in. Being a team player is crucial, and you need to be co-operative without being asked.' The outcome of 'liberalisation' has been the curtailment of individuality and inventiveness.

Managerialist approaches sought not only conformity and role interchangeability, but also 'performance management' in 'achieving' the

excluded young people. The advent of 'Connexions', a new service of personal advisers, aims to 'ensure success through learning and a smooth transition to adulthood and working life for every young person'.[6] And at the heart of 'Connexions' is the need for effective networks of practitioners who work as passionate advocates for young people.

While the financial viability of Connections needs addressing urgently, I warm to it. Indeed recently one of my informants joked that it was time to set up a 'full circle' club. This would be for people like ourselves, who had seen the systematic dismantling of an infrastructure capable of providing a very similar service to the one the Government now wants to set up. Good humour tempers cynicism, and the desire to provide an inclusive service for all young people might yet prevail.

Conclusion

Career Guidance turned out to have been a poor career for many that chose it. While they cherished the needs of young people as central their task, the cost to them was high. The turnover of careers advisers is extraordinary. Many of those who saw their role as advocates for young people and had creative ways of working were seen as individualistic and unmanageable after privatisation. Many left the service because of the baleful influence of managerialism. One should not revel in the fact, however, that many of those who came in to manage 'tightly controlled' and 'strictly monitored' services are finding it hard to adjust back to the need to work once more in unconventional, unconditional and innovative ways.

The shame was all the waste, the marginalisation and commodification of expertise, and the time, money and emotion spent in dismantling care-full work. But as an old-timer I like to think I am now in a good position to help.

6. DfES, *The Connexions Framework for Assessment, Planning, Implementation and Review*, DfES Publications, Nottingham 2001.

Unemployed and feeling worthless

Reflections on the emotional experience of unemployment

Maria Lorentzon

Maria Lorentzon looks at the effects of unemployment on mental health.

Ruskin's perception of separate gender spheres placed men in public work roles, with women in the nurturing and hidden world of home and hearth.[1] And though such Victorian ideas about the division of labour between men and women are gradually dying out, it remains true that many unemployed men in the late twentieth century still expressed shame and bitterness about their position. Men still commonly identify work roles as their chief source of prestige and intrinsic personal value. This was highlighted in series of *BMJ* editorials by Richard Smith in 1985, to which I will make reference in the first part of this article.[2] There is

1. J. Ruskin, *Sesame and Lilies*, G. Allen, Orpington 1898.
2. Most of the quotations in the first part of this essay are cited from Richard Smith's articles in the BMJ, as listed below: '"Bitterness, shame, emptiness, waste": an introduction to unemployment and health', 12.10.85; '"Please never let it happen again": lessons on unemployment from the 1930s', 26.10.85; '"Gissa job": the experience of unemployment', 2.11.85; '"What's the point. I'm no use to anybody": the psychological consequences of unemployment', 9.11.85; '"I feel really ashamed": how does unemployment lead to poorer mental health', 16.11.85; '"I couldn't stand it any more": suicide and unemployment', 30.11.85; '"We got on each other's nerves": unemployment and the family', 14.12.85. They are referenced in the text by the journal name, date and page.

now a debate about whether women's increasing involvement in the labour market is leading to a similar value system for them. Arguments have been made, by feminists and non-feminists alike, that women have an alternative 'career option' and source of self-worth in motherhood and home-making, and that they move more smoothly than men between the public world of work and private domesticity. Some current research seems to call this into question.

George Orwell recorded his observations about unemployed men in *The Road to Wigan Pier* in 1937: 'When I first saw unemployed men at close quarters, the thing that horrified and amazed me was that many of them were *ashamed* of being unemployed' (cited *BMJ*.2.11.85, p1263). Austrian researcher Marie Jahoda and colleagues also described catastrophic conditions in the early 1930s, in Marienthal, a small steel town near Vienna, where closure of the steel works had made almost every man unemployed. They wrote: '...we entered Marienthal as scientists; we leave it with only one desire: that the tragic opportunity for such an enquiry [into the effects of mass unemployment] may not recur in our time' (cited *BMJ* 26.10.85, p1191).

Catastrophic unemployment - producing conditions reminiscent of those in Marienthal - occurred in Britain during the early years of Conservative government; the mining industry was dealt a body-blow, with a massive programme of mine closures, from which it will not recover. During the prolonged miners' strike against the closures, miners supported by their wives and partners sought to preserve not just their jobs, but a way of life. Whole communities were experiencing virtual 'social death', of a similar kind to that of the people of 1930s Marienthal. The political climate of the early 1980s was harshly individualistic; Thatcher was propagating the belief that 'there was no such thing as society', in an ideological climate of Social Darwinism. The resulting conditions are exemplified in Beatrix Campbell's 1984 book *Wigan Pier Revisited*, in which a semi-skilled man, who had been unemployed for two years, is quoted as saying:

> I used to get up at 6 am like I was going to work ... when you are unemployed you feel you have committed a crime somewhere, but nobody tells you what you've done ... of course I get depressed ... sometimes I feel really ashamed ... this is the first time I've ever not given my sisters something for Christmas (cited *BMJ*, 16.11.85, p1405).

The feelings of an Asian unemployed man, as recorded in Fagin & Little's 1984 *The Forsaken Families*, are touchingly revealed in the following quotation: 'My wife she don't respect me any more … I can't maintain, can't buy presents for my son' (cited *BMJ*, 14.12.85, p1708). He remarked on his wife's changed attitude towards him: 'Indira treats me differently. If I asked her to do a job before, she did it. Nowadays she says she will do it later'. Thus unemployment was leading to a breakdown in family patterns. Sometimes the stress proved unendurable, as in the case of a 40 year old Welshman who was found hanged, having been unemployed for 10 months. A letter left by him stated: 'I can't go on … I'm drinking my unemployment money away' (cited *BMJ* 30.11.85, p1564).

These quotations sampled from editorials by Richard Smith have been presented as examples of the emotional experiences recorded by unemployed men. Significantly, none of these related to unemployed women. (It should be noted that in the 1970s and 1980s it became increasingly obvious that women who were out of paid employment did not always register as unemployed, and this might be taken as denoting their different attitude to the external employment market.) The main emotions highlighted in these editorials on 'occupation-less health' were:

- Bitterness/Anger
- Shame
- Emptiness/A sense of being wasted
- A sense of being mentally unwell/Hopelessness, leading to suicidal feelings.

The immediate shock of becoming unemployed is frequently followed by feelings of anger and bitterness - the 'why me?' reaction. Smith cites the results of a 1975 study in the UK of 100 cases of wife-battering, which found that 48 per cent of the husbands and cohabitees in these cases had been unemployed at some time, and 29 per cent of them were frequently or mostly unemployed (cited BMJ, 14.12.85, p1709). He also quotes from a similar study conducted by the Australian Royal Commission on Human Relationships in 1976, in which battered wives were asked to 'phone in'. Of the 56 respondents, 23 per cent had unemployed husbands. One woman stated: 'When he lost his job he went absolutely bonkers. He changed completely. He became depressed and snappy. Frustrated.'

Shame is a frequently recurring theme in reports on the feelings expressed by the unemployed. Smith notes from a number of sources that the unemployed are likely to suffer frequent humiliations and lose social status, and that, in particular, many of the long-term unemployed feel very ashamed of their position. Those who had been unemployed for a long time often reported that their lives, experiences and relationships began to 'empty and count for much less'. Prolonged unemployment was, for many people, a profoundly corrosive experience, which undermined their personality and could lead to a diminution in their capacity for work.

If the 'normal distress' associated with unemployment is not resolved, serious consequences may follow, including chronic alcoholism, mental illness and suicide. The example of the 40-year-old unemployed man killing himself has been cited above. In this man's case, alcoholic misuse was also part of the picture, and Smith debates which factors, or combination of factors, led his suicide. Such questions are difficult to answer with certainty, but it would seem likely that a combination of negative self-image and material poverty - caused by unemployment - led to alcoholism, and that all these factors were influential in pushing the man towards suicide. It is possible that preventive intervention could have been applied to avoid such desperate action. Smith observes that:

> in a recent survey of 954 men, unemployed on average for five months, a fifth said that their mental health had deteriorated since they lost their job. They reported increased anxiety, depression, insomnia, irritability, lack of confidence, listlesssness, inability to concentrate and general nervousness (*BMJ*, 9.11.85).

It would seem apt to conclude this discussion with Smith's quotation from Freud, from 'Civilisation and its Discontents'. Since work ties us to reality, 'if we are not obliged to get up in the morning and apply ourselves to a job then we are in danger of being overwhelmed by fantasy or emotion'.

The emotions of unemployment

It would seem clear from this brief review that strongly negative feelings accompany unemployment - though most of this material relates primarily to men. A number of questions can be posed about the level of emotional support that is provided, both on the journey towards unemployment and when this state becomes a reality. A number of pertinent questions and comments are summarised below.

1. The emotional labour input by human resources personnel and other work-based counsellors needs to be examined further in terms of the emotional effects on the person about to be made unemployed. Does the currently popular macho management style in many private and public sector organisations take account of the need for such support in order to prevent potentially disastrous consequences of stress in the future? How much heed is given to the point raised by Williams & Bendelow, that 'emotions have a fundamental impact for ... the social organisation of emotions in the workplace'.[3]

2. How realistic are expectations that female spouses will provide emotional support for their unemployed men, as inferred in the 1980s literature? There is evidence that female partners/wives of unemployed men often resent them as 'being under their feet' in the home. Examples have also been cited of women feeling that their own status is enhanced, when their previously dominant men are brought low through unemployment. Emotional labour input in regard to dependent children of unemployed men, as provided by mothers, is, undoubtedly, considerable. However, it appears that childless female spouses of men either unemployed or about to become so consult their GPs more than women in this position who have dependent children.[4] Why is this? Is the emotional support provided for children making mothers disregard their own stress-related complaints?

3. Most studies relate to unemployed men, as noted above. The assumption is often made that women are likely to revert to their 'natural' roles as mothers and home-makers. This takes no account of single, childless women who have worked in satisfying jobs and have no taste for domesticity. Would male

---

3. S. J. Williams and G. Bendelow, 'Emotions and "sociological imperialism" - a rejoinder to Craib', *Sociology*, 30, 1996, p151.
4. N. Beale and S, Nethercott, 'Job loss and morbidity: the influence of job tenure and previous work history', *Journal of the Royal College of General Practitioners*, 36, 1986.

partners be prepared to offer emotional support to their unemployed wives and partners on the same basis as they would expect to be supported?

There are clearly no easy answers in this area, which is affected by many complex trends within Western post-industrial society, including: the relationship between the public and private domains; gender perceptions of work-related self-esteem; the increasingly insecure world of work; and the decreasing stability of traditional, monogamous, heterosexual relationships. What does seem clear, however, is that more focused research concerning the effect of unemployment on women needs to be conducted. Svallfors et al, in their examination of employment commitment in Denmark, Norway and Sweden, found this to be *higher* among women than men in all three countries.[5] This discovery runs counter to the stereotype of women's 'natural' role as home-makers. In another study among unemployed men and women in Sweden, which linked employment commitment to psychological well-being, Nordenmark found that unemployment carried significantly higher risks of poor mental well-being for those who had strong work motivation for non-financial reasons - both women and men - as compared to those with a lower commitment to employment.[6] The status conveyed by work outside the home is clearly important for women as well as for men. As Arlie Hochschild has noted, researchers have consistently found that women who do paid work - however hectic their lives - feel less depressed, think better of themselves, and are more satisfied with life than women who don't do paid work.[7]

Employment status is clearly one important factor for the understanding of health inequalities.[8] Though biomedical researchers tend to be cautious about inferring direct causal links between unemployment and physical health status, there is general agreement that the long-term unemployed tend to have negative feelings about themselves and their immediate world; and this

5. S. Svallfors, K. Halvorsen and J. G. Andersen, 'Work orientations in Scandinavia: employment commitment and organisational commitment in Denmark, Norway and Sweden', *Acta Sociologica* (Norway), 44(2) 2001.
6. M. Nordenmark, 'Employment commitment and psychological well-being among unemployed men and women', *Acta Sociologica* (Norway), 42(2) 1999.
7. A. R. Hochschild, *The Time-bind; When Work Becomes Home and Home Becomes Work*, Metropolitan Books, New York 1997, p41.
8. For a wider discussion of the causes of health inequalities, see H. Graham (ed), *Understanding Health Inequalities*, Open University Press, Buckingham 2000.

is likely to impact on their mental health. These responses would appear to apply to both men and women, although fewer studies have, so far, been conducted on the latter. Assumptions that women are less affected than men by status derived from the 'public sphere' require careful re-examination. The Victorian 'angel in the house', as favoured by Ruskin and his ilk, is clearly not a role model for most women in the third millennium. The emotional satisfaction derived from home-based, nurturing activities no longer seems to compensate the majority of women for lack of paid work and its associated status and sociability. A question could, of course, be posed as to whether women in the past were ever 'satisfied' with their lot in the sense which we apply today.

A final reflection concerns the political will in today's Britain to deal with evidence of a lack of 'fit' between working life and home commitments, especially in the case of women. It is worth noting that 40 per cent of Swedish MPs are women, and their more 'family friendly' labour legislation is seen as resulting, at least partly, from the influence of women in Parliament. Political spin by the current New Labour government often appears to present unemployment as yesterday's problem, whereas it is in fact today's pain for workers in industries which have proved superfluous in the global market place. Weasel words and expressions, such as 'down-sizing' and 're-engineering', do not fool most of us, who know that they really mean redundancies, and their associated misery, which I hope I have illustrated in this paper.

Emotional labour and cancer work

Some reflections after a conference

Gay Lee

In this article, Gay Lee *reflects on the extent to which emotional labour as a concept can be usefully applied to the everyday practice of nursing.*

Once upon a time there was a patient - Joan - who was dying slowly of cancer. Her quality of life was not great. She couldn't walk, she was incontinent, and she felt sick so much of the time that she couldn't enjoy her food. No medicine seemed to help her very much.

The staff were good and kind. But the more they cared for Joan the more she demanded of them. Nothing was ever right and she was never grateful. She cried a lot about her situation and she shouted out for the nurses even when she didn't want anything. She craved attention and control.

At first her carers were pained by Joan's pain and did what they could to alleviate it. But because of her behaviour, feelings changed, and working with Joan became an act which had a personal cost - they had to put aside their own feelings of anger and frustration at her demands, and her lack of feeling for *them*. They had to smile and be nice to her.

Everyone had to work at this but they did it in different ways. *Acting* patiently and obligingly came easily to some and made them *feel* better towards Joan. Others had to really work on their feelings of resentment in order to nurse her well. For some it was all in an irksome day's work but they just got on and made light of it. Some got very upset and took their feelings home with them. There were very few carers who were free of feelings of conflict about her - a woman dying without much dignity, and with some of her problems self-inflicted.

The whole team of carers was engaged in a process which has been called 'emotional labour' - particularly hard work with Joan, but something people in caring and service jobs have to do to some degree or other most of the time. This can be unconscious, semi-conscious or completely conscious.

Arlie Hochschild, the sociologist who first coined the phrase, used it to describe the work of flight attendants. In her book *The Managed Heart*, she defines emotional labour as 'the management of feeling to create a publicly observable facial and bodily display'.[1] This is designed to produce an emotional state in the other, e.g. feelings of gratitude or a reduction of fear. For nurses it's about reducing patients' anxiety and giving them confidence in their care.

Last July I attended the second annual emotional labour conference, 'Emotional labour 2001: the public, private and professional self'. Most of the people making presentations were academics and researchers, who were applying this concept to the world of community work, business, politics and employment relations, as well as the caring professions. But can the term 'emotional labour' be usefully applied to the day-to-day practice of cancer and palliative care (or other) nursing - to familiar work situations?

People do manual work (in nursing this would be the physical work of looking after patients) and mental work (assessing the best treatment or care for the patient); so why not examine the idea of emotional work too? A nursing recruitment advert at the beginning of the 1990s asked nurses to consider whether the financial rewards of being a nurse matched the emotional ones. In Hochschild's study, paying flight attendants for their emotional labour to make passengers feel safe and cared for was recognised as having exchange value by the airlines. Put simply, if passengers opted to fly a particular airline because of its friendly flight attendants, then sales and ultimately profits would increase.

As a nurse I feel we don't talk very much about the emotional aspects of our work, as they affect us personally, and even less about their financial worth. So two questions arise: Is it useful to talk about the emotional aspects of our

---

1. A. Hochschild, *The Managed Heart: the commercialisation of human feeling*, University of California Press, Berkeley 1983.

work? And is the concept 'emotional labour' helpful to the discussion? The term was first used in *nursing* by Pam Smith in her book *The Emotional Labour of Nursing.*[2] The book examined 'the notion of emotional labour as a component of caring' in nursing. Smith says there is often a gap between what you feel and what you think you should feel, and so you may have to do 'work' on yourself in order to act appropriately with a patient or colleague.

You may have come on duty feeling upset by something that happened at home. You may not like the person you are caring for, or you may be very upset by the patient's distress (as, perhaps, with Joan). There may be too many distractions or hassles for you to be able to focus on the patient. Whatever - you often have to work hard at reducing any discrepancy between your pleasant, outward manner and your deeper feelings - because it's difficult to keep up a front for long. We work at this, as Arlie Hochschild says, 'either by changing what we feel or changing what we feign' .

Working on your feelings via your face is what Hochschild calls 'surface acting'. Here, the emotional labour you are doing is about 'putting on an act' and doing it well enough for any conflict with your feelings to disappear so you feel comfortable. But it doesn't always work because of the pressures mentioned above and you can end up feeling very stressed by the effort. But it is still often a good way of dealing with a difficult situation.

Hochschild also talks about 'deep acting'. This involves taking your feelings as the starting point for emotional labour and working 'outwards' towards your outward appearance, and has been compared to acting. Actors *become* the person they are playing but they preserve the core of their real 'self' at the edge of the stage. That way actors - or nurses - can actually put on a better show and also prevent emotional burn out.

In the 1999 Emotional Labour issue of *Soundings* Pam Smith quoted a nurse who described how she left her personal self at the door before going on the metaphorical ward 'stage'. She said: 'The minute I hit that door that's the stage, we're on show, and that's the way I've always been. I have gone into work depressed but the minute I go in the door the smile's on my face, and the patients don't know because I'm an actress as well'.

---

2. P. Smith, *The Emotional Labour of Nursing: How Nurses Care,* Macmillan, Basingstoke 1992.

If we give this concept of emotional labour a label, does it enable us to recognise and talk openly and deliberately about our emotions, to understand what we do - how we 'emotionally labour'? Would it be helpful if we learned to labour well emotionally just as we learn the practical and intellectual aspects of nursing?

The emotional labour of caring for Joan

We used different emotional labour 'strategies' when nursing Joan.

Surface acting

This could involve:

1. Feeling annoyed but being nice to her until the annoyed feelings subsided (successful!).
2. Being annoyed with her and trying your best ... but eventually speaking sternly to her because you can't keep up a front any more (you're having a bad day so it's unsuccessful).
3. Making an agreement between the staff and Joan about the nature and level of the care she will get (this is giving some structure to the surface acting - a realisation that it's very difficult and that it needs to be worked on as a team).

Deep acting

1. Doing some hard, reflective work with yourself so you don't let Joan 'get to you'.
2. Taking a deep breath, going to her, putting yourself alongside her in her misery and calmly doing and saying whatever needs to be done and said.

It's worth asking ourselves what kind of structures and support enable us to 'do' emotional work well? Should we have systematic training in how to 'do it better' - for the sake of patients and also for the sake of ourselves? Would this mean that anyone could do caring work if they were given suitable preparation and were suitably supported? Ultimately, would there no longer be the people who say: *'I don't know how you can do this kind of work - I couldn't do it'*?

Another aspect of emotional labour discussed at the conference was its relationship to the weak bargaining power of nurses and other carers when it comes to pay rises. Maybe this is due to emotional labour - traditionally women's work - being perceived as not requiring skill and effort (it's rarely a problem to smile). Technical skills and medical treatment are seen as the keys to making people better (death not being a good outcome); and if good caring is only the icing on the cake, there is no need to reward it well. How much is emotional labour worth? How much should we get paid for doing it? And is it significant that emotional labour is more often part of women's work than that of men's?

'I love ideas but do enough other people?': further reflections

Following a discussion I had with some colleagues who had read the above reflections, they were keen to embrace the term 'emotional labour'. It helped us to focus on the work we do which is unrecognised - it legitimises and pushes it forward in the list of priorities.

However other concepts which follow from it, like surface and deep acting, were not really addressed. Perhaps this is because we do not think, or have not thought, either sociologically or conceptually about this subject. Maybe it's not even relevant for us to do so. It's only functional for health care workers to think in this way if it helps them move on - otherwise it remains in the realms of a fascination with ideas.

Nurse communicating with older patient © Dympna Casey

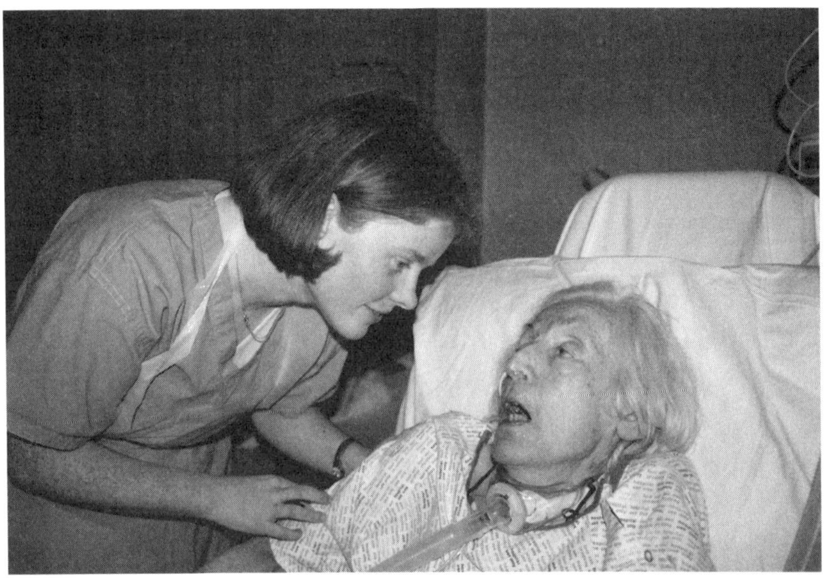

So can we make emotional labour and its associated concepts relevant to clinical practice? Could we use the terms surface and deep acting to move us on in terms of emotional support for one another when it gets down to the nitty gritty of support - or do we need other tools from counselling? There may be a fundamental 'gap' between the academic and the clinical at the root of some of the problems of trying to develop an academic approach to nursing and midwifery.

Involvement and emotional labour

Del Loewenthal

Del Loewenthal *argues that involvement at work can bring problems as well as benefits.*

Pam Smith, in her book *The Emotional Labour of Nursing: How Nurses Care*, found that emotionally supportive relationships were vital to the well being of both student nurses and patients.[1] So, being involved in emotional labour can sometimes be helpful. But what does this process involve? For example, do people sometimes submit to carrying out emotional labour that is detrimental to them, for economic reasons? Furthermore, how do they know whether emotional labour is in fact psychologically beneficial or detrimental? And what sort of emotional learning is most helpful to the individual in relation to emotional labour?

My research on involvement at work suggests that many of the concepts used in this field are devised from an organisational rather than an individual perspective.[2] Most academic definitions imply that work involvement is always of benefit to the individual. None of the studies I examined used the ordinary dictionary definitions of involvement - which I adopted for my study. In the dictionary, involvement is defined as occurring when an individual's experiences are 'twisted; complicated; intricate; confused, tangled, affected, implicated' (Penguin English Dictionary). This is not the kind of definition with which most academic studies are working.

I interviewed 56 people in my study, mainly nurses in the National Health

1. P. Smith, *The Emotional Labour of Nursing: How Nurses Care*, Macmillan, Basingstoke 1992.
2. Loewenthal, D (1979) *Productivity, involving the individual*, D. Phil. Thesis, Falmer: University of Sussex.

Service. I found that, as with stress, one can have too little and too much involvement. Through their involvement people may, over time, confuse their selves, by entangling what they want with what they are involved in. And there are forces within individuals motivating them to escape from their selves, in this case into emotional labour, which can result in inappropriate emotional learning. My research was an attempt to show what happens when an individual takes up an organisational role involving emotional labour, and to examine the ensuing socialisation process in all its complexity. Whilst there are subjective benefits, there are also losses for people who become socialised in this way.

The process of involvement

The idea that involvement in emotional labour can be can be harmful was partly demonstrated in answers to the question, 'In what ways, if any, has your experience as a nurse changed you as a person?' Amongst the most common responses I received was a concern about social life, particularly in relation to friends outside nursing. When I arranged responses from the interviewees according to seniority, starting with students and ending with senior nurse managers (as below), a pattern emerged:

> *Nurse A*: The hours are peculiar and sometimes there are social commitments I would rather go to.

> *Nurse B*: Well, I don't know if it adds an awful lot of joy outside working hours, because there aren't many people that you can mix with that have the same outlook as you, or do the same things that you do.

> *Nurse C*: Probably with my friends - I don't get to see them that much and they're thinking, 'Oh God, she sounds a bit of a drag - can't come out again, she's tired'. But I just don't have the time I did before for other people - well, I feel a bit sad about that but maybe I'll adjust myself.

> *Nurse D*: I don't think it's damaged me at all ... I used to grudge being at work and thinking my friends were having a good time, whereas now I don't even think about it. It doesn't seem like work anymore. I don't look on it as a job. A job to me is getting on a bus in the morning and sitting in an office and not

thinking any more of it, leaving and that's it for the day. But you still tend to think, you know - when I'm off duty I still tend to think about work ... even though I like to get away, it's still on your mind, it's not like an office where you can just tidy up the desk and put it all away ... you still have something at the back of your mind, like I must remember to do that. And all the time you are hoping whoever is ill on the ward is better by the time you go back. It still comes to you even though you try not to think about it.

Interviewer: You seem to mention that as something positive.

Nurse D: Yes, because I don't think it's boring. If something's boring, you switch off like that and you don't want to know anymore ... but I find it interesting, you know. If I want to find out more about a certain thing, then I can go and look into that when I get home.

Nurse E: I've got friends who have been in industry, and they don't understand why I'm not available at weekends, Christmas. It irks me rather that I've not put it over - and I can't be bothered to put it over if they can't understand that a hospital needs to be manned 24 hours a day.

These quotes suggest that nurses' involvement develops in a process similar to that described by Davis in her work on the 'doctrinal conversion' of student nurses.[3] Nurses A to E above can be seen to be going through Davis's progression: from 'initial innocence', 'labelled recognition of incongruity', 'psyching out', 'role simulation', 'provisional internalisation' to 'stable internalisation'.

Motivation for involvement

My research attempted to show that some of the features of work which are most frequently seen as conditions for meeting an individual's maintenance and self-actualisation needs (in humanistic models, for example) can in fact serve to subtract value from an individual's life. In particular, work involvement can be used as a means of escape from other areas of life.

3. F. Davis, 'Professional Socialization as Subjective Experience: The Process of Doctrinal Conservation among Student Nurses', in Becker et al (eds), *Institutions and the Person*, Aldine, Chicago 1968.

In my study, an example of someone whose involvement was used as a form of escape was Nurse G:

> … takes up much too much of my time … and it is a little bit difficult leading a social life as not everybody can understand my sort of timetable … but I know I overdo it far too often … I can actually withdraw from the things I very much don't want to do socially. I know this … People think, 'Oh, I must not interfere or phone her up or ask her out because she's probably asleep', and that is of certain value to me - which not everybody realises, though a few do I think … escapism.

These feelings can be seen as in line with Arlie Hochchild's understanding that 'we gladly surrender to absorption in our quest for "fulfilment", "self-actualisation" and "involvement"'. But they can also mean that the individual deliberately restricts the development of her self. This restrictive behaviour can be further subdivided into: (a) those whose motivation is based on work consciousness: i.e. their maintenance needs are perceived as being identical to those of their work organisation; (b) those whose motivation is based more on using work as a way of escaping their problems or development needs whether inside or outside work.

Hochschild's concept of 'emotional commodification', and her recognition that emotion is central to the economy, are also evident in nurses' involvement in their work.[4] As well as a personal motivation to become involved, there are also external pressures structuring the emotional responses of nurses. Emotional involvement can be a part of a disciplining process, either intentionally, through coercion, or unintentionally as a by-product of the technology used. Sometimes this involvement is not good for the individuals concerned - they may have to repress unwanted emotions or to display emotions they are not feeling.

A research method was devised which resulted in empirical evidence that showed that in order to maintain a process of 'coercion', work organisations provide the individual with a false sense of 'push' towards involvement - false

---

4. Hochchild, A (1983) *The Managed Heart: the commercialisation of human feeling*, Berkeley: University of California Press.

inasmuch as this sense of push is actually brought about by the 'pull' of the structure of the work environment. Furthermore, individuals who have a choice allow themselves to become involved in this way, thus avoiding realisation of their real maintenance needs and escaping the true actualisation of their selves (or to use a different language, they get even further away from the true nature of their desires).

The effects of emotional involvement

Hochchild writes about the effects of emotional labour on an individual's life when it is *deep-acted*. The following extracts from my study demonstrate that, underlying the interviewees' 'emotional' involvement, there was frequently confusion and contradiction (and this was often evident in statements volunteered after some supportive silence from the interviewer):

> *Nurse G:* I think - or I hope - I have become less of a snob. I was very naive, very prim, not knowing anything about the world, living a completely isolated little life, it was a very small convent and I suppose they breed you to think you're something rather special and precious. Coming here was quite a shock - I mean, you do meet people who swear, who spit, who wee on the floor, and all things like that and it's amazing how soon you accommodate to this, really. I think you also have to become unselfish. You have to be disciplined. When I started training the discipline was much tougher, I mean you didn't dare have one hair out of place, you didn't dare come on a minute late, and it was very sort of regimental - and I'm sure that did me a lot of good.
>
> ... When I said that one is unselfish, a lot of people think that I'm a little hard. I think people outside think that nurses and doctors must be hard to do this work. I don't think that's absolutely true. I think it means you have to control your emotions a lot more. I am in outside life a bit bossy - I suppose I am here too. But I think working in this regimental atmosphere does do this to you. I hope I can get out of this state because I myself can see myself like it. But it's very easy in nursing, it's one of the dangers of nursing.

> *Nurse H:* 'I think I've become much harder. You have to really, because you can't let every little thing upset you. Especially like people dying, it happens so often, but every time somebody dies you can't let it upset you. And you have

> to be so firm with some of the patients. You can't always be kind and soft with them, they take advantage of you. You learn responsibility because you have quite a lot of responsibility and learn how to cope with different situations as they come along.
>
> *Nurse I*: It's made me harder. My outlook on life has changed. I can stand up for myself.

As people lose the ability to realise their own needs - and any awareness of them - (through lack of practice), they end up with a vested interest in rationalising and anaesthetising their needs through further involvement; i.e., a consequence of being involved can be a need to carry on being involved. Furthermore, it is possible to speculate that those who felt that work provided all the inputs they needed, and that work did not subtract value from their lives, were in all likelihood feeling like this in order to protect and rationalise this 'intellectual' involvement. People keep themselves deliberately unaware of aspects of themselves that they have denied, or have been denied to them; and one mechanism through which this false sense of integration can be sustained is continued involvement.

Thus my research appears to challenge those who assume that involvement at work is always beneficial to an individual. There are a number of thinkers whose writings on involvement at work approach questions of emotional labour in an unhelpful way. Contrary to certain sociological assumptions, an individual might become involved at work, and be made to be involved, precisely in order *not* to question her 'sense of purposeful connection to the work enterprise'.[5] Furthermore, this time in contradiction of Blauner, it is not only 'alienated activity' which is 'not free and spontaneous activity, but ... compulsive and driven by necessity';[6] this also applies to involvement activity. In fact Etzioni's 'moral involvement', far from being the good to be aimed for, needs to be seen as the form in which some individuals experience their alienation. Etzioni's involvement continuum typologies need

5. A. Etzioni, A *Comparative Analysis of Complex Organisations*, The Free Press, Illinois 1975, p29.
6. R. Blauner, *Alienation and Freedom*, University of Chicago Press, Chicago 1964, p27.

to be redefined, such that his 'moral involvement' can be seen as 'involvement alienation', and his 'alienative involvement' redefined as 'calculative alienation'.

My research seemed to demonstrate that an individual's 'input selection' can lead to an involvement that has the potential to subtract value from her life, through a combination of factors - externally, from the work environment, and internally, through an escape motivation. It is possible to describe such an involvement process as a series of stages:

- The individual selects inputs from a range of options.
- She is motivated in both the selection of and continuation with these inputs by her need to reduce awareness of some other aspects of her work or non-work life.
- If these inputs become long-term work involvements, then she will come to associate the maintenance needs of the organisation with her own maintenance needs.
- Thus she will be involved in the maintenance of the organisation, since any threat to the organisation is a threat to her need to reduce awareness.
- As the involvement process continues she becomes more compartmentalised, such that she removes her self further away from being able to integrate her life without involvement supports.
- As her need to escape from awareness of her lack of integration increases, so does her need to become further involved, i.e. her present involvement increases the need for continual involvement.
- As this involvement becomes compulsive, her perceived choice of alternatives decreases, and with this she reduces her freedom to select new inputs and be involved with them if she wants to, i.e. there is a negative correlation between involvement and awareness of choice and of her own needs.

In my research I developed a change cycle, as a heuristic device for examining beneficial and detrimental involvement processes over time. The interview data was used to demonstrate the importance of the individual's need for integration, and the ways in which inappropriately involved people were more 'compartmentalised', to their own detriment. Attempts were then made to demonstrate empirically that when this psychological need for wholeness and integration is not satisfied, the individual cannot achieve self actualisation because her needs are tied to the survival and goals of the organisation. So she tries to escape, the key mechanism for this being her involvement. Furthermore, the internal and external forces that are directing the individual's activity attempt to sustain a false awareness through the continual involvement of the self. It seemed also that this false awareness was easier to achieve for individuals in more managerial jobs (as well as those in training). (This in turn raises the question of whether more and more people will have detrimental forms of involvement as a result of our increasingly managerialist culture.)

Some implications: the effects of involvement on the person who is a nurse

The nurse's relations with her self

It has been shown that for the compartmentalised individual, the role her occupation plays in giving organisation to her life is similar to that of people who work in total institutions, though she might try and sleep outside the institution. External factors - working shifts, wearing a uniform, the division of labour, expectations of maintaining optimism and deception (in sum the way she is involved and managed) - can combine with the inner motivation of escape to produce an involvement process which is detrimental to her.

Stages of 'doctrinal conversion' can be seen not only in student nurses but also in later stages of the nurse's career. Micro involvements both at work and outside work show changing patterns as the nurse moves up in the nursing hierarchy. Similarity was found with Sayle's study, in that staff nurses thought less about work when outside work than did either students or sisters.[7] It was also found that Menzies's argument, that nursing creates defence mechanisms which constrict nurses' relationships with patients, can be extended, to show that the involvement process can create defence mechanisms which constrict the person who is a nurse physically, intellectually, socially and emotionally.[8]

It had previously been considered that the principal reason for choosing nursing

---

7. D. Sayle, 'Nurses' Use of Leisure', *Nursing Times*, June 1972.
8. I. Menzies, *The Functioning of Social Systems as a Defence Against Anxiety: A Report on a Study on the Nursing Service of a General Hospital*, Tavistock Publications, London 1959.

was that it was seen as helping people in a practical way. This research has shown that money is also a significant reason given by nurses in response to the question 'Why do you work?'. However, perhaps a major contribution of this study is that it shows that monetary and other considerations can be more than outweighed by the individual's escape motivation. Such behaviour is reinforced by the way work is organised, and by the individual's need to maintain a reduced awareness of her lack of integration; it is most apparent in the compartmentalised individual - and it is towards this compartmentalised type that the majority of nurses are inclined.

For the compartmentalised type, one question that arises is what happens to the individual's escape motivation when the nurse becomes a manager. My research showed that more senior nurses occupy their selves with compulsive thoughts of the future. Furthermore, it is possible that the transition to management may initially be experienced as a threat, since the nurse will probably have to relinquish the compartmentalisation through which she has maintained a reduced awareness of her lack of integration. In fact, the behaviour of this compartmentalised type is reminiscent of Whyte's 'Organization Man'.[9]

That organisations encourage individuals to value highly compartmentalised behaviour, through such mechanisms as involving people in order to manage them, has been demonstrated by others as well as by this research. For example, Stewart and Liddell found that ward staff assessed as high ability those student nurses who were more conservative, religious, dogmatic, and lower on political and economic values.[10] As judged by the tutorial staff, the high ability student nurse was 'relaxed', higher on social values and tended to live in the past or future rather than in the present. Thus the compartmentalised type nurse is rewarded, and a morally involved nurse, with a low power of self direction, is legitimised. 'Calculative involvements', to use a term from Etzioni's involvement typologies, are less valued.

The cycle of involvement

Goffman's notion of an involvement cycle was reaffirmed, with one exception. Goffman suggests, with regard to involvement with inmates, that the cycle of contact and withdrawal can be repeated. However, my research showed that - and this varies with the direction, duration and intensity of a nurse's involvement

9. Whyte, W (1956) *The Organisation Man*, New York: Simon & Schuster.
10. Stewart, R and Liddell, J (1975) 'Where success lies', *New Zealand Nursing Journal*, Vol. 63, March, pp13-19.

- the individual's past involvement can restrict her freedom in relation to later patterns of 'contact and withdrawal'.

The nurse's relations with clients/patients

Ideally, a nurse is able to see both herself and those with whom she is interacting as people. And she is able to choose an 'appropriate distance' for each interaction. Thus the nurse is able to recognise and utilise her own and her patients' feelings, rather than denying such feelings and/or being trapped into a single pattern of responding, regardless of her self or the person who is her patient.

However, it is not only the nurse's training process, and other devices by which she is managed, that mitigate against such relative freedom of choice; choice is also limited by the conceptual tools available for examining possible types of patient involvement. For example, Habenstein and Christ's framework, which sees only a limited set of options for the nurse, is a conceptual trap with similarities to Etzioni's limiting approach to the study of people at work.[11]

Habenstein and Christ's notion of the 'utilizer' has similarities with Etzioni's notion of calculative involvement; their other interpretative categories - 'traditionalizers' and 'professionalizers' - are each seen as having specific forms of moral involvement. Their framework does not allow for a person to have humane concern without dedication, or to have the power of self direction as well as humane concern. They argue that it is the 'holistic' individual who is able to have such humane concern.

Relations with family members and friends

Although the emphasis in my research is on work involvement, the effects of work involvement need to be examined for partners, children and the relations between them (as with other forms of emotional labour). My findings suggested that there was an 'extension', as opposed to a 'compensation', between work and non-work involvements.

Relations with her own and other people's structures

11. Habenstein, R and Christ, E (1955) *Profesionalizer, Traditionalizer & Utilizer: An Interpretative Study of the Work of the General Duty Nurse in Non-Metropolitan Central Missouri General Hospitals*, Columbia: University of Missouri Press. For Etzioni see note 5.

The findings from my research suggest that whether an individual's involvement is self- or other-structured it can still lead to a restriction of choice. (An individual could initially have considerable power of self-direction, and yet become a long-stay prisoner of her own structure.) Escape motivation or the coercion of others can each lead to a dependence on structures which restrict choice; but the involvement process serves to decrease awareness of the nature of these restrictions, and of any loss of power. At the same these structures provide a false sense that an individual is making her own choice. Such structures may vary according to the particular speciality, the nursing hierarchy, whether staff are medical or administrative, the prevailing technology, etc.

Some further implications for emotional labour and emotional learning

My research seems to demonstrate that work involvement is not automatically beneficial for people who are nurses. In fact, it has challenged the widely held view that work involvement is something which, ideally, should always be aimed for by any individual who works. Similarly, emotional learning arising from involvement is usually regarded as personal to the individual, and as leading to 'intentional psychological change'. My study problematises this notion of 'intentionality', as also the idea that emotional learning enhances personal relationships; this is as deceptive as the view that involvement and emotional labour are always good for you. As Pam Smith argues with regard to emotional labour, it is possible that this way of learning can put one at risk of becoming detached and alienated.[12]

Examining the lives of nurses, and their involvement in emotional labour, suggests that there are benefits and costs - perhaps unseen costs - in becoming socialised as nurses. I am, of course, particularly valuing autonomy and heteronomy, and could be criticised for pathologising those whom I term as having 'escape motivation' in their choice (which can become no choice) of involvement. However, I hope this article has provided an initial exploration of how notions of involvement and emotional labour might inform each other.

---

12. Smith, P (1999) 'Logging Emotions: A Logbook of Personal Reflections', *Soundings*, Issue 11, pp128-137 p134).

Hands-on care: baby being bathed © Dympna Casey

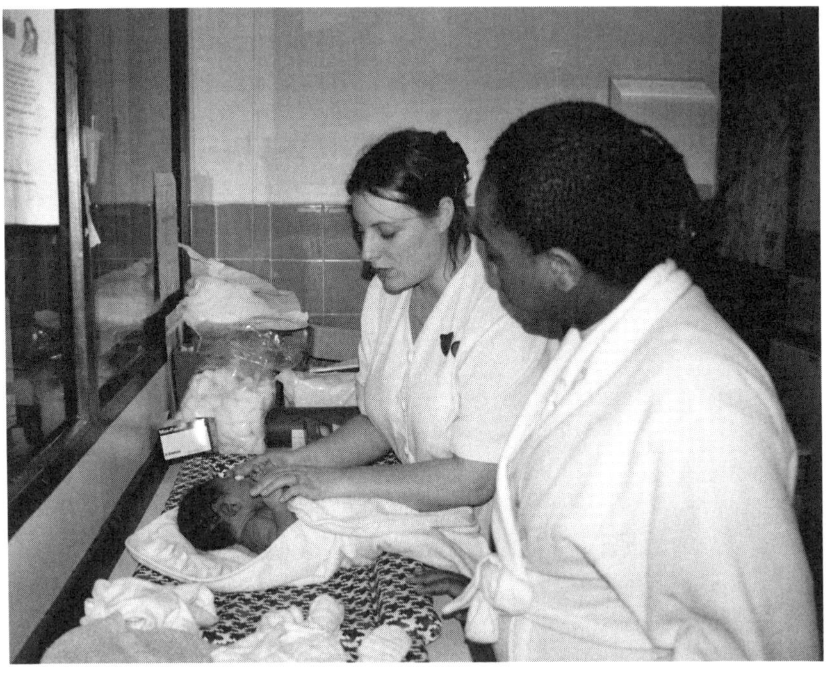

Therapeutic nursing, emotional labour, economic exchange

Is there a link?

David Newbold

Over the past fifteen or so years the pace of reform in the British health care system has been incredible. The rationale behind much of this change has been to maximise the efficient use of relatively scarce public resources, within a given budget, so as many people as possible can benefit from treatment.

No part of the system has been immune from the pressure to change. For instance, the 'clinical freedom' of the medical profession is subject to constant scrutiny, along with the drive to *consistently* provide forms of treatment based on evidence of effectiveness rather than opinions. There is pressure to examine different ways of funding health care to ensure efficiency and equity. Patients these days also tend to act as informed 'consumers' of their care rather than passive recipients. Furthermore, nurses are increasingly being pressurised to act as substitute labour for doctors on the grounds of efficiency. This latter point has been of significant interest to me since my early days as a staff nurse working on a cardiac surgical intensive care unit, providing the 'hi-tech' and 'emotional labour' aspects of care. I also often asked myself, 'what if anything is it that nurses do that is therapeutic in its own right?'

My purpose in this article is to begin to set out some of the parameters surrounding these issues and in particular to address the question of nurses' therapeutic role. Put another way, it appears that nursing practice today is potentially influenced by two different paradigms - nursing as 'health technology' and nursing as 'emotional labour' - which may clash!

The nursing as 'health technology' paradigm

Nurses have always been versatile and flexible workers, capable of taking on other roles and incorporating them into their workload. In this respect these human resources are considered by government planners to be a form of health technology. For example, according to the Health Technology Assessment Programme in the UK: 'health technologies are, therefore, not just new drugs or pieces of equipment. They cover the activities of all healthcare professionals'.

Some would argue that this flexibility is one of the more important nursing functions, even going so far as to describe nursing as the 'glue' holding the system together. In this paradigm, treatments shown by research to be effective need to be delivered at minimum cost, so that the most people possible can benefit. This efficiency point is rather like having a queue of one hundred people who need to make a journey from A to B, and a limited budget to spend on transport. If the budget was spent on five Rolls-Royce limousines, then five at a time could go in style, leaving a long queue. Alternatively, the budget could be spent on twenty 'Mini-Metro' saloon cars, meaning more people could make the journey and the queue would be shorter. Following on from this point, the question of what nurses - the largest body of clinical staff in the NHS - do in their daily roles has massive implications for the efficiency of the system.

The health technology paradigm has influenced the way nursing care is delivered in a number of ways. First there is the issue of a cost effective 'skill-mix' within the nursing profession itself. Thus the more 'fundamental' aspects of the nurse's role - often inaccurately labelled 'basic' nursing care - can be delegated to care assistants, allowing qualified staff to act in more managerial roles. Second, there is a similar issue of skill-mix and labour substitution between doctor and nurse, with medical tasks being delegated to nurses. Taken together, these influences from above and below have significantly altered the role and function of nurses working in hospitals. Third, changes to care have involved altering the throughput of patients within the system. Clearly, this has efficiency potential in terms of the quicker freeing up of beds; and because the patient has a shorter length of stay, the risk of hospital acquired infection is potentially lower. Throughput can be enhanced by the use of 'Integrated Care Pathways'. Fourth, and linked to throughput and the scale of provision, there is evidence to suggest there is a relationship between the volume of cases treated and the outcome. Aneurin Bevan, regarded as the Father of the NHS, neatly summarised this point with reference to the closure of the cottage hospitals in favour of large hospitals:

> I would rather be kept alive in the efficient if rather cold altruism of a large hospital than expire in a gush of warm sympathy in a small one.[1]

Here Bevan appears to be supporting the health technology paradigm as the preferred approach to patient care.

The nursing as 'emotional labour' paradigm

Emotional labour is arguably the more traditional paradigm of nursing, with its own body of evidence, mainly qualitative in nature. The paradigm is represented in the literature by a number of constructs and concepts, such as the 'therapeutic use of self', or 'caring as therapy'. More recently, nursing students have been taught to deliver emotional labour consistent with mainstream psychological interventions such as counselling, based on Egan's classic book *The Skilled Helper*, and there are parallels which can be drawn to psychological constructs such as emotional support and social support.

Recent qualitative work has sought to establish the nature of the emotional labour component of nursing. For instance, Smith and Gray suggest that, 'The emotional labour of nursing involves feelings of care and support that nurses are constantly called on to instil in their patients'.[2]

---

1. A. Bevan, Speech, 30.4.46, House of Commons.
2. P. Smith and B. Gray, 'The emotional labour of nursing: how student and qualified nurses learn to care. A report on nurse education, nursing practice, and emotional labour in the contemporary NHS', South Bank University, London 2000.

Other researchers have built an emotional labour dimension into their quality assurance measurement tools. Koerner, for instance, has developed the SERVQAL questionnaire, which has five dimensions including: compassion, close relationships, uncertainty reduction, reliability, and individualised care.[3] The emotional labour component has a clear linkage to the first two of these dimensions.

Until recently, there was little quantitative evidence to suggest that emotional labour may have measurable physiological benefits. If such evidence were to exist, this would strengthen the case for nurses providing emotional labour as a viable input in its own right. However, a detailed review by Uchino et al has provided a significant step towards providing such evidence.[4] Their review of 81 studies demonstrated a direct link between social support (arguably linked with emotional labour) and improved physiological status in terms of cardiovascular, immunological, and endocrine outcome measures.

A paradigm clash

So is there indeed a paradigm clash between approaches based on the paradigm of health technology and the emotional labour paradigm? And is it in the nature of paradigms to clash? I would suggest that it is from such colliding trajectories that the direction for practice is derived. Furthermore, it is helpful to think of the clash between these two paradigms, and the resultant dilemma about what nurses should do in their daily work, in terms of the economics of *complements* and *substitutes*.

The labour substitution argument described above links in with the health technology paradigm. Here, it is medical inputs which generate the outcome, whilst the emotional labour (nursing) aspects impact only on process. On this account, substitution could take place on cost effectiveness grounds, without loss of outcome.

But the argument for nursing as a *complementary* input means that, in order to generate the outcome, both medical *and* nursing inputs *must be provided*

3. M. M. Koerner, 'The conceptual domain of service quality for inpatient nursing services', *Journal of Business Research*, Vol 48, 2000.
4. B. N. Uchino, J.T. Cacioppo, J. K. Kiecolt Glaser, 'The relationship between social support and physiological processes: A review with emphasis on underlying mechanisms and implications for health', *Psychological Bulletin*, Vol 119(3), 1995.

together. The outcome is the *joint product of medicine and nursing*. Thus if nurses simply substitute for doctors, the outcome is sub-optimal, because the nursing component is missing. It is here that the evidence on the impact of social support on patient outcome is useful, because it indicates a measurable impact across a variety of physiological parameters. So, Bevan's 'gush of warm sympathy' may actually be a valuable therapeutic input.

Therapeutic nursing and economic exchange

In economics, for any exchange of goods or services to occur, there should be a mutual gain from the trade for both parties, in terms of an improvement in their welfare. As we have seen earlier, nurses, in providing emotional labour in the form of social and emotional support, may induce a feeling of well being and measurable physiological change in their clients; this is one half of the improvement in welfare that is involved in economic exchange. But is there an improvement for the caregiver? According to Grant - and many others - caregivers looking after sufferers with chronic health conditions may experience a deterioration in their health status as measured by their immune, endocrine and cardiovascular status - which is precisely the opposite result![5]

On this reckoning, the mutual gain necessary for exchange to happen is clearly not present, since the patient's health may improve at the expense of the carer's. Within a traditional economic approach this would be remarkable. To analyse and explain nurse-patient interaction we thus need a different approach. Not much work has been done in this respect, but one possibility would be to draw the work of Nobel Laureate Amartya Sen. Sen distinguishes between 'sympathy' - being pleased at another's pleasure and pained at their pain - and 'commitment' - choosing to act in such a way that one's own personal welfare is lowered in helping another.

I propose that there is a clear connection between theories of caring in nursing and Sen's notion of caring, and also between the concept of commitment and emotional labour in nursing. Thus caregivers and nurses committed to improving the welfare of others will employ emotional labour skills, arguably at the expense of their own well-being. Further work is needed to develop this

5. I. Grant, 'Caregiving may be hazardous to your health', *Psychosomatic Medicine*, Vol 61, (4) July-August 1999.

idea, however.

This short article has set out a physiological rationale for the provision by nurses of emotional labour, and suggests that this may actually be a viable input in its own right. If this is so, and some nurses are not currently providing emotional support because they are required to provide substitute medical labour, outcomes may be sub-optimal. Emotional labour inputs appear not to be valued by current health managers, due perhaps to the dominant health technology paradigm. However, this would be in marked contrast to Arlie Hochschild's notion of employers asking employees such as flight attendants to use emotional labour to address the needs of their clients - and rewarding them for doing so.[6] Nurse-patient interaction is also problematic if it is analysed within the conventional economic paradigm of rational, self-interested 'man'. To analyse nursing exchange in economic terms it may be necessary to use more modern notions of exchange. These ideas represent exciting and promising future lines of enquiry, and the links between them need to be made explicit if a case is to be made for nursing to have an autonomous input into health care processes in the twenty-first century.

---

6. A. Hochschild, *The managed heart - the commercialisation of human feeling*, Berkeley, University of California Press 1983.

Nursing the machine © Dympna Casey

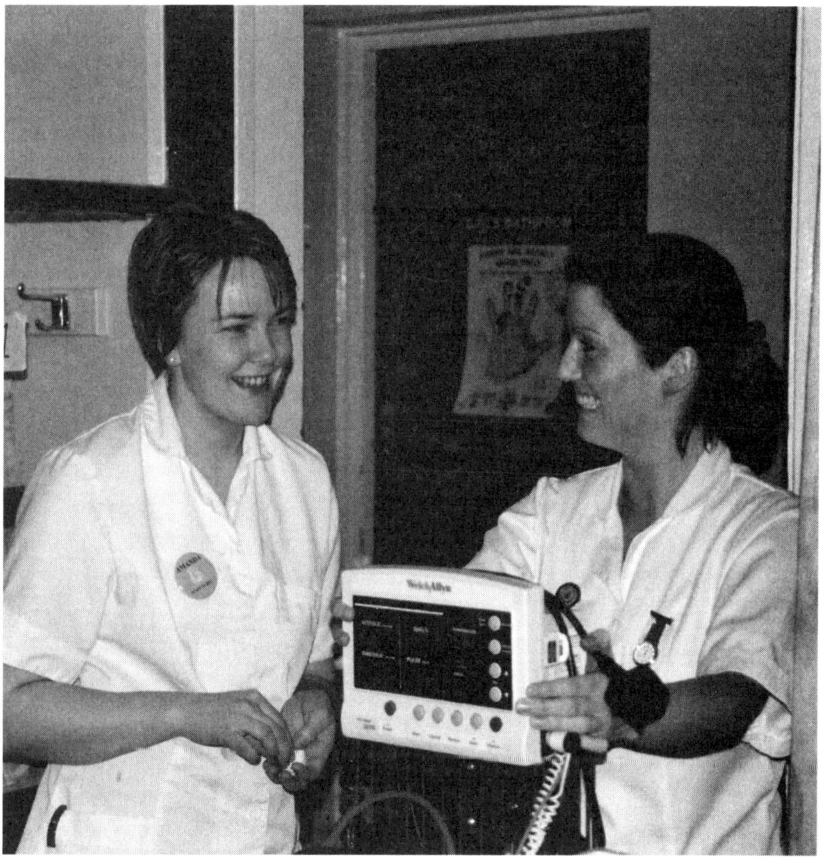

Hi-tech care © Dympna Casey

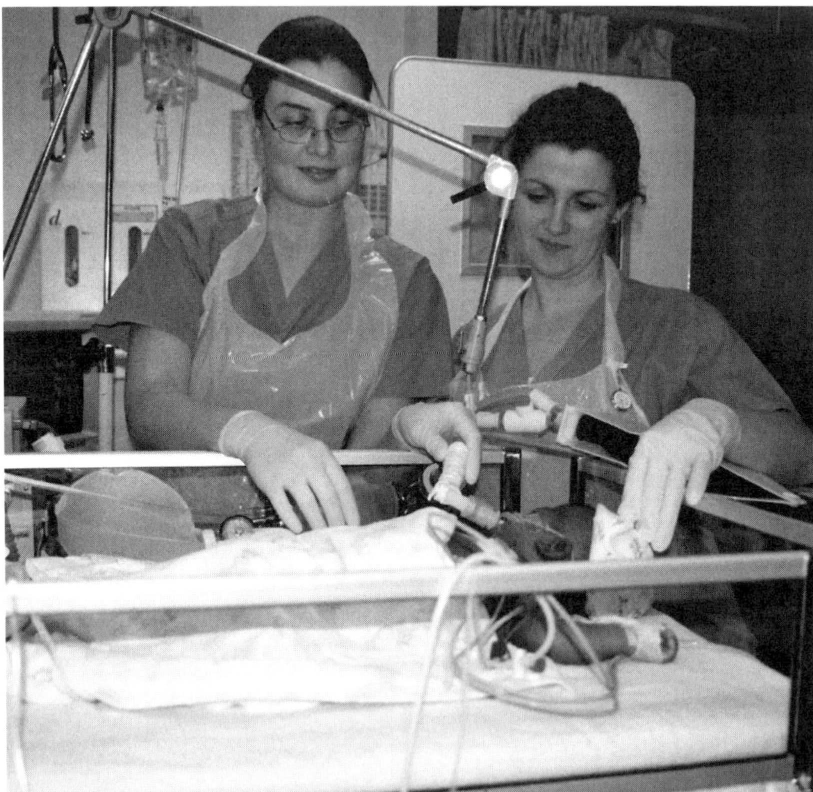

The disappearance of convalescence

Bridget Towers

Bridget Towers *looks at historical changes in convalescence provision. After being gradually dropped from the NHS in the postwar period, it may be due for a comeback.*

Many medical historians and sociologists would recognise the indirect reference in my title to Jewson's classic article of 1976, 'The Disappearance of the Sick Man from Medical Cosmologies' (*Sociology* 10). Jewson claimed that medical therapeutic practice had shifted its focus; from a concern with bedside medical presence with a holistic subject person, to the laboratory-based formulaic diagnosis of pathogens present within an object 'body'.

Whilst I am not treading the same path as Jewson, I acknowledge that his work has been very influential in my own thinking, particularly his situation of the 'liturgy' of these therapeutic encounters within discrete cosmologies.

However I am not an 'historian of ideas'. I spend a large part of my life as a researcher operating in the ugly world of the contemporary health service, evaluating policy implementation and designing pilot initiatives. Amongst the many disquieting transformations in our national health care system is the relentless pressure from health care managers to reduce the amount of publicly resourced health care given to any illness episode, be it in terms of the length of hospital admission, or certificated illness periods. The impact of this pressure is experienced not just as an absolute loss of health care, but also in a confused sense of illness and recovery as people strive to negotiate their own events of sickness without the legitimating frameworks of medical attendance, certification or hospitalisation. Frequently older people invoke a past in which particularly serious illness events were structured by medical and nursing care presence, and formally closed by a convalescence period.

These invocations have led me to explore a territory in which I grew up in the early 1950s - a seaside town landscaped with convalescent homes, sanatoria, open air schools for delicate children, seaside holiday homes for maladjusted children, and discrete little psychiatric rest homes for the war-wounded officer classes. These were not just rather splendid buildings, they embodied the irrefutable proof that there was a tangible 'thing' of great therapeutic value that was somehow present in our town; and these institutions with their visitors managed to tap into this, in a way that, self-evidently, we completely failed to do. I grew up with a sense that 'convalescence' was something people came to our town to 'get'. There was another dimension to this experience, and that was the social and economic impact of these homes on our lives. We could recognise the visitors instantly, and classify and allocate them to respective homes; we had local names for the residents according to the homes; 'the men' from the large Metropolitan Convalescent Home; the 'little folks' for the delicate children; the Winsbies for the maladjusted children.

The homes also provided our earliest holiday employment and we rapidly acquired knowledge, and increasingly expertise, about the 'convalescent regimes'. But by the early 1970s all these homes had closed. Most were demolished and replaced by luxury flats for the elderly; a few rematerialised as institutional care facilities for new health care groups. And last month I stood on the balcony of what is now a specialist unit for the elderly mentally ill, which in the 1920s had been one of the largest open air hospitals for delicate children in England, and in the intervening years had been a British Legion convalescent home and then a rehabilitative home for the disabled.

Historians of medical architecture would note that the original name of the building has remained, as has the complete frontage, gardens, reception halls and balconies. My interest, however, lies in exploring the imprints and transformations of the practices and social organisation that sustain the concept of convalescence, despite its disappearance as an institutional material form.

The beginnings

My narrative begins with the establishment of a London charity in 1844, the Metropolitan Convalescent Institution of London, established to:

> provide a home in the country for the temporary residence of the convalescent and debilitated poor, whose restoration to health is impractical in the hospitals and at their own often unhealthy and ill-provided homes, but may be speedily effected by Pure Air, Rest and Nutritious Diet.

In this essay I am not going back to the beginnings of the notion of convalescence, as alluded to in these articles of association; rather I want to look at the beginnings of the idea that convalescence should be seen as part of a gradually universalised health and welfare entitlement.

Dr Robertson, the shadowy medical philanthropist who was the major publicist for the launch of the charity, articulated this view in the particular class language of altruism of his time:

> if then the opulent have, long since, discovered that a convalescent's retreat is good for them, will any venture to say that it is not equally good, and infinitely more necessary for the feeble and disabled of our manufacturing population.

The original plan was to build four 100-bed homes, close to the seaside, which would be 'specifically inaccessible to friends and visitors' ... 'Patients would be referred by the Charity directly from Hospital but would exclude all those with active illness'.

However a barracks-like model quickly became adopted, and the 250-bed home became the norm. The convalescents were segregated into three categories, each with their separate homes - men, women and children. They were located in three areas, Broadstairs and Bexhill-on-sea for the adults, and Walton for the children. I believe that this was the beginning of the landscaping of the public sector seaside convalescent home.

Asked to contextualise this development, I would point to developments in France. France had been the reference point for the introduction of 'preventoriums' - open air schools and institutions for the social/health care of groups who were at the boundaries of psychological/physical and moral diagnostic categories. In 1855 we find a Napoleonic (III) decree establishing the foundation of special hospitals for the care of working-class convalescent patients (interestingly, the right of admission could also be converted into a monthly or annual grant). It was, however, the Hospital of Vincennes (500 beds) which was the great French landmark in convalescent care. Controlled by the Ministry of the Interior and built by state funds in the Vincennes Park, it was an astonishingly magnificent building. (But of course that is another subplot in the story of French hospital building, and its significance for the development of medical conceptualisations. I believe that Foucault's great works, 'The Birth of the Clinic', and - up to a point – 'Madness and Civilisation', are made comprehensible only within an understanding of his own mental mapping of French institutional health care.)

The charity provision of convalescent homes gradually became supplemented with trade union homes funded by benevolent funds, and, later, friendly society and approved societies benefit entitlements. The British Legion and the King Edward Fund also moved into the field.

The interwar years

After the 1914-18 war another key element enters the story - tuberculosis, and the sanatoria movement for its care and containment. The state became involved in the financing of this area, providing special sanatorium benefit, and embarking on a large scale sanatorium building programme; the state was also concerned with resourcing health care at the earliest signs of what might be perceived as tubercular illness. Convalescent homes therefore begin to have a premium, in terms of their essential role in the prevention both of the activation of the dreaded TB bacillus, and of its seizing a hold during periods of vulnerability after serious illness. Hence an entering of the moral dimension, which mandated compliance with strict and regulated convalescent care - because otherwise one might be culpable of 'wilful negligence', leading to self inflicted TB.

I have written elsewhere about the ways in which the adaptation of the sanatoria and the institutional homes from the private bourgeois model to that of the publicly provided facility was not just about a transformation of structure. It reflected a change from a primarily passive treatment rationale, based on rest, fresh air, and good nutrition, to one of protection, isolation as a form of social defence and health education. Plentiful, lightly nuanced food, selected from an open menu and dictated by personal appetite; rest, reading, moderate exercise with convivial company - this was little more than the lifestyle of the wealthy bourgeoisie; in the public institutions, the bourgeois material comforts that had sustained this approach started to slip away, and this increasingly exposed its medical legitimacy to criticism. Altitude and/or sea air became reduced to 'being in the country or near the sea' (echoes of our modern 'Sea view B&B'). Private rooms with balconies became Wards with an entire side (sometimes both) open to the air; country and seaside walks became flagged routes to be taken in crocodiles; leisure to occupy the mind became work to occupy the hands and labour discipline to retain the deference of class; for the staff of doctors, housekeepers and chambermaids there was substituted the superintendent, matron and a regime of self service; the informal rules of class etiquette became codified practices and regulations which were enforced with penalties. Smoking and drinking became proscribed; social exchange gave way to the segregation of the sexes.

During the inter-war years the convalescent homes expanded their provision, and there was a gradual differentiation between types of convalescent care; some institutions provided quite substantial levels of medical care and would even take patients in quite advanced stages of terminal illness, for whom palliative care was all that was required; in others, the main function was simply to provide a period of recuperative rest, something which rapidly became characterised as a 'convalescent holiday'. This latter group was particularly well represented in the provision by the friendly societies and the trade union benevolent funds.

There was a problem here, however, as the plans for the development of a health care system based upon national insurance meant the incorporation, or at the least the preservation, of the rights and entitlements of those who were covered by the Approved Societies; but these members would also expect their convalescent benefit and entitlements to be covered in the national health insurance scheme. The ministry of health on the other hand was not minded to build into a national health care service a 'convalescent holiday scheme'. This point was raised time and again during the 1930s as the Dawson plans were developed. During this time issues of health care finance began to call into question the concept of convalescence.

There were also epidemiological developments in the inter-war period that began to change the picture of potential demand for convalescent care. Tuberculosis morbidity and mortality had declined by the early 1930s; practices of management of infectious disease shifted from long term isolation and convalescence towards shorter isolation periods and local clinic management. Outpatient attendance began to supplement in hospital inpatient treatment, and therefore, paradoxically, for a period of time there was no great pressure on hospital beds; there was a brief period during which hospital stays increased very substantially. These were all straws in the wind that by the postwar period had become supplemented by other changes.

Post war and early 1950s

After the establishment of the 1946 legislation, while operational aspects were being organised, the ministry of health, at that time an expanding and very strong ministry, began to consider the future of convalescent homes, and whether or not they would be retained as part of the NHS. They were in three major groups: the private homes, those which were trade union owned and those that were associated with hospitals. A policy decision was taken not to plan for their continued funding and provision, and to gradually allow for the capital assets of these homes to fall into the hands of the regional or district hospital authorities.

Separate benefit funding had ended, and there was a new focus upon a clear demarcation between periods of sickness certification and benefit, and being functionally well and available for work.

Interestingly, at this time the only occupational group who lobbied for the maintenance of the convalescent homes as an integral part of the new health service were the Almoners (the hospital social workers), who saw this as a sphere which would give them some control over hospital discharge; it was also a knowledge field into which they were inclined to move - the psycho-social aspects of rehabilitation.

We also need to note that at this time there was another shift in the epidemiological picture, and that the development of antibiotics, and INH, had an impact on case fatalities and patient case management. The demand for convalescent care came increasingly from an older population, who tended to suffer from chronic illness and might be expected to have numerous periods of convalescence.

The convalescent home for children disappeared as the separation of children under 12 years of age from their families became increasingly resisted; the Curis report had documented its adverse affects (and note here the impact of Bowlby's work!).

The 1950s saw these homes gradually deteriorate in terms of staffing levels, rates of pay and standards of care; the patient population became older and therapeutic optimism gave way to a warehousing mentality. The Ministry of Health expected them to fold, with the buildings accruing to the local or regional hospital board.

The 1960s-1970s

The decline continued, and the first wave of the reorganisation of the NHS meant that local hospitals no longer had the degree of power that they had had to control the local convalescent homes; in practice this meant that some of the local hospitals on the coast had very considerable managerial responsibility. Decision-making about the future of the homes became a regional matter, and the start of the rationalisation of 'beds' as the units of provision and managerial responsibility meant that separate costing of convalescent care disappeared.

The impact this would have on local economies was recognised, and closure decisions were accompanied by planning for the transformation of the homes into other publicly funded health care facilities; this was seen as important to safeguard local employment. This practice, however, has meant (and continues to mean) that the same staff, employed in the same institution, have served different client groups with ostensibly different health care needs; at that period these were not workers for whom intensive training programmes were established, and they therefore transferred their patient management skills from one context to another. Today these workers act as important oral history sources on the transformations of these homes.

The recent past

This was the period of the rapid escalation of attempts to control and contain rising health care costs. In the early 1980s the focus was upon hospital health care, and there was pressure on hospitals to reduce the length of hospitalisation for each illness episode. Clinical audit was becoming a tool of financial management, to pressurise health care professionals to evaluate their own work in terms of quantifiable comparisons and normative standards.

The experience from the United States with Diagnostically Related Groups was gradually introduced, and hospitals now began to work with 'anticipated Patient Recovery Times' as indicators of efficient deployment of health care resources. These can be finely calibrated. And they have a logic that leads to the definition of convalescence as 'recovery', with recovery starting from the point when the intended medical/surgical intervention has been completed; i.e. as the trolley moves out of the theatre. You have a 'predicted pathway', deviations from which become matters of concern and enquiry.

So we have moved to a concept of 'recovery' that takes place in the hospital; what has happened to the post-hospital experience - the transition period between being well and being sick?

Since the motivating force is cost-control we would expect to find that this post-hospital period is not publicly resourced, and that is precisely what is happening. We have 'The Hospital at Home' schemes, and the 'Intensive Home Care' packages, which are staffed by skill mix teams of 'informal carers' (untrained, unpaid) and community nurses.

To see this in practice we might look at what happens to you if you go to your local hospital for a 'total hip replacement'; you can expect a hospitalisation period of 10 days, followed by 'hospital at home', jointly resourced by social services home helps and Health Authority district nurses.

I am aware that I am moving into areas of detailed health care policy and management, and rather than dwelling on these I will point to one final twist in the story.

As the costs of rehabilitation and recovery in the community fall on primary care providers, there is an increasing incentive for them to pool their resources to fund specialised rehabilitative provision for their patients; and, unsurprisingly, they are beginning to plan for the building of new rehabilitative units (using PFI funding). Are we about to reinvent the convalescent home?

Concluding themes

What is this concept of convalescence? Without being remotely nostalgic for a past they had few illusions about, my interviewees spoke in a language and used concepts that would have resonated across the last century:

> Yes, in some sense I felt better, but I just needed a little time to get myself together, to allow my body to readjust and to enjoy a real rest from looking after everything and everyone (Dorothy (55) recovering from a mastectomy (Interview 2001)).

Is this simply the language of debilitation, or is it an expression of a need to claim a special space and time in which to negotiate transition, a safe 'crossing-place'?

Whose concept of 'convalescence' is at issue? We can see huge class and cultural variations in lay beliefs about the meaning of this transitional period. And yet it is in the 'soft' areas of health care that we might anticipate the emergence of new experts and their knowledge claims. And the historical record shows just how easily crude knowledge claim-making succeeded in medicalising moral exhortations.

Where does this deeply anchored proprietorial sense of convalescent time stem from? Does it reside in the public domain of popular culture? Or is it perhaps part of an invented past? Certainly I interviewed people who would in one breath castigate the class discrimination of the convalescent homes, whilst in another they would visibly reconnect to a time of gentle therapeutic space.

We cannot fail to recognise that, in a very real materialist sense, convalescence is a class differentiated concept and set of practices. Whose practices are we thinking about when we talk about the need for publicly funded convalescent care?

There is currently no convalescence in our health care system, or in its budgetary allocations. But there is strong evidence that we cling to a notion of 'recovery' - a period of time in which to negotiate the experience; the problem for us is how to negotiate, valorise and accredit it.

Narrating the emergency

Heroism and horror

Stuart Nairn

Stuart Nairn *looks at the difficult emotional labour involved in emergency work.*

> The man was ashen when I got to him, and I simply stuck the needle into his chest. Air hissed out of him like a bicycle tire, in little bubbles of bloody froth ... It was as dramatic an act as any I was likely to accomplish again, blood pressure rising to normal, heart rate falling to normal, all of us breathing hard. Almost as an afterthought I realized that I had saved him, that he was alive because of me.
>
> Late that night, after my shift, I went to see him in the ICU. He was already off the ventilator and breathing on his own, waking up, coming back, making dim animal noises through a haze of morphine and Valium. I knew that he would leave whole, and I sat there in the dark for a while, watching the red and blue lights of the monitor, savoring him, taking something for myself.[1]

This story is one of many Huyler relates in his book, but what characterises this story is that a successful intervention is seen to be unusual. While this kind of dramatic rescue is an everyday event in TV soaps, Huyler is surprised by his success, to the extent that he went to sit with the semi-conscious patient, 'taking

1. F. Huyler, *The Blood of Strangers: Stories from Emergency Medicine*, University of Chicago Press, Chicago 1999.

something for myself'. This is an ideal example of an aesthetic of rescue, but a more typical story is entitled 'The Bleeding Girl'. In this story, a girl with juvenile rheumatoid arthritis bleeds to death, despite intensive treatment and multiple blood transfusions. Huyler performed a difficult intubation for which he received praise from his colleagues and the mother; but it was a hollow victory. His technical success simply prolonged the agony and eventually it was the mother - who had become hardened towards him - who stopped further treatment.

Although the image of emergency care is heroic - even a failure can be seen as heroic failure - it is in narratives that the complexity of emergency care is displayed. That emergency care can do more harm than good is an unsettling presence in professional narratives.

While working as an emergency nurse, I remember successfully defibrillating a patient, only for her to continue flipping in and out of cardiac arrest for the next two hours. Each successful shock produced a more and more terrified and anxious patient, so that when she finally died, I could only feel relief. Emergency care is an active, interventionist and optimistic speciality, but its practice can be problematic.

These types of stories reflect a contemporary interest in trauma, and in narrative knowledge. Trauma is now a central feature of the way that the world is understood. But there is an inherent difficulty in defining the traumatic experience; trauma is about the memory of an event that was never understood in the first place - traumatised victims are usually unable to grasp the reality of what happened to them, although the memories continue to plague them. There has also been a growing interest in narrative, which is now finding its way into some clinical areas, such as psychiatry, general medicine and nursing. This may in part be a reaction to a growing emphasis on quantitative evidence-based models. Whatever the reasons, I will develop these themes, and advocate the use of such knowledge to understand the nature of the emotional labour of emergency professionals.

Narratives are not simply the telling and re-telling of events; they are interpretations, which symbolically recreate these events. What is included and excluded entails an editing process on the part of the teller. This editing process is influenced by perceptions of the events themselves, the context in which the story is told, the cultural values about what is acceptable or unacceptable, and finally the intended audience. The shape and texture of the narrative is not a seamless mirror on reality, but rather the interplay of bodily experiences, social circumstances and cultural values. There is a time when stories can be told and a time when they remain untold or hidden in private worlds

Heroic medicine

Stacey argues that western culture prioritises stories of success and progress. Crises occur within a framework of transcendence, from chaos to control, and where suffering is reconstituted as wisdom. But what, she asks, of the others?: those that did not 'smile bravely', 'who cried with fear and terror in the face of death', those who did not feel wiser, only more bitter or confused:

> Theirs may not have been the story of discovering the generosity of the human spirit, of the bountiful goodness of friends and family. Perhaps they discovered new depths to loneliness and depression, or felt betrayed and abandoned by those they relied upon. What if everyone around them was not so wonderful? And what if there was not anyone around, wonderful or not?[2]

Stacey's point is that there are preferred narratives, ways that we are expected to behave and respond. We not only become ill, we must also learn how to be ill. But this is threatened by the contingency of life-threatening events, which can produce chaos, either temporary or prolonged, a chaos that exists on the edge of language - a muteness or a scream - which inhibits a coherent narrative and becomes an anti-narrative. To contain this there is the medical emergency, which is more than a set of protocols and technical interventions: it is also an aesthetic of rescue and cultural management.

This aesthetic of rescue is demonstrated in images of disaster. The semiotics of professionalism and care are framed in images of rescue workers clambering over wreckage, leading or stretchering survivors from the scene, and carrying out first aid on blood-stained bodies. The one positive note struck by the media after the carnage of 11 September was in accounts of fire fighters who symbolised the heroic against the traumatic impact of terrorism.

These stories are embedded in a cultural context - a culture saturated by images of trauma - where authenticity and justification for a particular use of

---

2. J. Stacey, *Teratologies: A Cultural Study of Cancer*, Routledge, London 1997, p15.

language are conducted through the shock and tears of emergency personnel. There has been a shift in emphasis towards more emotional reporting. For example, in newspaper reports of a train crash in December 1927, rescuers are plucky and heroic, nurses put aside their femininity to help, but at the Ladbroke Grove rail disaster (5.10.99), where 31 people died, one of the key images was of firewoman Sally Cox, wiping a tear away from her eye. A shocked policeman was said to be in tears, 'unable to bear the sight that confronted him' (*Sun*, 7.10.99). The emphasis was on how, despite this emotional trauma, they nonetheless did their job. By focusing on how upsetting it was, even for those used to death and injury, the horror of the incident could be more forcefully expressed.

These signs of emergency care are flexible products of professional narratives, and become incorporated into occupational cultures. Implicit to professionalism is the control of emotions. This does not mean neutrality. In the therapeutic relationship, the professional can display irritation and anger as well as care and attention. So a nurse can display emotional concern at a client's behaviour, but these emotional displays are *controlled* expressions, not temper tantrums or indications of disgust, horror or contempt. But this does not mean that such raw emotions are absent, and if they are repressed in the professional/user relationship they nonetheless find expression elsewhere. In a popular book on the narratives of emergency workers, these themes are explored in a non-professional context.[3] There is much here about death and failure, and unrewarded efforts at saving lives. There is also a bias towards children as the more extreme and disturbing subjects. Success, when it comes, is presented as a relief rather than some heroic victory. One story relates how a doctor felt after struggling to ventilate a woman:

> As I drive home that night, I'm depressed. I wonder why I'm not elated. I just saved a life. I had prepared for this moment for years and tonight it all came together. I should be elated, but I am depleted. Drained. I realise why. I never want to be that scared again as long as I live (p55).

---

3. M. Brown (ed), *The Real ER: True Stories from the Emergency Room*, Virgin, London 1996.

There is an attempt to distance their work from the heroic, all-knowledgeable and all-confident images of popular fiction; to place themselves in a more fragile light, as people who learn and make mistakes; to undermine the over-confidence that the public (or litigious consumers) are supposed to believe in. In short, these narrators are not miracle workers and do not wish to be seen as such.

In another book on the tradition of storytelling among paramedics, one respondent complains that the media:

> ... always want to show paramedics running. And then you get the call and people on the scene, they expect you to run. You're lugging seventy pounds of equipment and people expect you to run up ten flights of stairs because they do it on TV. Then you're working on some patient, and the crowd around you goes 'You've gotta save them! Do some of that *Rescue 911* shit!'[4]

Popular representations celebrate emergency work as heroic, but for emergency workers this produces unrealistic expectations. Escaping from these discourses is not easy. Even the book from which the quote above is taken advertises itself on the back cover in the following way:

> In this extraordinary world their stories intentionally trivialize pain and horror. Since the gothic gore they meet every day is business-as-usual, their tales can be cynical, flip, even profane and in-your-face. Their repertoires afford a shocking glimpse into a chaotic urban underworld where prostitution, drug abuse, assault, and murder are daily fare.

Despite one of the central themes of the book being a critique of how popular programmes represent paramedics, it is nonetheless advertised with due attention to the clichés of emergency work. On the one hand the stories undermine heroic representations, but on the other they reinforce them. This is reflected in the way that their tales are saturated with irony and sardonic humour. The straight hero narrative is nearly always derided, but they still manage to emerge as 'urban warriors' (p89). For example in one story (pp56-59) a crew is called to a shooting.

---

4. Cited in T.R. Tangherlini, *Talking Trauma: Paramedics and Their Stories*, University Press of Mississippi Jackson, 1998, pxix.

They find the patient before police backup arrives. He is in a smashed up car with 'fifteen bullet holes in the front door'. They hear some loud bangs and dive for cover before realising that it is the car backfiring. Then the car bursts into flames and the man has to be dragged out. Then two 'black guys' walk up looking like 'gangsters' - one of them holding a newspaper as though hiding a pistol, and looking 'mean and nasty' - only to politely ask if they can give any help. They leave as quickly as they can because: 'God knows who's gonna show next to our party here! We're by ourselves in the ghetto, you know'. The denouement comes when they visit the recovering patient, who is only interested if they found a gold chain that he had lost: 'No "thank you", no nothing'.

Horror stories

What also characterises these stories is a detailed focus on physical injury. Tangherlini notes an emphasis on the face and head in horror stories, because in the West the face and brain are connected to self-identity. This point is reinforced by social attitudes to traumatic brain injury. Cognitive deficits resulting from trauma raise concerns about how much of a person's identity remains.

Stories are therefore part of an informal de-briefing exercise, but they are also an exploration of horror, a focus on the body that emphasises the horrific for comic effect. They are entertaining stories that defer the subjectivity of the victim and place the smashed up body at the centre of attention. For example, in *Talking Trauma* two paramedics describe a successful suicide where the person has shot himself in the head:

> *Steve Y*: There was steam coming out of the top of his head. I mean he looked like a little smokestack that had fallen over. It was real *Night of the Living Dead* shit.
> *Lars*: He had put a double-barrel shotgun in the back of his mouth and he had just blown the entire back of his head off! It was - blam - blown out. There was no brain skull. I mean, we didn't even see where the brain was. We couldn't even find the brain bits ...
> *Steve*: Yeah, everything from his forehead back, kind of in a concave ... It would've made a nice salad bowl! (p130).

But they can also draw attention to socio-political issues, as in the story of a call where the neglect of an elderly woman symbolised family breakdown and urban violence:

> … his mother was lying on just this spring box mattress in the middle of the floor. No sheets, nothing, just lying in feces and urine. And she had a bilateral femur fracture. And her skin was just rotting basically. And there was this trail of ants leading up to her legs and carrying pieces of flesh away (p165).

The fractures had been caused by her son and the woman died three days later. Broader policy issues also emerge in paramedics' relationship to mental health. On the one hand their stories reflect a contemptuous attitude to such patients who provide comically entertaining stories, on the other they generate a critique of a poorly executed policy of de-institutionalisation that has left desperate people on the streets.

The socio-political context

One of the prevailing themes of emergency narratives is how factors external to medicine undermine its practice. Waitzkin argues that doctors reproduce a capitalist ideology by isolating the individual from the social context, which implies a level of power in the medical encounter.[5] But doctors' stories in emergency rooms often express a frustration with their efforts.

> I'd become a doctor for the gratitude I once had seen in the eyes of healed patients. But in the emergency room, the only looks I got were those of anger, denial, resignation, disgust, and annoyance. I'd gone on to residency because I wanted to deliver healthy babies for happy couples. Instead, I'd just held up a husky boy to a mother who lay on a bare black plastic pad with the sheet twisted up under bloody buttocks, who lay with one arm over her closed eyes, muttering 'Oh shit' again and again, like it was the mantra for the new age.[6]

In this story, the doctor cannot reconstitute a successful delivery into a happy

---

5. H. Waitzkin, *The Politics of Medical Encounters: How Doctors Deal with Social Problems*, Yale University Press, London 1991.
6. Cited in D. Sachs (ed), *Emergency Room: Lives Saved and Lost: Doctors Tell Their Stories*, Little, Brown and Company, London 1996, p5.

mother. A healthy baby is not a cause for celebration, merely the realisation of more problems. The person's subjectivity disappears into the 'mantra of the age' and the bloody physicality of birth. The messiness of the social world overwhelms the technical efforts of doctors as they respond to unwanted pregnancies, urban violence, mental problems, reckless behaviour and ungrateful patients. In these narratives doctors present themselves less as heroes than as battle scarred veterans on the frontline of care. As such these narratives are symbolic ways of addressing their frustrations and personal distress. They are not accurate descriptions of a reality, but occupational myths that humanise their relationship with the work. As Gabriel puts it:

> In the last resort, these myths are efforts to deal with life's harshness, unpredictability, and arbitrariness and to make bearable something which is even harder to endure than the unequal distribution of wealth and power, the unequal distribution of suffering. The first two may invite social political solutions, but not the last. Here only symbols can offer consolation.[7]

Emergency care attempts to assert itself as an effective biomedical practice, but its discursive power confronts a social world that resists the quick fix. In effect, it is constantly traumatised by a reality it is unable to contain. The focus is on extremes, from the horror of disasters, to the sardonic humour of paramedics, to the emotional labour of death and the limits of medicine. But where are the stories from middle-class or rural areas, or of the elderly struggling to cope with a multitude of social and physical problems, who turn up in emergency departments with frustratingly unclear but real problems? The emergency trope seems to be most culturally useful as a medium to contain - via an aesthetic of rescue - the social problems of disorder that erase collective solutions. Medicine is often practised less as a solution than as a highly visible and technical expression of concern that offsets a commitment to more durable solutions. The emergency aestheticises an urban underclass, sidelining deviant behaviour.

The emergency carries with it the cultural baggage of emotional scripts. These scripts are shaped by a culture that prioritises success and progress

7. Y. Gabriel, 'Turning Facts into Stories and Stories into Facts: A Hermeneutic Exploration of Organizational Folklore', *Human Relations*, 44(8) (1991), p873, pp50-1.

narratives. But trauma shatters such categories. The emotional aftermath is only partly contained by professional 'feeling rules'. Consequently, these stories reflect an ambiguous anxiety and fascination with the worst the world can throw at us. But they often represent an aesthetic short cut, which allows us to explore that world without proposing any coherent moral or political response.

Indeed much of the narrative content is about burnout and stress, of feeling numbed and helpless, of how they broke bad news to relatives and their reactions. There is a feeling of helplessness in the face of social problems. The work is largely reactive when confronted with societal violence, domestic abuse, alcoholism and neglect. The result is often a cynicism towards patients as these problems are individualised and extracted from their socio-political context, resulting in a world-weary apathy, punctuated by the adrenaline rush of the emergency.

The emotional labour of police work

Rick Rattue and
Nelarine Cornelius

Emotional labour should not be seen as something only women do. Police work, for example, also involves emotional labour: and an analysis which acknowledged this might enable radical improvements in the service.

According to Marx, 'The tradition of all the dead generations weighs like a nightmare on the brain of the living'. For Helvetius: 'Any idea foreign to our way of looking at things and feeling them always seems incongruous to us'. And for Koestler: 'Every creative act involves ... a new innocence of perception, liberated from the cataract of accepted belief'. Ours is perhaps a small attempt to suggest a new perception of police work.

The difficulty for us was trying to get beyond a number of entrenched (and polarised) accounts of the police, to try out the fairly recent vocabulary of 'emotional labour' upon 'street' police work.[1] Our hope is that through understanding the *emotional* (as well as physical and intellectual) labour

1. Policing is an extremely diverse set of activities. By 'street' policing we mean the activities that surround the investigation of burglary, theft, murder and other crimes of violence, and the 'maintenance of public order and decency'.

processes of police work we might help to re-frame discussion and explore ways in which the service might be developed and delivered.

What we will do is sketch out a series of promising approaches, all of which have something to offer but also have something wrong about them, before returning to the details of police work, and the implications for police practice.

Promising approaches

The work of Arlie Hochschild

Arlie Hochschild's defining study of flight attendants, *The Managed Heart*, was concerned with both the value and the cost of heart-felt emotion work done for money: *emotional labour*.[2] Worse than manual labour, for her the 'commercialisation of human feeling' involves alienating the self, the 'core of being'. Hochschild's later essays on working for the love of working focused on the 'care deficit' that this creates at home, particularly a deficit of care towards children and elders and 'cold-modern' institutional care.

The way in which all-hours police work puts a strain on home life - a care deficit if you like - is the stuff of TV fiction. But while much uniformed security work such as payroll protection and guarding warehouses is, like the work of cabin crew, commercialised, policing is not.

The special issue of *Soundings* on emotional labour in 1999 marked an important increase in interest in emotional labour. Two UK conferences and a workshop series which continues have enabled valuable exchanges among academics and practitioners, especially nurses. However, we are worried that there are large sections of emotional labourers that are being neglected. In particular it strikes us that we are in danger of reproducing the popular assumption that emotional labour is mostly 'something women do'.

Although interest in emotional labour in the UK is led by those involved in and studying nursing, nursing shows the same specific lack-of-fit with Hochschild's flight attendants as does policing: in the UK nursing and policing is emotion work done for pay, but neither are done for profit. It is public work. On the face of it, then, in terms of emotional labour, policing should

2. A. R. Hochschild, *The Managed Heart: the Commercialisation of Human Feeling*, University of California Press. See also Steve Smith's 'Arlie Hochschild: soft spoken conservationist of emotions: review and assessment of Arlie Hochschild's work', *Soundings* No.11 Spring 1999.

receive roughly the same attention as nursing. Why should the emotional labour of police work be left off the agenda?

Furthermore, in contrast to the work of flight attendants, nursing and policing are both recognised *professions*. But what kind of professions?

Professionalism, 'caring' and 'non-caring' work

Keith MacDonald's *The Sociology of the Professions* (Sage 1999) contains some powerful observations about different kinds of professions, which hint at the presence or absence of emotional labour. For example he associates *personal service professions* with 'human' or 'caring' activity like nursing and social work; on the other hand, presumably, in *impersonal service professions*, including law and accountancy, emotions are not central to the primary task.

MacDonald's distinction is also 'gendered': he calls the caring professions *matriarchal*, *meditative* and *'middling'* in terms of class. The state or other professions usually mediate between carers and their clients; for example, doctors mediate between nurses and patients, greatly reducing their autonomy.

On the other hand, *non-meditative*, *middle-class* professions, like medicine, accountancy and the law are more typically *patriarchal* and less mediated by other professions.

MacDonald argues that patriarchy, like class, is rather diffuse, but has specific structures that constitute a *system of production*, *patriarchal violence* (physical or psychological) and *patriarchal relations at work*. Class matters, MacDonald believes, but *patriarchy* is the most powerful organising principle.

Where does policing fit? For example it might be seen as *patriarchal*. As a profession it is *middling*, but it recruits strongly from the working classes. Is it, and should it be, *meditative*?

The 'gender segregation' of the emotional labour concept?

Most research on emotional labour concentrates fairly narrowly on 'feminised' and hospitable professions, notably nursing. This is valuable in that it highlights the level of challenge and the value of women's work and because it moves us away from 'masculine' views of labour and labour process.

But there is paradox and danger here. The paradox is that emotional labour might start to be stereotyped as *only* concerned with the feminised, gender segregated and caring professions. This would substitute a new gender bias in understanding labour processes to replace the old ones. There is a risk that the message becomes 'gendering is good'!

The point is that there are very large male dominated professions in police and prison work and in the armed services that *also* engage in emotional labour, albeit that the 'services' that they offer are rather different. Do they fit MacDonald or Hochschild? Or are they cross-cutting groups: *patriarchal, recruited more from the working class than the middling classes*? Are they *meditative or non-meditative*? In what sense are they *hospitable* or *hostile*? What else is special about their work?

The danger is that if we don't have the right language to describe it, we will not examine the emotional labour of male uniformed front line services properly. Real harm to communities and to workers will persist.

Public tragedies and police work

Most of the dialogue about policing is about things going wrong; it is especially about racism, failed prosecutions and miscarriages of justice, again and again. Would the vocabulary of emotional labour help in understanding recent and distressing public accounts of the failings of the police service, as well as the more occasional, but equally damming revelations about injurious prison regimes? It seems foolish to disregard the emotion work that takes place in encounters between police constables and witnesses, victims, informants, or suspects and within the court process generally. (This applies equally to the relationships between prisoners and prison officers.)

The tragedy at the centre of the MacPherson report - the bungled police investigation of the murder of the black teenager Stephen Lawrence - highlighted failings that were attributed to unwitting or institutional racism in The Metropolitan Police, which compromised their engagement with members of ethnic minorities. But MacPherson's recommendations are strikingly similar to those offered *twenty-five years earlier* by Lord Scarman following the Brixton riots. Why had there been such limited progress in behaviour and outlook?

The case of the murder of the schoolboy Damilola Taylor was also widely reported, with the work of the police service again coming under public scrutiny, and rightly so. But the ease with which the actions of the police were derided in this case cast a long and worrying a shadow with regards to understanding what went wrong specifically in the Damilola case. The Metropolitan Police devoted the maximum of resources to the investigation. Yet the unthinking and un-*self*-critical way in which the media derided police action risks creating new, uninformed and uninformative myths about police work, which get us no nearer to understanding why things still go wrong. In fairness it must be said that it was not for lack of trying that the police found *no* forensic evidence and were unable to produce a credible court witness. The danger is that the police will feel not just beleaguered and embattled, but also bewildered and embittered. This is not a healthy basis for change.

Sometimes a swing *in favour* of a service is no better informed. In the aftermath of 11 September US fire-fighters who had been targeted as 'bad guy' union-militants and subject to cuts in spending, became public heroes overnight. Obviously, the celebration of the NY Fire Department and NYPD blue was a simple public response to the heroism and nobility of disciplined work undertaken in atrocious conditions. But such a mood-swing is indicative of only one aspect of the emotion work that is performed by such groups. Elsewhere in this edition of *Soundings* Stuart Nairn finds that the relationship of emergency workers to their clients can be complex and highly ambivalent.

There are other observations that can be usefully made about this area of work, in particular in relation to their role in contributing to *social capital*. Policing, fire-fighting, prison-guarding and paramedic work involve more than just a labour process of enforcement, control, aid or emotion work. These groups are empowered to undertake *virtuous work* in an Aristotelian sense - to do good, in spite of personal danger. This is sacred work. It enhances the community's sense of security, belongingness and freedom from fear; that is it contributes much of its stock of social capital. Thus stories and reports of ineffective and dysfunctional service delivery, whether fair or unfair, well informed or misplaced, are often fuelled by anxieties over deficiencies in social capital - and not just deficiencies, but also severe inequalities.

Discourses on inequality

Inequality can be defined in different ways, which then lead to very different policies, and to interventions which could be either corrective or damaging.

Sen argues in *Inequality Re-examined* (Oxford University Press 1992) that many different models of inequality show a sameness of response. *Income egalitarians* demand 'equality of incomes'; *welfare-egalitarians* demand 'equal welfare levels'; *classical utilitarians* insist on 'equal weights on utilities' and *pure libertarians* demand 'equality of rights and liberties'. He and Nussbaum argue that we should depart from these approaches, by acknowledging the diversity of each individual's characteristics (age, gender, aptitudes, talents, proneness to illnesses ...), including their circumstantial characteristics (ownership of assets, social backgrounds, environmental predicaments...): for them it is important for all to be able to be or do what they have reason to value, and they emphasise potentiality, flourishing, individual and collective voice and agency.[3]

Crucially, the concept of *capability equality* addresses the interactions between individuals, groups, institutions and cultures that enable or impede 'full citizenship' within society. It does not concern itself primarily with attaining any of the types of equality referred to in the paragraph above. Indeed equality of income, welfare, rights and so on, are seen as absurd and probably damaging. All this is a useful approach when considering policing.

The modern UK police service

Some kind of official policing has existed in Britain for over seven hundred years. The modern service was established in nineteenth century, however, by Robert Peel's Metropolitan Police Act of 1829. The recruitment of '3000 strong men of good intelligence and with a written recommendation as to good character' met with public suspicion. It was feared that the Met would be a repressive militia similar to revolutionary militias in France. However, its 'maintenance of the peace' through the quelling of fierce riots, by reducing fear, gradually began to win public respect for the Met. The CID was also set up in the nineteenth century, though most specialist branches did not appear until the twentieth century.

Originally middle management was recruited from the working-class lower ranks, on an officer's attainment of the correct qualifications, while upper management ranks were populated from outside the police, by high-status, middle-class groups. But after emergency wartime regulations in 1939, all appointments were made from the lower ranks. In the 1970s, 'fast track' graduate

3. M. Nussbaum and A. Sen, *The Quality of Life*, Clarendon 1993.

and 'high flyers' schemes turned the clock back in the name of 'professionalisation'. Non-graduate officers are also able to obtain degrees, with support of the service, and many do. However, universal appointment by steady progress from the lower ranks has largely disappeared.

During this period a number of problems emerged, especially in relation to race. A superintendent later recalled:

> We took anyone, if they had two arms and two legs. That brought an influx of aggressive young men joining for the money and the excitement, not public service. They soon were embroiled in their own turf war: blue versus black, on the streets of Bristol, Brixton and Toxteth (*Guardian*, May 2001).

Racism and sexism have been a problem in the police force for a long period; successive reports and inquiries have attempted to address these issues, with varying degrees of success. As Sue Lees, in commenting on the McPherson report in *The Guardian* in 1999, argued:

> Racism and sexism function to both create and enhance solidarity. If this is questioned - when, for example, women enter the force - the level often increases. Addressing sexism, like addressing racism, is no easy task as it is embedded in both internal processes and the service delivery of the police. In other words, it is institutional. Any attempt to contest such attitudes is likely to meet a backlash aimed at preserving the status quo. Those who hold sexist and racist attitudes, therefore, rather than being bad apples, are conformists.

Emotional labour in police work

Over a period of six months, we undertook a small exploratory research project in constabularies in the south of England, to capture police accounts of their work. Access was excellent. Telephone and face-to-face interviews and 'shadowing' were used. Time was also spent in interview rooms, in police cars, in a canteen and even on the beat. There were extended interviews with two black male officers, four white female officers and thirteen white males, mostly 'front-line' officers. Overlapping themes emerged:

Emotional detachment and repression

Unsurprisingly in a service largely staffed by men, when asked about how best to deal with crime scenes, responses tended to feature themes influenced by discourses of masculinity and patriarchy. To do the job well officers needed to take part in banter - responding quickly to derogatory comments - and to be capable of robust rebuttals of suspects' 'verbals'. Women officers agreed that having a 'thick skin' and 'not being sensitive' to verbal abuse was important.

All officers felt *emotional detachment* and *repression* was necessary. Emotional expression was reserved for informal arenas. 'Real' policing was learned in the canteen, police cars and vans, during after-hours drinking and eating, and on shift completing paperwork. Here there were 'safety valves' where officers swapped stories. One white female officer argued that:

> You should be able to talk about all sorts of things ... I think that if there is something wrong in the group they should sort it out themselves and not go to the boss. Laughing and joking is part of being a police officer. If you don't that's when you end up being stressed and then you are off sick. It's all like an extended family.

The psychologist George Kelly would call these arenas *learning laboratories*. This is where officers learn about dealing with their differences.

One white male officer described his experience of working in vans with his shift team.

> I've spent a lot of time in the van and it's both male and female officers having a laugh and a joke and a jovial time. If I were ever offended, I would point it out and so would someone else if they were. When there's a female though, it's a different kind of banter. There are certain things you wouldn't say to a female that you would say to others. Males give as good as they get. In the van you get to know people well.

His black colleague, however, described further differences - of walking into rooms full of lively conversations and then of everything 'going quiet'...: 'This can have a cumulative effect of eroding your confidence'. And one of the female officers described more overt bullying by male officers because she was 'female and well educated'; she eventually moved.

Care

Most front-line officers talked of 'us and them'; senior management neglect; being overstretched and under-resourced; poor working conditions including long and difficult shift-patterns; and being undermined by a self-serving legal profession, 'running with the hare and the hounds'. They felt senior management should show more proactive and supportive leadership. It was felt that many senior officers did not care, focusing on their own interests, not the front line.

Our limited research into rank and file disposition indicates that positive action in favour of disadvantaged groups might be mistrusted as 'favourable treatment' in an already inequitable working environment. Another interpretation, however, is that public scrutiny of the front line has been increased, and it seems to beat officers that higher-level officers enjoy status, power, and invisibility of action. The mystique and status of beat officers had been stripped away.

Professionalism and 'emotional detachment' at the crime scene

Asked what the most demanding aspect of their job was, most answered sudden deaths and assaults. They all said that it was important to detach themselves emotionally from crime scenes. They repressed emotions so that they would not 'get in the way'. The accounts were fascinating:

> As a professional, you put emotion aside ... you have to detach yourself. After all, you are the one in uniform and people are looking at you to take control. Emotional values can't come into play.

> You can't allow your feelings to influence you. Whether it's a rape victim or someone who's got damage to their car. You can't let it affect the way you deal with it. The human side of you is affected by what you see and deal with. For example, if it's a horrific car accident you will hold your emotions till later. When you sit down about it later, then you get upset.

Care reduced when the going gets tough?

Although half of the officers coped with the intensity of policing by talking to colleagues at work, the rest 'dealt with things' by 'having a drink', 'going to the gym', 'gardening', or 'just coping'. It was more difficult to unearth detailed accounts of this than of the emotional challenge of the work itself.

What of officers away from work? Robert Jackal's research on detectives in the New York Police Department states that detectives felt their interactions with criminals coarsened their view of human nature, creating suspicions of everyone's motives and actions.[4] Numbed or terrified by encounters with extreme violence, they did not or could not reveal these feelings to others. Jackal writes:

> The whole construction of the police world depends on officers maintaining the appearance of rugged emotional distance, especially from the most emotion-laden and draining experiences of their work.

The consequences extend beyond work:

> [the job's] rhythms, its languages, its images, its ugliness, its secrecy find their ways under tightly closed doors and come to stand between husbands and wives or between lovers, subtly eroding the delicate frameworks that sustain intimacy and trust.

Closing thoughts

Arlie Hochschild suggests that 'emotional numbness' may reduce stress by reducing access to feelings through which the stress introduces itself. The worker becomes accustomed to the dimming or numbing of inner signals. But she adds that the same strategy may reduce the acuity of the emotional labourer. The refusal to put the 'inner self' to work means feeling less, but also noticing less.

This is a 'feeling rule' that is sustained by the informal organisation: operational front-line culture provides the feeling rule 'don't feel (at least for now)'. Make no mistake, mutual care does take place, but it is dressed up and expressed in the solidarity of jokes and horseplay. One officer said of police college training that they 'weeded out' those that did not *feel* the way that the force wanted them to. Masculinity and patriarchy help to reinforce this way of

---

4. R. Jackal, 'A detective's lot: contours of morality and emotion in police work', in S. Fineman (ed), *Emotions at Work*, Sage, London 2000.

dealing with emotion, but they might also make straightforward (un-coded) mutual care less valuable than it could be.

Not all policing is about highly emotional scenes. Many officers gained satisfaction by helping people in high visibility policing, and in successfully dealing with minor disputes. Police investigations at the scene of a burglary have been described as 'social work on the road'. Social validation counteracts some of the estrangement, lack of care and numbing.

Disengagement at the crime scene might be linked with more intensive - if camouflaged - mutual care away from it; it could also be linked to a culture that tends towards isolationism, and is particularly sensitive about any challenges. This may contribute to informal and unwitting discrimination: 'closing down' works against empathy with witnesses or officers who have different 'feeling rules'. If Hochschild is right, disengagement at the crime scene may result in loss of acuity and also of information - which could be catastrophic to police investigations.

Does it have to be this way? One of the surprises of our work is that officers have no difficulty in grasping Hochschild's terminology of deep and surface acted emotional labour. They say, 'It is what we do'. There is an opportunity here to give a voice to new practices, by giving a language within which the problem can be recast. This has already been the case in nursing.

There is also a message to be carried from the junior to the senior ranks, 'show leadership and concern for us'. This is not that far away from saying 'equip us to show leadership and concern for ourselves'.

There is some force in MacDonald's observation that 'gender matters'. The inclusion of women has already shifted the way policing is done. But there is nothing essential to male gender which means that policing cannot be meditative in the presence of distress, suffering and death - as nursing most certainly *is* (and about which many nurses have written at length). Indeed if policing was more meditative, officers might have to take *less*, not more 'baggage' home with them at the end of a shift.

It may also be helpful to tease out the practical implications of Sen and Nussbaum's claim that the most viable and defensible form of equality means 'being able to be or do what one has reason to value', and their emphasis on potentiality, flourishing, individual and collective voice and agency. This provides a model of equality that has the potential to redefine the problem and take new initiatives. The question of initiative brings us directly to our last point:

We are in no doubt that, like nursing, police work involves very high and frequent levels of challenge, and authentic bravery. Acknowledgement of this in nursing - of the sheer, transcending, intrinsic value of nursing care - has led to the influential and successful *Clinical Leadership Development Programme* which, after an emotionally unsettling process of reflection and measurement, enables nurses of any 'rank' to show 'transformational leadership', 'adulthood', 'political astuteness', 'networking', 'influence' and 'wellness'.[5] It is intriguing to imagine what the police equivalent might be. Rank and file police officers might also like to know that *Clinical Leadership Development* enables nurses precisely to challenge the powers-that-be, in the pursuit of service ideals in which they and their patients could share confidence.

Our police stories of alienation from the hierarchy, and the headline stories of aggrieved victims, are not unlike problems which nurses are already putting right.

---

5. See S. Smith, C. Ashburner, P. Smith, G. Cunningham, B. Gray, S. Lister, and S. Nash, '"Cognitive Sculpting": the RCN Clinical Leadership Development Programme; emotion strategies in leadership development', paper to the International Conference on Organisational Behaviour in Health, Oxford March 2002.

The refugee experience

Ian Robbins

Ian Robbins, who runs an NHS traumatic stress clinic, discusses the emotional experiences of refugees, and the difficult emotional regime they face in the United Kingdom.

I have been involved in working with refugees for a number of years both in the UK and in a number of African countries. This has always left me impressed by the extent of individual resilience, but surprised at the lack of knowledge in host countries about the refugee experience. To appreciate the current dilemmas of refugees it is worth thinking about what their experience consists of. This is particularly important as ever larger numbers of people are becoming refugees, or are being displaced within their own country, while host countries are becoming increasingly reluctant to accept any but the most desperate of refugees. Refugees who leave their countries typically do so as a consequence of having their basic human rights violated, usually by totalitarian regimes. Current media stories would have us believe that the decision to leave their countries was an easy one, but the reality is often very different.

The refugee experience

For most there have been increasing cycles of political repression in their country of origin. This starts with limits to freedom of speech, tight censorship of the press and limitations placed on centres of higher education. It may also involve access to normal public services being denied on the basis of religion, ethnic origin or political allegiance. In some instances the cycle of repression may initially be disguised as an attempt to improve public order. Refugees are often bitter about what they subsequently come to see as their short-sightedness in not recognising the significance of the early changes. By the time the direction of the changes becomes more apparent there is little chance to reverse them.

A good example of this is the changes introduced into Germany in the 1930s. The increasingly draconian legislation contained in the Nuremberg Laws was tolerated with little awareness of where it might lead. By the time it became obvious that genocide was likely it was not possible to leave. Furthermore many felt that if they had taken action earlier on, the increasing repression would have been averted. Many survivors blame themselves for not recognising the direction which the repression was taking. The end result of this is a sense of guilt for what happened to themselves or their families.

Marie, who was originally from Kinshasa in the Democratic Republic of Congo, was very bitter about her perceived lack of foresight:

> I was so pleased when Mobutu was finished. Many of my family had suffered because of him so when Kabila came to power I celebrated and at first gave my active support. It was only when I got involved in politics when I went to the university that I was made personally aware of what was happening.

She was arrested, tortured and raped as a result of normal student politics.

Her family paid a large amount of money in bribes for her release and rapidly arranged for her to leave her country. They reasoned that were she to stay she would be either detained again or killed. For others there may be considerable indecision until events force them to leave. In deciding to go, they are accepting that they will leave behind family and friends whom they may never see again.

The process of leaving is both expensive and dangerous. An agent is used to get papers and tickets, and to procure a smooth passage through customs. This may cost US$10,000 or more. If caught in the process of leaving, arrest, further torture or death may follow. There may also be little choice as to final destination. The alternative is to leave by land. But border areas are dangerous places. When refugees are leaving they typically take small items of high value with them, such as jewellery, bullion or cash. Both border guards and local bands of robbers prey on refugees around the border areas because they offer rich pickings. Rape and murder are also common. The onward journey may continue to be very frightening. One Albanian woman recently told me:

> I travelled by lorry for over two weeks with my children. I was the only woman among over twenty men. Even though they behaved very properly there was no privacy and I was afraid that I would be raped again.

While she arrive unhurt, she was very shaken by the journey.

Many refugees have been exposed to major trauma. They have often been subject to detention following arrest or abduction, and to violence and threats. But perhaps the most difficult aspect of detention is its indefinite nature. With a prison sentence there is at least some end point, but detention can last days or years. It is difficult to know what the rules are, and there is no process of judicial review.

While in detention many are tortured. Torture is the deliberate attempt to damage the mental and physical well being of others, and usually includes both physical and psychological elements. Among the psychological elements are prolonged solitary confinement, sleep deprivation and sensory deprivation. Detainees may also have to listen to or watch the torture of others, and may be subject to mock executions. Often there will be intense degradation and humiliation, where people may be forced to eat excrement or participate in the abuse of others.

Sexual violence is common, with elements of both psychological and physical torture. This may include being subject to sexual remarks with the threat of rape being made explicit. Prisoners are forced to undress in front of guards; and also, as in the case of the husband of Marie, who was mentioned earlier, in front of their wives. They may be touched, raped or made to perform sexual acts with other prisoners. There may be sexualised attacks in the form of beatings to, or mutilation of, genitals. Foreign objects or shock batons may be inserted into the rectum and vagina. Prisoners are made aware that there is an explicit wish to damage their future sexual functioning, or to 'contaminate them' and make them unacceptable to their partners or families.

There may also be intense physical pain inflicted through beatings with rifles, whips or clubs. Electric shocks are often used to the genitals and burning with cigarettes or other heat sources is common. Suffocation may be induced by immersion under water, often polluted with excrement, or by hanging people in positions which compromise the chest muscles. This produces intense panic. People may be kept naked, often in cold environments, or may be soaked with water. Acids or chillies may be used on eyes or genitals.

Torture works in part because of what may be done as well as what is actually done. Skilled torturers rely on anticipatory dread and vary what they do accordingly. They often present false choices to the victim, who is made to feel that if they had given the right answer they would have avoided the pain. In reality they would be tortured whatever they said, but the false choices lead to them accepting a degree of responsibility for their own suffering. Perhaps the worst torture for most is to watch their partners or children being tortured or raped in front of them.

Refugees are also exposed to other forms of violence. This may be systematic, aimed at inducing terror in a whole population, or it may be more random. Random violence may occur in war zones, where it may be intentional, or what is increasingly referred to by the military as collateral damage. There is exposure to dead and mutilated bodies. Alongside this may be the loss of all property and possessions.

Associated with the violence is the disappearance of friends or relatives. In many countries such as Argentina, Chile and Sri Lanka, people have waited for many years to find out what happened to their families. Although they may believe that their relatives are dead, there may also be a lingering hope. There is also an endless list of gruesome fates to haunt them, which are impossible to get rid of without knowing what happened.

There is loss on a large scale. Not only is there loss of family and friends, there is also loss of most possessions. This may be accompanied by loss of status. Many refugees come from affluent families, and may have had professions with high social status in their country of origin. A relative of mine who became a refugee from Austria in 1938 went from being an art historian and part of a wealthy family to working in a munitions factory in South London. Since she had never had to deal with even normal domestic activities, the dramatic change in circumstances had a profound impact on her well being and mental health. Current refugees are often in a similar position, and the loss of status may be very damaging.

Arrival

On arrival in the UK the process of claiming asylum starts with the immigration officials, whose approach spans a wide range of styles with differing levels of compassion. Often the individual is shocked, fearful and apprehensive. They may fail to declare much of the trauma which they have experienced, especially if they have been raped or tortured. This is usually the result of a sense of shame. It would be unusual for a complete story to be told at the port of entry. Unfortunately any failure to declare information at this point may be part of the grounds for refusal of the application. The initial interview is very important.

One refugee from central Africa, who was 15 on arrival, had lost substantial amounts of weight prior to her journey. As a consequence she looked very haggard. It was remarked at her initial interview that she looked older than 15. Since then she has returned to normal weight, and certainly looks no older than her stated age. But the accusation of being older than she says continues to blight her progress. Currently, as an unaccompanied minor she has a degree of protection against being returned, and indeed her case should not be heard until she is no longer a minor. But if it is decided that she is older, the responsibility of the government is different and she may be returned to her country of origin following her case being heard.

The initial interview may also result in the refugee being put into detention. Detention may be in a dedicated detention centre or, in a small number of cases, in a prison. Given the captivity experiences which have forced many to become refugees, this can have a damaging effect on mental health and well-being, and may exacerbate existing problems. It may also lead to a sense of injustice for those who had high expectations of natural justice in the UK. There may also be continued bad news from home, which increases the problems of adjustment to a new country, with vastly different values and culture.

Adjustment is also in part determined by where refugees are placed. Previously 80 per cent or more of refugees to the UK would settle in or around the London area. While this undoubtedly placed strain on services, it did afford the possibility of joining a community of people from the same country who shared a common identity. Now refugees to the UK are dispersed throughout the country. This may include areas where there is no history of substantial numbers of immigrants. As a consequence there is no experience in these areas of dealing with the health needs of refugees, of integrating non-English speaking children into mainstream education, or even of having sufficient people who can interpret. This serves to increase an already marked sense of social isolation. This may be exacerbated when the process of dispersal occurs after an initial period of settlement in London. This may have allowed the formation of the beginnings of a social network. Once dispersed they may be reluctant to try to create a new network. There is often overt racism at local community level.

The dispersal programme is driven by the availability of housing stock. It is often available in areas with pre-existing high levels of deprivation, and there may be resentment among the local community. Experiences with the local community are reinforced by contact with social services, education or housing officers who may fail to understand their needs and thus respond adversely.

Asylum status

The difficulties in adjustment are exacerbated by continued uncertainty over asylum status. Decisions about asylum applications may take many years. During this time the possibility of a return and all this entails may have a very damaging effect on mental health. A number of refugees have found the whole process very humiliating, especially when events which they regard as very shaming become public knowledge. During the time they are waiting for a decision they are unable to work and as a consequence are reliant on the state. This is particularly galling for those with professional qualifications which are in demand. Once a decision is made, it may appear as if this is the end of a process, but in reality it is only the beginning of starting to rebuild a life. However, at this stage there may be no help available.

Some of this may be due to a lack of knowledge about refugee needs rather than deliberate indifference. The effect, however, is to create a high level of frustration and anger. It is difficult to express this anger when it exists alongside a belief in the refugees themselves that they should be grateful for being allowed to be refugees. Such a view is reinforced by current government rhetoric, which proves its no-nonsense credentials by 'being tough' on refugees. The current Home Secretary recently gave examples of refugees allegedly overwhelming local services such as schools or doctor's surgeries. In reality, since placement of refugees is decided by the government's own department, it is they themselves who determine which areas are to be 'overwhelmed'.

The failure of many - including health professionals - to engage with refugees may result from a wish to avoid the emotional distress of entering into their experience. Were we able to do so, it would be difficult to sustain current approaches. Similarly, there is little if any time in professional curricula devoted to refugee issues. As a consequence there is little real knowledge of what refugees may have gone through, a gap not filled by the media; and there is no knowledge of what could ease their progress into the UK. In describing the refugee experience I myself feel uncomfortable. Their experiences are often horrific, but describing them in detail has an almost voyeuristic element to it. Without describing them in some detail, however, the unremitting misery which is part of being a refugee is lost.

Perhaps what is most depressing about current government discourses on refugees is the lack of any recognition that they may bring value to the country in terms of skills and experiences. Many refugees are from skilled professions, and those who are not are often willing to accept menial jobs as a means of rebuilding their lives. The UK has been enriched in the past by waves of immigration. A change in mindset would benefit the UK; and it would not only improve the lot of refugees, it could also bring a sense of morality to a process which appears to have lost it.

'Down on the Farm'

Reflections on emotional labour and regeneration

Marjorie Mayo, Trudi James and Pam Smith

There has been a proliferation of regeneration projects since the election of New Labour in 1997. Here Marjorie Mayo, Trudi James *and* Pam Smith *comment and reflect on a portfolio of photographs and newspaper clippings which show the changing face of regeneration on the Broadwater Farm Estate in Tottenham. The images and words - whose content ranges from late nineteenth century rural harmony to the riot torn community of the 1980s - evoke powerful emotions. The emotional labour of regeneration is seen through a series of snapshots, from municipal commitment to promote healthy living to the emotional labour of individuals who have helped to transform the Broadwater Farm, to make it 'happy and secure'.*

In the last year Trudi James has been working as a Sure Start Health Visitor in Haringey, where her patch includes the Broadwater Farm Estate, referred to locally as 'The Farm'. The Sure Start programme is a government initiative aimed at improving the lives of under-fours and their parents. Local councils make bids for monies to set up partnerships with a variety of organisations and people to support innovative projects.

When we were thinking about this second Soundings *special issue on emotional labour, the link between regeneration and emotional labour emerged as an important theme. After a discussion with Marjorie Mayo, who had presented a thought-provoking paper on the complex emotional demands on workers involved in regeneration projects at the 2001 Emotional Labour conference, Trudi collected together a portfolio of images that linked into this theme. These images were assembled from the Haringey Museum archives, the Sure Start office records, and an exhibition on the Broadwater Farm estate to commemorate the life and death of the much-loved caretaker, Russ Simper. The images include a powerful mix of photographs and newspaper clippings.*

As a result of further discussions with Trudi and Marjorie, Pam Smith has made an attempt to chart the emotional labour and regeneration themes that emerged from the collection of material.

The Original Broadwater Farm (1892). As the photograph illustrates, Broadwater Farm really did begin life as a prosperous diary farm. The milk churns in the cart drawn by animals knee-deep in the picturesquely named River Moselle convey an image of rural bliss. Judging from that splendid building that was no ordinary farm and probably owned by a gentleman farmer.

The Lido site in the 1930s - a wide open grassy space with the Lido in the distance. The construction of Lidos to provide outdoor bathing was part of a movement to promote healthy living, which was epitomised by the Peckham experiment in South London. This municipality decided to make provision for the wellbeing of its inhabitants. Good diet and exercise were part of the package. Although there was a positive side to these endeavours, there was also an authoritarian element of an external authority knowing 'what is best for you'. Such initiatives were early examples of urban renewal.

The Broadwater Farm Estate

By the 1960s open spaces and public bathing had been replaced by public housing. The Broadwater estate, with its covered walkways, low rise buildings and construction on stilts above the Moselle River, could be seen as a regeneration project of its day. The tenants were enthusiastic because moving to the Farm gave them new opportunities and 'high hopes' for a better standard of living than they had had in the former South Tottenham slums they left behind. On the negative side, this already stigmatised them, and the Farm acquired a bad reputation before it even began.

The idea had been that the Farm would be a model for integrated living, with shops, a creche and social amenities. In the event this never happened and the facilities were inadequate; the people of Broadwater Farm became quite isolated. Requests to London Transport to run buses to the estate were never heeded. Racist labels also began to be attached to the tenants, who were stereotyped as 'poor black people' with high unemployment and large numbers of 'unmarried mothers'. This is a big issue in regeneration: people get stigmatised and labelled because of where they live. When they apply for jobs, for example, their postcodes conjure up in employers' minds an image of who they are, and may seriously reduce their chances of getting an interview, let alone employment.

Broadwater Farm Estate 1974

By the 1970s there are overtones of surveillance. A sociologist brought in on behalf of the local liberal parliamentary candidate to study the local environment provided what is clearly a partisan report of the estate. Its findings were summarised in the local newspaper *The Weekly Herald*. The headlines of

6 October 1978 read, 'Expert raps terror flats' - countered by a more positive police view: 'It's not so bad'. Many argued that local press coverage dealt the Farm 'a bad deal'; there were reports such as 'Fear haunts the gloomy passages, lifts and entrances' amid a 'sub-culture of violence'. Local tenants spoke out against the 'total misrepresentation of the facts'.

A resident, John Marshall, expressed his views of the estate in a poem published in the *Herald* on 13 October 1978:

> Of course the sociologist isn't right -
> Broadwater is such a beautiful sight:
> The estate has a design unique -
> Yet, it really must be pique
> That has led to criticisms
> For the opposite witticisms
> Come from the vandals who care
> To embellish beauty so rare -
> With their blue and white spray cans
> And their explicitly stated plans
> To take the 'North Bank' or 'the Shed'
> And misspelled in letters of red
> Arsenal are ****, the police stink -
> And further down, in lurid pink,
> Messages of Love, - just wait till Anne's dad
> Finds out about the times she's apparently had,
> Yes, go take a look - no muggers will harm,
> For this is the perfectly designed Broadwater Farm.

It's clear that the sociologist was not reporting the concerns of local people. His report spoke of rubbish, vomit and other indicators of urban decay. The poet challenges this sense that some external authority knows what is best for the people of Broadwater Farm. He is clearly of the opinion that the sociologist just doesn't understand what is going on. Take the interpretation of crime, for example: though crime was prevalent on the estate it was likely to be petty at that time rather than violent. A decade later, the Inquiry following the riots found widespread unjust labelling of Broadwater Farm from outsiders, for both people and buildings.

During the 1970s the post-war commitment to regeneration was waning, and public sector spending really began to be curbed, especially in housing. The cutbacks in education and health were slower to impact, perhaps partly because they were more likely to affect the middle classes, who were less affected by cutbacks in social housing because they were more likely to be owner-occupiers. The working classes on the other hand were much more dependent on the availability of public housing. Consequently, they were really badly affected by the drastic reduction in social housing. In London in particular this resulted in growing pressure on public housing, which meant that people who were housed by local councils were often in dire poverty with a variety of social needs. Also, because the level of funding was so low, housing maintenance suffered and the houses and flats in which the people lived were in a state of extreme disrepair. I think you can see therefore why Broadwater Farm Estate became stigmatised and labelled a 'sink estate', and why tensions built up and ultimately created the conditions that contributed to the riots.

In the 1980s, at the height of the Thatcher years, the all too familiar images and emotive language used by the media to describe the Broadwater Farm riots and death of PC Keith Blakelock convey a sense of lawlessness, racial tensions, police abuse and government neglect. Terms such as 'Butchered' (The *Sun*, 8 October 1985) and 'Rioting Mob shoot police' (*The Daily Mail*, 7 October 1985) bear testimony to this. Douglas Hurd, the Home Secretary of the day, was said not to be welcome to view the damage (*Daily Telegraph*, 8 October 1985). Councillor Sharon Lawrence was quoted as saying, 'His government has done enough damage to this borough. My message to him is to stay away and send the money'.

Heroines and heroes of Broadwater Farm

Finally, in the 1990s, the cycle of regeneration comes full circle. Recent media images present the Broadwater Farm as a happy place for children, not least because of the kindly attention of caretaker Russ Simper. The headlines of the *News of the World*, 4 April 1999, read 'Miracle of Broadwater Farm: How £50m and a Lot of Love Transformed Riot Estate. Children used

Princess Diana's visit to the estate. Her visit in the wake of the riots, as on so many other occasions, was a symbol of hope and deliverance for many. This was a really powerful image, coupled with the fact that a local artist drew a picture of Princess Diana and Prince Charles to welcome them to the estate.

to stone the police when they came ... now they greet them with smiles'. Russ was said to have decided to stay in the area 'to help rebuild the multi-cultural community he loves'.

Research undertaken by Ann Power and colleagues at the London School of Economics has shown the important role caretakers play on estates in building up relationships and continuity over long periods of time. The cutbacks in housing from the 1970s onwards drastically reduced the numbers of caretakers available to the local community.

Princess Diana and Russ Simper both played their parts in bringing Broadwater Farm back from the brink. But on reading the newspaper cuttings it is apparent that a heroine not yet mentioned is Dolly Kiffin. The 1980s Inquiry was told by local councillors that: 'The dynamism and enthusiasm

Sure start paddling pool. Sure Start initiatives are part of the 'transformation' referred to in the News of the World. This paddling pool from one of Sure Start's publicity photographs brings new opportunities to promote children's health and wellbeing, in an area and activity which are not so far away, either geographically or ideologically, from the 1930s Lido.

of Dolly Kiffin has everything to do with the way in which progress has been made on Broadwater Farm Estate'. Dolly was a local Afro-Caribbean woman who played a really important role. She worked with the local Youth Association, and councillors attributed the turnaround on the estate to her. Yet it is interesting she is not mentioned in the 1999 *News of the World* article. Is this another example of women, and especially black women, hidden from history?

Reflections on emotional labour and regeneration

The language of regeneration talks about urban renewal, health and wellbeing. By inference this also implies emotional wellbeing. The language of the Sure Start delivery plan very clearly states:

> We [the Sure Start workers] need local people to contribute to and *feel ownership* of initiatives if we are to succeed in opening up access to opportunities and resources, which can make a significant difference to them and the lives of their children. This aim relates to the goal *of creating a stable and sustainable community* where families are *genuine* and respected stakeholders ... [it is] not about doing things for people, but doing things with people (my emphasis).

So the local people need to *feel ownership* and to be *genuine* stakeholders. This requires the Sure Start workers to do emotion work to produce these positive feelings among local people. The goal of Sure Start is to create a stable and sustainable community, just as the goal of emotional labour is make others feel safe and cared for. Using participatory appraisal, workshops have been organised with local parents, professionals and volunteers to bring people together to investigate local problems and negotiate solutions. These workshops aim to build up a feeling of collectivity, reciprocal learning and joint action.

Pictures courtesy Haringey Museum Services and Sure Start Programmes Haringey. Thanks to Rita Reed, Sarah Hargreaves, the Sure Start Programme Haringey and the Bruce Castle Museum. You can contact the Bruce Castle Museum at Lordship Lane, Tottenham, London N17 8NU; tel 0202 8808 8772; Website: www.haringey.gov.uk; E-mail museum.services@haringey.gov.uk

ESRC SEMINAR SERIES ON EMOTIONAL LEARNING

Following earlier discussions on emotional labour, a seminar series is being organised by Pam Smith, Del Loewenthal (both University of Surrey) Stephen Smith (Brunel University) and Michael Rustin (University of East London), on the topic of Emotional Learning. This series is funded by the ESRC.

Four seminars will be held in this series on the following topics:

21 June 2002
UNIVERSITY OF EAST LONDON
(Convenor Michael Rustin)
Theoretical Foundations for the Study of Emotional Learning

17 January 2003
UNIVERSITY OF SURREY
(Convenor Pam Smith)
Emotional Learning as Critique

20 June 2003
BRUNEL UNIVERSITY
(Convenor Steve Smith)
Reparative Forms of Emotional Learning

17 October 2003
UNIVERSITY OF SURREY
(Convenor Del Lowenthal)
Education and Training for Emotional Learning

If you would be interested in attending the seminars in this series, which will all be one-day events, would you please contact any of the four convenors at their University email addresses: D.Loewenthal@surrey.ac.uk; P.A.Smith@surrey.ac.uk; Stephen.Smith@brunel.ac.uk; m.j.rustin@uel.ac.uk

Soundings back issues

Issue 1 - Launch Issue - Stuart Hall on New Labour / Beatrix Campbell on communitarianism / Fred Halliday on the international order / Mae-Wan Ho on genetic engineering / Barbara Castle on Labour / Simon Edge on gay politics.

Issue 2 - Law & Justice, edited by Bill Bowring - contributors - Kate Markus, Keir Starmer, Ken Wiwa, Kader Asmal, Mike Mansfield, Jonathan Cooper, Ethan Raup, John Griffith, Keith Ewing, Ruth Lister and Anna Coote. Plus Steven Rose on neurogenetic determinism / Jeffrey Weeks on sexual communities / David Bell on Dennis Potter.

Issue 3 - Heroes & Heroines - contributors - Barbara Taylor, Jonathan Rutherford, Graham Dawson, Becky Hall, Anna Grimshaw, Simon Edge, Kirsten Notten, Susannah Radstone, Graham Martin and Cynthia Cockburn. Plus Anthony Barnett on Di's Divorce / David Donnison on New Labour / John Gill and Nick Hallam on Euro '96.

Issue 4 - The Public Good - edited by Maureen Mackintosh - contributors - Gail Lewis, Francie Lund, Pam Smith, Loretta Loach, John Clarke, Jane Falkingham, Paul Johnson, Will Hutton, Charlie King, Anne Simpson, Brigid Benson, Candy Stokes, Anne Showstack Sassoon, Sarabajaya Kumar, Ann Hudock, Carlo Borzaga and John Stewart. Plus Paul Hirst and Grahame Thompson on globalisation / Anne Phillips on socialism and equality / Richard Levins on critical science.

Issue 5 - Media Worlds - edited by Bill Schwarz and David Morley - contributors - James Curran, Sarah Benton, Esther Leslie, Angela McRobbie, David Hesmondhalgh, Jonathan Burston, Kevin Robins, Tony Dowmunt and Tim O'Sullivan. Plus Phil Cohen on community / Duncan Green on Latin America / Cynthia Cockburn on women in Israel.

Issue 6 - 'Young Britain' - edited by Jonathan Rutherford - contributors - Jonathan Keane, Bilkis Malek, Elaine Pennicott, Ian Brinkley, John Healey, Frances O'Grady, Rupa Huq, Michael Kenny and Peter Gartside. Plus Miriam Glucksmann on Berlin Memories / Costis Hadjimichalis on Europe / Joanna Moncrieff on psychiatric imperialism.

Issue 7 - States of Africa - edited by Victoria Brittain and Rakiya Omaar - contributors - Basil Davidson, Augustin Ndahimana Buranga, Kathurima M'Inoti, Lucy Hannan, Jenny Matthews, Ngugi Wa Mirii, Kevin Watkins, Joseph Hanlon, Laurence Cockcroft, Joseph Warioba, Vic Allen and James Motlasi. Plus Bill Schwarz on the Conservatives / Wendy Wheeler on 'uncanny families' / Dave Featherstone on 'Pure Genius'.

Issue 8 - Active Welfare - edited by Andrew Cooper - contributors - Rachel Hetherington and Helen Morgan John Pitts, Angela Leopold, Hassan Ezzedine, Alain Grevot, Margherita Gobbi, Angelo Cassin and Monica Savio. Plus Michael Rustin on higher education / Colette Harris on Tajikistan / Patrick Wright interview.

Issue 9 - European Left - edited by Martin Peterson - contributors - Branka Likic-Brboric, Mate Szabo, Leonadis Donskis, Peter Weinreich, Alain Caille, John Crowley, Ove Sernhede and Alexandra Alund. Plus Angela McRobbie on the music industry / Mario Petrucci on responsibility for future generations / Philip Arestis and Malcolm Sawyer on the new monetarism.

Issue 10 - Windrush Echoes - edited by Gail Lewis and Lola Young - contributors - Anne Phoenix, Jackie Kay, Julia Sudbury, Femi Franklin, David Sibley, Mike Phillips, Phil Cole, Bilkis Malek, Sonia Boyce, Roshi Naidoo, Val Wilmer and Stuart Hall. Plus Alan Finlayson on Labour and modernisation / Richard Moncrieff on the Ivory Coast / Mario Pianta on Italy.

Issue 11 - Emotional Labour - edited by Pam Smith - contributors - Stephen Lloyd Smith, Dympna Casey, Marjorie Mayo, Minoo Moallem, Prue Chamberlayne, Rosy Martin, Sue Williams and Gillian Clarke. Plus Andreas Hess on individualism and identity/ T. V. Sathyamurthy on South Asia / Les Black, Tim Crabbe and John Solomos on 'Reggae Boyz'.

Issue 12 - Transversal Politics - edited by Cynthia Cockburn and Lynette Hunter - contributors - Nira Yuval-Davis, Pragna Patel, Marie Mulholland, Rebecca O'Rourke, Gerri Moriarty, Jane Plastow and Rosie. Plus Bruno Latour on the Left / Gerry Hassan on Scotland / Nick Jeffrey on racism in South East London.

Issue 13 - These Sporting Times - edited by Andrew Blake - contributors - Carol Smith, Simon Cook, Adam Brown, Steve Greenfield, Guy Osborne, Gemma Bryden, Steve Hawes, Alan Tomlinson and Adam Locks. Plus Geoff Andrews on New Labour / Fred Halliday on Turkey / Nick Henry and Adrian Passmore on Birmingham.

Issue 14 - One-Dimensional Politics - edited by Wendy Wheeler and Michael Rustin - contributors - Wendy Wheeler, Michael Rustin, Dave Byrne, Gavin Poynter, Barry Richards and Mario Petrucci. Plus Ann Briggs on Bullying / David Renton on South Africa / Isaac Balbus on the 1960s/ Laura Dubinsky on US trade unions.

Issue 15 - States of Mind - edited by Michael Rustin - contributors - Alan Shuttleworth, Andrew Cooper, Helen Lucey, Diane Reay, Richard Graham and Jennifer Wakelyn. Plus Nancy Fraser on the left/ Stephen Wilkinson on Cuba/ Mike Waite on social entrepreneurs/ Kate Young on violence against women in Bangladesh.

Issue 16 - Civil Society - edited by Andreas Hess - contributors - Jeffrey C. Alexander, Robert Fine, Maria Pia Lara, William Outhwaite, Claire Wallace, Grazyna Kubica-Heller, Jonathan Freedland. Plus Peter Howells on wealth and money/ G. C.Harcourt on compulsory voting/ Emma Satyamurti on living with difference/ Simon Lewis on South Africa/ Paulette Goudge on third world emergencies/ Tom Wengraf on Bourdieu.

Issue 17 - New Political Directions - edited by Michael Rustin and Doreen Massey - contributors - Sarah Benton on inclusive citizenship/ Giulio Marcon and Mario Pianta on Italian peace movements/ Massimo Cacciari interview/ Sue Tibballs on sex and the left/ Richard Minns on pensions and the capital market business/ Ian Taylor on the Canadian Right/ John Calmore on race in the US/ Judith Rugg and Michele Sedgwick on Budapest's statue park/ Ruby Millington on young offender institutions/ Merilyn Moos on her mother's life. Plus Jon Bloomfield, Nick Henry, Phil Hubbard, Kevin Ward and David Donnison on the future of cities.

Issue 18 - A Very British Affair - edited by Gerry Hassan - contributors - Gerry Hassan, Jim McCormick, Mark Perryman, Katie Grant, Cathal McCall, Charlotte Williams, Paul Chaney, John Coakley, Kevin Howard, Mary-Ann Stephenson, David T. Evans. Plus Hilary Wainwright, Angie Birtill, Beatrix Campbell, Jane Foot and Csaba Deak on cities and democracy/ Geoff Andrews on Berlusconi/ Glyn Ford on North Korea and Jane Desmarais on literature and anorexia.

Issue 19 - New World Disorder - edited by Stuart Hall, Michael Rustin and Doreen Massey - contributors Stuart Hall, Chantal Mouffe, Gary Yonge, Eli Zaretsky, David Slater, Bob Hackett. Plus Jonathan Rutherford on the new politics of knowledge, Les Back on asylum, Anne Costello and Les Levidow on flexploitation in the EU, Linda McDowell on boys, and Grazyna Kubica's London diaries.

SPECIAL ISSUE: THE NEXT TEN YEARS
Sarah Benton on people and government/ Anthony Barnett on constitutional reform/ Mary Hickman on Northern Ireland/ Ash Amin on regional inequality/ Jean Gardner on women / Tim Lang on food/ Kerry Hamilton and Susan Hoyle on transport/ Bill Bowring on law and order/ Gavi Poynter on unions/ Richard Wilkinson on health.

All back issues cost £9.99, post-free. *The Next Ten Years* costs £7.99, post-free.

Send your orders to Soundings, Lawrence and Wishart, 99a Wallis Road, London E9 5LN. Or email to soundings@l-w-bks.demon.co.uk. Tel 020 8533 2506 Fax 020 8533 7369
